AT THE EDGE OF A DREAM

A LOWER EAST SIDE TENEMENT MUSEUM BOOK

AT THE EDGE *of* A DREAM

The Story of Jewish Immigrants on New York's Lower East Side 1880–1920

LAWRENCE J. EPSTEIN

AN ARTHUR KURZWEIL BOOK

JB JOSSEY-BASS

BICENTENNIAL
1807
WILEY
2007
BICENTENNIAL

Published by Jossey-Bass
A Wiley Imprint
989 Market Street, San Francisco, CA 94103-1741   www.josseybass.com

Wiley Bicentennial logo—Richard J. Pacifico

Jossey-Bass books and products are available through most bookstores. To contact Jossey-Bass directly call our Customer Care Department within the U.S. at 800-956-7739, outside the U.S. at 317-572-3986, or fax 317-572-4002.

Jossey-Bass also publishes its books in a variety of electronic formats. Some content that appears in print may not be available in electronic books.

LIBRARY OF CONGRESS CATALOGING-IN-PUBLICATION DATA

Epstein, Lawrence J. (Lawrence Jeffrey)

At the edge of a dream : the story of Jewish immigrants on New York's

Lower East Side / Lawrence J. Epstein. — 1st ed.

p. cm.

"An Arthur Kurzweil Book."

"A Lower East Side Tenement Museum Book."

Includes bibliographical references and index.

ISBN 978-0-7879-8622-3 (cloth)

1. Jews—New York (State)—New York—History 2. Jews—Migrations. 3. Jews, East European—New York (State)—New York—History. 4. New York (N.Y.)—Emigration and immigration—History. 5. Lower East Side (New York, N.Y.)—Ethnic relations. I. Title.

F128.9.J5E67 2007

305.892'40747—dc22   2007004000

Printed in the United States of America

FIRST EDITION

HB Printing 10 9 8 7 6 5 4 3 2 1

CONTENTS

ACKNOWLEDGMENTS

⤜⤛

A
NYONE WHO writes about the Lower East Side stands on the shoulders of the
enormous number of writers and researchers who wrote about the area. The
books, articles, archival materials, and films were in many places, and I
thank all those who helped me obtain the materials.

I want in particular to thank Ruth J. Abram, president of the Lower East Side
Tenement Museum, not only for her tireless work in creating the Museum but also
for her support of this project. Stephen Long was constantly helpful in providing
archival assistance and much else. Derya Golpinar was especially valuable in helping locate crucial graphics materials. Indeed, I'd like to thank all the people at the
Tenement Museum for their help.

Many scholars were extremely kind in providing help. Ken Libo and Daniel
Soyer were very patient in making bibliographic and other suggestions. Tony
Michels provided extraordinarily valuable insights into political life on the Lower
East Side. Hasia Diner's original contribution to this volume is deeply appreciated.
Joan Micklin Silver was characteristically kind in our discussion of the making of
Hester Street.

The contributions and help these people gave should not be considered as
endorsements for the ideas and interpretations in this book. I alone remain responsible for any errors or historical evaluations.

When I first had the idea for this book, I turned to my longtime friend and editor Arthur Kurzweil, who knows more than anyone about Jewish books. Arthur

brought the idea to Alan Rinzler, Jossey-Bass's executive editor. Alan was immediately enthusiastic and enormously perceptive and helpful throughout the entire life of the manuscript's preparation. Together, Arthur and Alan provided valuable editorial guidance. In addition, the staff at Jossey-Bass and John Wiley & Sons—including Seth Schwartz and Joanne Clapp Fullagar—contributed valuable professional aid during the process of editing, producing, and marketing the book.

I got help also from many other people. In particular, I want to thank Susan Lustig for all sorts of assistance. Stewart Ain and Jonathan Mark of *The Jewish Week* had useful suggestions. I always turn to Renee Steinig for ongoing genealogical advice. Phyllis Simon provided wonderful family stories. I also want to thank all who provided graphics material for the book.

The National Center for Jewish Film at Brandeis University was extremely helpful in providing access to films that were difficult to locate.

Grateful thanks to my great friends who provided much needed solace and advice. Assemblyman Mike Fitzpatrick is simply irreplaceable as an extraordinarily kind person and dedicated public servant. He; his wife, Lorena; and his brother, John, are like members of my own family.

Doug Rathgeb and I have been discussing writing for more than forty years. He lived through all the stories I had about this book, and I thank him for his patience, intelligent comments, and just being there.

I want to thank my colleagues in the English Department at Suffolk County Community College who provide a perfect environment for a writer. Dr. Sandra Sprows, the academic chair, and her assistants, Dr. Doug Howard and Prof. John Parbst, were enormously helpful in many ways. Sandra has become a sounding board for ideas in my last few books, and I deeply appreciate her insights.

Thanks to my literary agent, Don Gastwirth; his brother, Dr. Joseph L. Gastwirth; my cousins Toby Everett and Dr. Sheldon Scheinert, who are always great sources of family stories; and other members of my family, including Harvey and Marsha Selib and Judith Marshall and their various children and grandchildren.

My grandfather, Josef Scheinert, was the first in our family to arrive here. He went back to Eastern Europe and then returned again before his wife, Liebe, and their children joined him. My mother, Lillian Scheinert Epstein, was born on East Houston Street a few years after the family settled in the United States. My grandfather, Louis Epstein, arrived in New York in 1898. The woman he would marry, my grandmother, Rose Knopf Epstein, immigrated as a self-described "servant girl" in 1899. A few years later, Louis brought his parents, Feivel and Hinda, to live on the

Lower East Side. This book—and this author—simply would not have existed if these ancestors had not journeyed to America's shores.

The intriguing family tales my mother told me piqued my lifelong interest in the Lower East Side, and my father, Frederick Epstein, always encouraged my writing.

My brother, Richard, is the first reader of my books. His constant enthusiasm and remarkable memory are deeply needed and deeply appreciated. His wife, Perla, and their family, Adam and his wife Jayne and daughter Allyson, and Sondra, always listen to my tales of writing with interest.

My dedicating this book to my children, Michael, Elana, Rachel, and Lisa, is a small expression of how proud I am of their extraordinary accomplishments and, even more important, their kindness.

None of my work would be possible without the endless help of my wife, Sharon, who has the unenviable task of providing me with constant guidance and support. That she does it so well, with love and care, is a perpetual blessing.

L.J.E.

INTRODUCTION

IT WAS Plymouth Rock for much of the American Jewish community. It was the place where time began for many Jewish immigrants. It was the setting for the very first full-length sound motion picture and an episode of *The Simpsons*. New York's Lower East Side has achieved mythic status not just in Jewish life but also in American history.

The Jewish immigrants who fled Eastern Europe found refuge there as they learned English and discovered in their golden new land a place of unparalleled freedom and opportunity. But the Lower East Side was also a place of grinding poverty, unendurable sweatshops, vicious crime, and tiny, vermin-infested tenement flats.

Whatever the hardships may have been, however, Jews kept arriving. In 1882, about 15,000 Jews immigrated to the United States. Between 1886 and 1898, some 380,278 Jewish immigrants entered just through New York. Between 1881 and 1910, a total of 1,562,800 Jewish immigrants entered the country—1906 was the peak year, welcoming 153,748 new American Jews. By 1920, there were about 3.6 million Jews on these shores, making up 3.41 percent of the U.S. population; 22.86 percent of the Jews in the world now lived in America. By contrast, in 1800, America held only 0.06 percent of world Jewry, and eighty years later, just 3.27 percent. Altogether, between 1880 and 1920, more than two million Jews immigrated to the United States.

The immigrant Jews weren't wandering. They came to America with the purpose of starting their lives over. Theirs was a mythic heroic journey, and they were heroes both individually and as a people. Together, they built great institutions and families and found the common bonds needed to endure and ultimately triumph.

Their heroism lay not just in their initial courage to leave their families and homes but also in facing down all the powerful forces arrayed against them: hunger, heat, crowds, a new language, new customs, and some Americans who opposed Jews either as immigrants or as Jews or both, who regarded them as foreign invaders, criminals and radicals, who, left unchecked, would destroy American culture.

Ultimately, though, this story is not just Jewish and not just about immigrants. Rather, it is a metaphor for the human journey all people take across life as they struggle, leaving one world to enter another and encounter bone-rattling hardships as they do. The lessons the immigrants taught of belonging to a people, of endurance, courage, common effort, humor, and family ties, are the very lessons all humans need to survive the struggles of their existence. In that sense, I hope that the audience for this book will include not just American Jews with family ties to the Lower East Side but all others who have an interest in history and in the dramatic struggles of the human heart.

The purpose of this book is to provide gritty yet uplifting real stories of deprivation, survival, and triumph. Many books have been written about the Lower East Side. It has been a generation since the publication of the best-known of those books, *World of Our Fathers* by Irving Howe with the assistance of Kenneth Libo. That magnificent work, published in 1976, focused especially on political struggles and the labor movement as well as Yiddish culture. But every generation needs to make the story of the Lower East Side its own in its own way. It is such shared memories that bind the Jewish people together.

I intend for this book to provide readers with experience more than analysis. I want you to feel what it was like to shop on Hester Street on a Thursday night when the street was ablaze with the light of hundreds of burning torches on pushcarts whose fifteen hundred peddlers paid $25 a year for their licenses, where a shopper could buy for 50 cents a pair of lace curtains that she had seen on sale in a store for $75, and where one could obtain fish, fresh fruit, seltzer "for 2 cents plain" and 3 cents with flavoring, and so much else right at one's doorstep. I want to take you into the sweatshops and see the sixty thousand hardworking children with their dulled faces and bent backs and to an unventilated, unbearably hot room in a tenement with four men, two women, several young girls aged nine to fourteen and a boy of eleven all working in knee pants, sewing and pressing. I want you to share in the story of George Burns, Fanny Brice, Irving Berlin, George Gershwin, and the many other entertainers who spent part of their childhood on the Lower East Side.

I want the book to provide a complete tour of the Lower East Side, showing its beauty and its ugliness, its great energy and its depravity. It is the story of crowded tenement blocks that included 2,781 people—and no bathtubs. It is a small place where between 1885 and 1900 one hundred Jewish newspapers circulated, where in 1918 there were twenty Yiddish theaters, and where one could find hundreds of synagogues, many in storefronts or flats. It is the story of a place where Jews arrived as refugees with an average of $15 in their pockets and from where most of them emerged successful and American.

The book tells why immigrants left Eastern Europe, how they came here, and what they found when they arrived. The journey across the Atlantic in steerage, the arrival at Ellis Island, and the trip to the Lower East Side were their preface to life in the Golden Land of America.

And once they were here, Jewish immigrants had to live in tenements, find jobs, in some cases find spouses, raise their children, form a community, find a synagogue, seek entertainment, and so much else. All the details of their lives are to be found in these pages.

AT THE EDGE OF A DREAM

Jewish immigrants arriving in New York. *Source: Courtesy of Brown Brothers.*

ONE

ESCAPING FROM THE OLD WORLD

>⟶×⟵<

T HE DEATH of one man in 1881 changed Jewish history. Tsar Alexander II of
Russia was assassinated that year, on March 13 (March 1 on the Julian calendar then in use in that country). The reaction and counterreaction to his
assassination, in combination with the accumulated heartaches and economic burdens of the Jews of Eastern Europe, forced Jews to make a fateful choice regarding
their future.

Two-thirds of the Jews living in Eastern Europe decided to remain. Of the one-
third that left, the overwhelming number came to the United States. Of those, 73
percent came from the Russian Empire. A very few went to the Land of Israel, then
under Turkish control.

The choices these people made would shape their lives and the lives of their
descendants. Those who stayed, or their children, eventually came under Soviet
rule or were swept up in the whirlwind of the Holocaust. Those who went to the
Land of Israel faced decades of struggle to establish the nation of Israel, achieved in
1948. For those who came to America, the struggle was first played out for many on
the streets of the Lower East Side.

And although history has yet to decide the full implications of the choices made
by those Eastern European Jews at the end of the nineteenth century and in the early
years of the twentieth, it was clear that the decision to stay or go and the decision

about where to go would affect not just individuals or families but the very fate of the Jewish people.

The Eastern European Jews were not the first group of Jewish people to emigrate to America. Sephardic Jews had come much earlier, and a great many German Jews arrived in the nineteenth century. The Eastern European Jews, though, came in the largest numbers.

The tsar's assassination took place against the backdrop of a long history of Jewish life in Eastern Europe. Jews had lived there since the thirteenth century, when persecution in Western Europe had become unbearable and a Polish king invited them to journey east. Their lives in Poland and Romania, Hungary, and Russia remained the same for centuries. The Jews characteristically lived in a *shtetl*, a village, and regulated their lives by Jewish religious law. The joys of a Sabbath meal, a prayer, a birth, a wedding, and other happy events punctuated what was generally a burdensome life. It was a life marked by poverty and persecution.

FROM DISCRIMINATION TO ASSASSINATION

By the late nineteenth century, there were many sources of discontent among the Jews of Eastern Europe. In Poland, the government had put the shtetl community councils in charge of collecting oppressive taxes. As Russia annexed more and more of Polish territory, additional young Jews became subject to the Russian military draft. More subtle in effect, the modern world was finding its way even to the small Jewish towns of Eastern Europe, and the economic and religious dislocations of modernity would undermine the long-standing traditional way of life. In short, the Jews were living in a tinderbox of problems waiting for a match to ignite them.

WITHOUT OPPORTUNITY OR HOPE

There were approximately 7.7 million Jews in the world in 1880. Three-quarters of them lived in Eastern Europe; only 3 percent lived in the United States. Most lived in the Pale of Settlement, 386,000 square miles between the Baltic and the Black Sea that included the Ukraine, Byelorussia (modern Belarus), Lithuania, and a large part of Poland. Poland itself had been carved up and parceled out among Russia, Prussia, and Austria at the end of the eighteenth century. The Austrians renamed their part Galicia.

There were sometimes rivalries and disputes among Jews from these different communities. There was, for example, a mutual feeling of distaste between Litvaks—Jews living in the northern part of the Pale of Settlement—and Galitzianers—those living in the southern part, primarily Galicia. Although eventually the conflict became less rancorous and even a source of good-natured ribbing, the two groups were originally filled with mistrust, a feeling that spilled over once they found themselves sharing the small world of the Lower East Side.

The divisions would remain precisely because Jewish life would be organized according to the town of origin in Eastern Europe. The Litvaks saw themselves as bearers of the Enlightenment, filled with modern culture to supplement their Jewishness. They saw themselves as the scholars of Judaism and the Galitzianers as backward mystics. In turn, the Galitzianers thought of the Litvaks as having abandoned Judaism.

But Jews had to face more than rivalries with each other. The industrialization that accompanied modernity meant that the traditional peasant economies, of which Jews in Eastern Europe were all a part, were no longer as stable as they had been. Jews, for example, often went to local fairs and relied on selling their goods. But the emergence of railroads put an end to fairs. Jews, living on the economic margins at best because of religious persecution, found themselves now in dire poverty. They had to compete with each other and their Gentile neighbors. The communal ties were loosened by such circumstances.

The pervasive economic fears, mirrored in the numerous Yiddish synonyms for *poverty* and in the Yiddish literature of such writers as Sholem Aleichem and I. L. Peretz, led to other sorts of fears.

As is often the case in times of economic uncertainty, the government sought to deflect peasant anger away from political leadership and so sought a scapegoat. The Jews became that scapegoat, and even before the famous widespread series of pogroms, or organized attacks on Jews, in the 1880s, members of the Jewish community were subject to attacks.

Many of the peasants found it all too easy to believe stories about the Jews. For example, at one time Jews in Russia were permitted to be innkeepers and bartenders. Their very success doomed them. Soon rumors began circulating that the Jews planned to weaken Russian minds using vodka and take over the country.

There were physical dangers as well. As an immigrant named Mollie Hyman recalled, "In 1904, Russia lost the Russo-Japanese War. The soldiers were coming back home. Before they passed through our little town, there was always a messenger from the little town before that let the Jews know that the soldiers are coming. If you had any girls, hide them. They used to rape them and kill them."

Jews had no means of organized communal self-defense. They relied for strength on their religion and their learning, valuable internal weapons but not very powerful against a peasant with a drink and a gun. They had a vibrant language as well in Yiddish, a language that became a substitute weapon, filled with wisdom in its proverbs and fire in its curses.

All these conditions left the Jewish community with ever-decreasing opportunities. The young, who had grown up hearing of the modern world and the Enlightenment in Europe, wondered why it had not found its way to their corner of the world. Desperate not to have to live as they did, in poverty and fear, and able to see nothing better in the future, they grew up in hopelessness. In many ways, they remained inheritors of a medieval world, one that excluded learning, especially for women, and included a lot of superstitions.

Perhaps the most pervasive of the various superstitions of the Eastern European Jews centered on diligent efforts to avoid the "evil eye," the *ayin hara*. The fear focused on the belief that some people had the malevolent power to cause harm to others merely with a glance. It was out of fear of such harm that the Jews of Eastern Europe developed various folk beliefs. They thought that if a child's physical appearance was praised too much, the evil eye might appear. Indeed, revealing too much personal information about the child—the height or weight, for example—might prove dangerous. There were ways of protecting children. A common custom was to place *a royte bendl*—a red ribbon—near the baby, perhaps on its cradle or carriage, to provide protection. Some mothers put a knife under the baby's pillow.

Various linguistic incantations were developed to avoid the evil eye. It was from such efforts that the widespread expression *kennehara* (elided from *kine ayin hara*) developed; it meant "no evil eye."

They had other burdens as well that shaped their views.

MILITARY SERVICE

The Jews living in various empires in Eastern Europe were subject to different sorts of military drafts. In Russia, young Jews at the age of twelve began being drafted in 1827. Conscripting Jewish boys at that age, prior to their bar mitzvah, was meant to force them to leave their religion. Later, the boys were drafted at age eight and sent

PROVERBS AND CURSES

SOME YIDDISH PROVERBS

When a father must help his son, both laugh; when a son must help his father, both cry.

God could not be everywhere, and therefore he created mothers.

A half-truth is a whole lie.

A chip on the shoulder indicates wood higher up.

A man is not honest simply because he never had a chance to steal.

The face is the worst informer.

The highest wisdom is kindness.

Better to suffer an injustice than to do an injustice.

For dying, you always have time.

Which king is the best in the world? A dead one.

A wise man hears one word and understands two.

SOME YIDDISH CURSES

They should free a madman and lock him up.

Hang yourself with a sugar rope, and you'll have a sweet death.

He should be transformed into a chandelier, to hang by day and to burn by night.

May all your teeth fall out—except one, so that you may have toothaches!

Let him suffer and remember.

SUPERSTITIONS

If a person breaks two glasses in a day, a third must be broken to avoid evil.

If you put clothes on inside out, you will have bad luck all day.

A kitten that enters a house brings good luck.

If your right eye itches, you'll have good luck, but if your left eye itches, bad luck will follow.

If a young woman sings while she sweeps the floor, she will marry a man who stammers.

A pregnant woman can determine the sex of her child. She must leave the room. Then someone puts a fork on one chair and a spoon on another. Both are covered. The woman then returns to choose a chair. If she chooses the fork, the child will be a boy, and if she chooses the spoon, she will have a girl.

It was bad luck to name a person after someone still alive or someone who died young.

to schools where they received military and Christian religious training. They went directly into the army after their training, entering service at the age of eighteen and being obligated for many years of service.

Once in the army, Jewish newcomers came under tremendous pressure to join the Russian Orthodox Church. In a few cases, Jews who refused were dragged into churches to undergo forced conversion. Golda Meir, the former prime minister of Israel, recalled that her grandfather served in the army from age thirteen until twenty-six, trying to remain kosher by surviving on raw vegetables and bread. He was forced to kneel for hours at a time as officers pressed for his conversion. He resisted, but many others could not withstand the pressure of being denied food or being forced to remain outside in the winter.

A SISTER'S BRAVERY

On a cold winter night, a young boy did not return home from religious school. His agitated parents and sister finally spoke to a classmate of the boy's. A renegade Jew who captured boys for the army had grabbed the child.

The sister discovered that the boys were being held in a camp just a few miles from their village. The Jewish holiday of Simchat Torah was approaching when she came up with a plan. She gathered food and also took a bottle of vodka to bribe the sentries. She got into her wagon and rode to the camp.

As she arrived, a sentry approached her. She did a little curtsy and explained her simple desire to give her brother a present for the holiday. The guard remained uncertain until she handed him the gift of a honey cake. He allowed her in, admonishing her that she could stay for no longer than a half hour.

Quickly she found her brother, Velvel. She spoke in a hushed tone: "At the very bottom of my bag is a dress and a girl's hat and shoes. Put the clothes on and wait for ten minutes after I leave. Then just walk right out of the camp. The sentry will believe that you are me leaving. I'll wait for you on the road." The frightened boy did as his sister said.

The girl left, waiting for the sentry to be busy. When he was turned away, she sneaked out of the camp. A half hour later, her brother trudged along the road walking slowly in his dress. The two arrived home safely. Eventually the entire family escaped Russia and journeyed to the United States.

⚔

In an interesting historical footnote, Israeli immigration authorities noted that when emigration from the former Soviet Union began, some of those leaving were the great-grandchildren of Jews who had been forced to convert and had intermarried, yet they still considered themselves Jews.

Young Jews and their families sought ways to avoid the draft, although that was difficult because at first the various Jewish communities had quotas of recruits, quotas that were double those for the general Russian population. When, for a time, eldest sons could avoid conscription, families without any sons adopted the second sons of families. The film producer Samuel Goldwyn recalled that in his hometown, two brothers had shot each other, one in the arm and the other in the leg, each attempting to cripple the other so as to avoid service. In more common cases, a cleaver was used to cut off the index finger—the trigger finger, rendering the young man unfit to serve.

In 1874, the quota system was replaced, and all Jews had to serve starting at age twenty-one. In reaction, at least one Jewish community sought to evade conscription by reporting an unusually high number of deaths among twenty-year-old males. As noted, some Jewish males mutilated themselves so that they would be declared unfit to serve, but starting in 1876, communities had to provide another soldier for each unfit potential recruit. Furthermore, any Jewish subject who had given shelter to a Jewish army deserter was arrested and forced to do hard labor. The Jewish community that knew of a runaway and didn't report him could be fined as much as 300 rubles.

THE ASSASSINATION

There was a military parade in Saint Petersburg, Russia, on March 13, 1881. Tsar Alexander II was to ride in the parade, and a group of anarchists, who had been plotting to kill him, chose the date to make an attempt. The conspirators mined a tunnel under Malaya Sadovaya Street. Then four of them, each holding a bomb wrapped in a handkerchief or newspaper, went to various spots on the parade route.

The tsar arrived at the parade by a route that avoided Malaya Sadovaya Street, and Sophia Perovskaya, the worried leader of the group, watched in anger as he turned to go back the way he had arrived, bypassing the mines. She sent a signal to two of the men with her to go to another spot along the Yekaterininsky Canal.

They dashed away and got there before the imperial carriage arrived only because the tsar had stopped to visit his cousin. When the carriage finally appeared, one conspirator, nineteen-year-old Nikolai Rysakov, ran up to it and forcefully threw his bomb at the horses' legs.

The bomb exploded. Two people were killed, and the carriage was damaged, but the tsar survived. Rysakov was immediately captured. The tsar, refusing the advice of his guards, insisted on stopping to examine the scene. As he walked around, another bomber, Ignaty Grinevitsky, lurched toward him and threw his bomb. It exploded, killing the assassin and wounding his target. The guards lifted Alexander and rode toward the palace. There was a trail of blood in the street as the carriage drove madly. The tsar died several hours later.

POGROMS

None of the four assassins was Jewish; the actual killer was Polish. All of them were put to death. However, a Jewish woman named Hessia Helfman had helped rent the apartment that served as the headquarters for the conspiracy. She was found guilty as well. But she gave birth after her trial, and her death sentence was then commuted to life in prison. She and her infant daughter died there. Her participation inflamed those who already hated the Jews.

Alexander III became the new emperor. Konstantin Pobedonostev, the new tsar's teacher, was a fanatical hater of Jews who now had the power to put his hatred into political action. He declared that one-third of Russia's Jews would emigrate, one-third would convert to Russian Orthodoxy, and one-third would starve to death.

THE ATTACKS

The first organized pogrom (a word derived from the Russian *pogromit*, meaning "demolish") began in Elizavetgrad (today's Kirovograd) at the end of April 1881. There were thirty more attacks in three days. In 1881, twenty thousand Jewish homes were destroyed. By 1882, more than two hundred communities had been attacked.

A new and even worse series of pogroms took place between 1903 and 1906. The most infamous of these occurred in a town called Kishinev. In February 1903, a boy with multiple knife wounds was found in Kishinev. Articles were published that the Jews had killed the boy to get his blood to make matzoh—an absurd but long-standing anti-Jewish charge. There was a growing chorus within the town calling for revenge.

The pogrom began on April 19 (April 6 on the Julian calendar), which was Easter Sunday and also the last day of Passover. Twenty groups, each with between twenty and twenty-five people, headed toward the Jewish area of the town. They broke windows and began robbing shops and houses. The police did not stop them. The marauders stopped their attacks at dusk.

Cities and towns where Jews fled pogroms between 1881 and 1906. Most took place in the Pale of Settlement, a region where Jews had been officially allowed to reside since 1825.

The crowds came back the following morning. Boys tossing stones came first. They were followed by adults, armed with crowbars, who attempted to destroy all they could find. They were followed by others who carried off Jewish goods. By eleven in the morning, the streets of the Jewish section of the city were littered with broken furniture and glass. Pillow feathers covered the roads. The archbishop of the area traveled through the crowd. The police refused to interfere, though they did direct some rioters to houses owned by particular Jews.

It was about noon when the crowd began to murder Jews and rape women and young girls. Some Jews began to gather objects to be used as weapons of self-defense. These men were arrested.

When the pogrom ended that evening, forty-nine Jews had been killed and more than five hundred injured. Seven hundred houses and six hundred businesses were destroyed. In all, about two thousand families were left homeless.

The story of the pogrom made its way around the world. As the April 28, 1903, *New York Times,* which overstated the number of dead, put it:

> The anti-Jewish riots in Kishinev, Bessarabia [modern Moldova], are worse than the censor will permit to publish. There was a well-laid-out plan for the general massacre of Jews on the day following the Russian Easter. The mob was led by priests, and the general cry, "Kill the Jews," was taken up all over the city.
>
> The Jews were taken wholly unaware and were slaughtered like sheep. The dead number 120 and the injured about 500. The scenes of horror attending this massacre are beyond description. Babes were literally torn to pieces by the frenzied and bloodthirsty mob. The local police made no attempt to check the reign of terror. At sunset the streets were piled with corpses and wounded. Those who could make their escape fled in terror, and the city is now practically deserted of Jews.

MAY LAWS AND OFFICIAL DISCRIMINATION

The Jewish victims became identified as the very cause of their own misery. In 1881, the new tsar, claiming he needed to protect Russian peasants from economic control by Jews, instituted a new series of laws in May. Jews were no longer allowed to live in any area or town with fewer than ten thousand inhabitants, even in the Pale of Settlement.

This was nothing less than a legal attempt to destroy the shtetl existence of the Jews. Their access to higher education was severely restricted by a quota imposed on Jews who wished to enter secondary education. Similar quotas were placed on various professions. Russians were permitted to expel the "vicious" in the villages—most of whom the judges found to be Jews. If Jews left their village for a short trip, they had trouble reentering to see their families. Jews could not take a widowed parent to his or her home village. They could not inherit a business in another village. If they got sick, they were not allowed to go to a hospital in another village. Any violation of these could lead to the loss of their right to live in their home village.

Having made higher education in Russia impossible, later steps sought to deprive many Jews of a professional livelihood. Jewish lawyers, who had made up 22 percent of the members of the Russian bar, were now allowed to constitute no more than 9 percent. Jews who lived outside the Pale of Settlement were suddenly targeted

THE ODESSA POGROM

A pogrom in Odessa took place October 18–22, 1905. Crowds attacked the Jews in their poor neighborhood known as the Moldvanko for three days and nights. There were 299 Jews murdered. A Jewish nurse working in a local hospital recorded what happened when the hospital staff went to visit the site of the pogrom. The nurse described the initial sights as they arrived.

"About ten Catholic [Greek] Sisters with about forty or fifty of their schoolchildren led the procession. They carried ikons or pictures of Jesus and sang "God Save the Tsar." They were followed by a crowd containing hundreds of men and women murderers. . . . They ran into the yards where there were fifty or a hundred tenants. . . . They began to throw children out of the windows of the second, third, or fourth stories. They would take a poor, innocent six-months-old baby . . . and throw it down to the pavement. You can imagine it could not live after it struck the ground, but this did not satisfy the stony-hearted murderers. They then rushed up [to] the child, seized it and broke its little arm and leg bones into three or four pieces, then wrung its neck too. They laughed and yelled. . . .

It was not enough for them to open up a woman's abdomen and take out the child which she carried, but they took time to stuff the abdomen with straw and fill it up. . . . It was not enough for them to cut out an old man's tongue and cut off his nose, but they drove nails into the eyes also."

⟶✕⟵

so that they would be forced to return there. Many Jewish artisans suddenly faced a law that if they used a machine in their trade, they could no longer be called an "artisan" and had to leave to return to the Jewish area. If Jewish jewelers sold chains they had not manufactured themselves, they were reclassified as merchants and told to return to the Pale. Such forced exits often came with a single day's notice.

An entire Jewish way of life was ending. The shock to the Jewish social system was enormous.

THE DECISION TO LEAVE

The pogroms and the May Laws were the tipping point, the moment that all the built-up fears, the economic dislocations, the loss of hope, and the belief that the past was the prologue to the future combined to give a final push. But it is important to emphasize that the pogroms alone did not cause mass Jewish emigration. The departures, which had begun in Eastern Europe in the 1870s before the pogroms and in Germany decades earlier, were motivated by economic factors. The pogroms remain large in the Jewish imagination of the era, but they should not be considered the exclusive reason for leaving.

The Kishinev pogrom was a profound prod for those who wanted to leave but weren't sure about the future of Russia. However, any decision to go into exile—to leave their native land; cross an ocean; surrender Yiddish, the *mamaloshen* (mother tongue)—and live in a foreign and forbidding world, was not an easy decision.

Students in particular were changed by the pogroms. Jewish students had a profound belief that education combined with social revolution would fundamentally alter Russian society, making it a far better place with a real future. Yet their revolutionary "friends" had supported the attacks on the Jews. Abandoned by their friends, they were losing what was left of their self-identity, their belief in the future, and their hope. More than their parents, who found it difficult to leave settled lives, and far more than their Orthodox Jewish neighbors, who saw the Russian outbreaks as yet another example of the age-old hatred of Jews that would have to be endured by remaining faithful to God and Jewish law, the young students were shocked into action.

THE DREAM OF AMERICA

Some of the students believed that wherever the Jews went, hatred would inevitably follow. Therefore, influenced by such nationalist thinkers as Moses Hess, they concluded that they had to create their own homeland where they could be in charge of self-defense. This tiny minority of students focused on a return to the Land of Israel, the historical homeland of the Jews.

But among the common folk and most students, the talk everywhere in Eastern Europe was of the United States, the "Goldene Medina," the Golden Land, which was really less a description of reality than the embodiment of a dream. They wanted to believe, needed to believe, that the streets were paved with gold, that the gates

THE GOLDENE MEDINA

Mary Antin, most famous as the author of *The Promised Land,* explained the attractions of emigration in her book *From Plotzk to Boston:*

> America was in everybody's mouth. Businessmen talked of it over their accounts; the market women made up their quarrels that they might discuss it from stall to stall; people who had relatives in the famous land went around reading their letters for the enlightenment of less fortunate folk. . . . Children played at emigrating; old folks shook their sage heads over the evening fire, and prophesied no good for those who braved the terrors of the sea and the foreign goal beyond it; all talked of it, but scarcely anyone knew one true fact about this magic land.

of the New World would open wide for them and lead to the lush fields of freedom. It was a land where even the Cossacks could not ride their horses and where people could become rich overnight. As the immigrant Marcus Ravage's uncle told him, people in America got paid for everything—even for voting.

Of course, the reality would be different. As one wry immigrant observed, "When I left for America, I was told the streets were paved with gold. When I got here, I found that not only were they not paved with gold, they weren't paved at all. And not only weren't they paved, but I was expected to pave them!"

But it was the dream that the Jews needed to sustain them through a dangerous and unsettling present and provide a vision of an alternative future. And unlike members of other national groups, Jews who went to America planned to stay. The trip was not simply an economic adventure leading to a return to Europe with money. Instead, the journey to America was mythic—it was a trip laden with danger but, once survived, it would lead to nothing short of a rebirth, the start of a new life.

Although it was mostly the young who went, they were not the only immigrants. Jewish families frequently traveled together, certainly much more commonly than other ethnic or religious immigrants. Parents concerned about the future of their very young children made the journey.

Some women went to America because "that's where all the Jewish young men had gone," leaving none to marry back home. Because many married men went to America first, intending to save enough money to bring over their wives and children—and often their parents—there were many married women, called "American widows," who stayed behind in Europe. In some cases, husbands who had gone to America sent letters back to the Old Country demanding a divorce.

Not all Eastern European Jews were so smitten with America. For every one eager to get to the Goldene Medina, two others thought of the faraway land as the Treyfene Medina, the unkosher land. One rabbi declared that anyone who left for America was living in sin. The majority of traditional Jews were concerned that in such a country, people would turn to money, not God, that soon all the treasures of the Talmud would be forsaken for more worldly treasures, and that Jews would forget *halachah*, Jewish law that guided their lives and those of their ancestors for generations.

THE ECONOMIC LURE

The various push factors of economic hardship and physical attack were complemented by the pull factor of the dream of America. For its part, America contributed to that dream by its very real economic and demographic situation. The Civil War had resulted in six hundred thousand American deaths. That meant that beyond the human tragedy, there was an incredible shortage of workers.

This shortage came at the very same time as the Industrial Revolution was transforming the American economy. The country had always an abundance of natural resources, but in the era between the end of the Civil War and the beginning of the twentieth century, America's economy exploded. There was a 700 percent increase in manufactured goods. The country's national wealth quadrupled. America needed workers if this boom were to continue.

Despite this attraction, the poverty-stricken Jews in Eastern Europe might still have been unable to afford the journey had it not been for the emerging use of steamships. Such ships could normally cross the Atlantic in eight to fourteen days, depending on the weather, whereas previous sailing vessels could take as long as three months to make the voyage.

The new steamships made money by bringing freight they collected in America back to Europe. However, that meant that the trip to America was wasted because the ships were empty. Once the steamship lines realized they could make additional money by carrying passengers on the voyage to the United States, even the low fares they charged added considerably to their overall profits. The companies courted potential travelers, creating alluring posters portraying lavish parties on board the ship that would bring travelers to the land of freedom and gold.

THE JOURNEY

The decision to leave, as wrenching as it sometimes was, as necessary as it was thought to be, was only the beginning. Once the choice had been made and sufficient money had been saved, the journey itself had to begin. That journey was often fraught with danger. Indeed, most accounts of the arrival of Eastern European Jews emphasize the difficulty of traveling by ship or the indignities suffered at Ellis Island, but it is crucial to recall that by far the most dangerous part of the trip was getting from a hometown to one of the ports of embarkation.

DANGEROUS TRAVEL

Leaving Russia legally was costly. Bribes were needed to get the necessary visas and other travel documents. These frequently took months, and sometimes years, to obtain. Illegal emigration was just as expensive because similar bribes were needed, and danger was a constant companion of the journey.

For example, the comedian Jack Benny's father, Meyer Kubelsky, had been smuggled out of Lithuania. Meyer's father had gotten a passport for his son, but the young man was then told he was still not allowed to leave. The desperate father owned a tavern and wine shop and spoke to the man who delivered empty bottles. Meyer hid under the bottles to make his escape.

The travelers didn't take much. Mostly, they tied their few belongings in a blanket or a sheet. They took a pillow—goosefeather pillows were prized—along with a souvenir from the Old Country, some religious item perhaps, and some food.

Many of the travelers went by train when they could afford it, but most could not. The train ride itself was rarely enjoyable. Many Jews had never even seen a train before, and suddenly they were in boxcars, some with benches, some without. On some trains, men and women had to travel separately. To escape to the border town of Brody, many riders in third-class railroad cars had to travel for twenty to sixty hours.

There were also thieves and scoundrels ready to cheat the would-be travelers. Sometimes travel agents sold tickets to London but charged for a journey to New York.

And the travelers never knew what would happen along the way. The singer Sophie Tucker was born on such a voyage. Her mother and two-year-old brother were making the trip. Sophie's mother, realizing she was about to give birth, tapped the driver of their cart on his shoulder and told him of her condition. The driver stopped and let her off. But then he drove away. The desperate woman found a house nearby, and the baby was born. Sophie Tucker's mother was seventeen.

In general, Jews from Eastern Europe left by one of four principal routes: (1) Jews from the Ukraine and southern Russia crossed into the Austro-Hungarian Empire (mostly illegally), traveled to Berlin or Vienna by train, and from there went to one of the ports where they could get on a ship to America. The main ports were Bremen and Hamburg in Germany, Amsterdam and Rotterdam in the Netherlands, and Antwerp in Belgium. (2) Jews in western Russia crossed the German border and headed for Berlin and then one of the ports. (3) Jews who lived in the Austro-Hungarian Empire were allowed to cross the German border legally and would then go to Berlin and on to one of the ports. (4) Romanian Jews mostly traveled to Vienna and then to one of the ports in the Netherlands.

Many departing Jews embarked on foot to the German ports, where they would get a boat for America. They were known as the *fusgeyer*, the wayfarers. They had sold their valuables, joined together often with others who came from the same community or had the same trade or were of the same gender (there were groups made up exclusively of women), and made a common fund to ensure that all in the group could make the journey.

This journey was often perilous. For some who were of military age, passing through customs was impossible. They were compelled to cross the border at night. For this, they relied on professional smugglers. One trick was to stand at a border crossing and wait for the soldiers to go after thieves, who constantly sought to smuggle illegal goods. While the guards were otherwise occupied, the escaping Jews made their way across.

Abraham Cahan (pronounced Cahn), editor of the *Jewish Daily Forward* and author of *The Education of David Levinsky*, the most famous of the immigrant novels, recalls his own perilous border crossing.

We were to leave the train at Dubno where we were to take a wagon through the region around Radzivil on our way to the Austrian border. That would be our last city in Russia; across the border was . . . Brody.

In the evening we followed two young Ukrainian peasants to a small, freshly plastered hut. One of the peasants was tall and barefooted and carried a small cask at his side. In Austria, there was no tax on brandy, so he smuggled it into Russia; on his return trip, he carried tobacco, more expensive in Austria, out of Russia.

We waited a long time in the hut before realizing we were being held for more money. Having paid, we moved on. We made a strange group going across fields and meadows in the night, halted suddenly every few minutes by the tall peasant holding up his finger and pausing to listen for god-knows-what disaster. . . .

We stumbled on endlessly. It seemed as if the border were miles away. Then the peasant straightened up and announced we were already well inside Austria.

Legal emigrants faced German guards concerned that the poor Jews were bringing diseases into their country. They therefore subjected the Jews to lengthy personal inspections.

TO THE PORTS OF DEPARTURE

The very first waves of the emigration affected by the pogroms began in the summer of 1881. The fleeing Jews went to the town of Brody, a center of departure located between Russia and Galicia, under the control of the Austro-Hungarian Empire. Charles Netter was sent from France to oversee relief efforts at Brody and get the refugees from there to Hamburg.

At Hamburg and other ports, the Jews faced additional problems. First of all, they endured additional inspections. Although steamship companies had a tremendous economic incentive to lure passengers, there was a catch. If, when the immigrants arrived in America, they were deemed unsuitable for immigration, the steamship companies had to take them back free of charge and in space that would otherwise be available for cargo.

Therefore, the companies made sure that inspectors at the docks were extremely careful in their choice of customers. Those who intended to travel were disinfected, and questionable ones were quarantined. They commonly stayed, hundreds of them, sleeping in rows for two weeks until they could be inspected again. Families, of course, were deeply concerned that one member would be left behind while others were allowed to travel.

Jews in ports were also subject to thieves. Hostel owners overcharged. Ticket agents either overcharged or gave too little change. Professionals stole baggage. There were the usual assortment of con artists and white slave traders who promised young women marriage or employment but gave them a harsh life in prostitution instead. Young men were told the voyage was long and they would need enormous amounts of food; unnecessary supplies were sold at exorbitant prices.

PROVIDING AID

Most of the abuses and difficulties did get better—especially after the turn of the twentieth century, when there was help. French Jews established the Alliance Israélite Universelle, British Jews the Anglo-Jewish Association, and German Jews the Hilfverein der deutschen Juden. Agents of these various groups were at ports and railroad stations. The groups worked to get reduced train fares and provided food and sometimes money.

Hamburg was one of the principal embarkation points for travelers, so emigrating Jews were met at the trains arriving there by representatives of the Hilfverein— which took control of travelers from the moment they entered Germany until they left on ships—and taken to a special immigration house, where there was a large room with benches along each wall.

Once there, all the travelers got coffee and rolls. A clerk, sitting at a desk in the center of the room, took down the travelers' names and examined their steamship tickets. The date was given for the next sailing of the ship.

But even after they had escaped the Russian or Polish rulers, the Jews had to face thieves among themselves. One traveler, Benjamin Gordon, told of being approached by a man in Hamburg. The man claimed to come from a town near Gordon's. As the two spoke, Gordon revealed that his boat needed repair and he would have to wait. The stranger suggested that Gordon exchange his ticket for that of the stranger's friend, whose boat was leaving in two days. The stranger only asked for $5 in addition to the ticket. Gordon said he had only $3, and the two agreed on the price.

The stranger told Gordon where to meet him the next day to get the ticket. Gordon found out the next day that the stranger had checked out. Gordon reported the incident and was told the city was filled with confidence tricksters. Luckily, Gordon had registered the ticket number, so the fraudulent user was arrested—but he was not the thief who had tricked him into buying the stolen ticket. Gordon got his ticket back and was pleased when he learned that the thief had finally been arrested.

Finally, however they did it, Jews from Eastern Europe found their way to the ports and onto steamships. They were about to begin a very adventurous ocean journey.

STEERAGE: THE LONG JOURNEY

The voyage across the ocean was a journey deeply embedded in the memory of the immigrants. For all of their lives, they would remember the name of the ship they came on, the date they finally reached America, and the shudder-inducing details of the voyage itself.

Many of them had youth on their side. They came from a people that specialized in survival. Their particular personalities thrived on adventure, on jumping into the unknown. Still, whatever personal or cultural skills and enthusiasm they brought with them, all these were tested by the harrowing conditions of the voyage across the ocean toward a new life in the Golden Land.

The irony of such trips is that, perhaps because of the limited duration of the travel, perhaps because of vivid memories of what they were fleeing from, the immigrants had surprisingly positive memories of the journey. Perhaps they saw it as a test or a pain like childbirth before they could be reborn as Americans. Perhaps they were glad to be anywhere but their former homeland. Whatever the reason, it should be remembered that, as would happen on the Lower East Side, the painful realities were often recalled with a fondness seemingly at odds with what the experience was actually like.

THE SHIPS

The cost of a trip across the Atlantic varied from $12 to $35, including food. This was more than the average Jew's annual income, so savings had to be accumulated over several years, or more typically, a relative in America bought the *shifskart*, the steamship ticket.

A STORMY CROSSING

Benjamin L. Gordon recorded his memories of storms during his trip across the Atlantic in his memoir *Between Two Worlds:*

One day before the ship was scheduled to land, we ran into a mighty north-eastern storm. The sky became black as Stygian night and the sea became more and more turbulent, dashing up fierce gray waves. The ship quivered, creaked, and wheezed, and the high waves slapped viciously against the small portholes of the cabins. It was impossible to stand or even recline without having a strong grip on some fixed object. Many people rolled on the floor amidst tables, chairs, and luggage. I became violently ill during the eight hours that the storm lasted.

>━◆━<

The ships sought maximum profit, which meant that they wanted to carry the most people possible in the least possible space. The poor Jews had to travel not as first- or second-class passengers but in steerage. Steerage was the name given to the area below the ship's decks where the steering mechanisms at the ship's stern had once been housed. Passengers in this area would feel more acutely each pitch and toss on the ocean's waves than they would in other parts of the ship. Steamships never ceased rolling on the ocean, so the voyage was extremely difficult for many passengers. Seasickness was a common ailment. Of course, almost none of the Jewish passengers had been on ships before, and so the movements were unfamiliar. Furthermore, the winds were frequently chilly, which kept passengers below decks, as did any rain.

Travel conditions varied considerably, depending on the ship and when the immigrants made their voyage. Before 1900, conditions were considerably worse than afterward because of new regulations and oversight. Some of the German vessels

Jewish immigrants on their way to America around the turn of the century. *Source: Courtesy of Brown Brothers.*

got better, eventually even installing kosher kitchens. By general consent, the *Staatendam* was the worst of the ships. There were reports of the passengers in steerage on that ship needing to steal water just to survive.

LIVING ON BOARD

Benjamin Gordon had made his shaky journey on the *Bohemia*. What he recalled most was the shouting, the cries of tiny children, and the musical instruments, played especially by Hungarian and Slovak passengers. The music brought with it hand clapping and foot stomping. The sound was overwhelming. The nights, though, were worse.

Because of the crowding, passengers stayed seated on their own luggage or on the decks. Gordon spent his nights on a chair on a deck. Most passengers did not wash or shave for the entire voyage. The avoidance of washing, of course, led to a pungent, pervasive smell of sweat throughout the area. The steerage area was almost never washed except at the end of the trip when the ship would be inspected.

A typical immigrant slept on a cot; cots were stacked three high. A passenger's berth was in the shape of an oblong box that measured 2 feet 6 inches by 6 feet 2 inches. An iron pipe sometimes separated the berths. Passengers frequently were so close that they touched shoulders while lying in their berths. This proximity had an ironic effect: the very tightness provided protection from the waves. Had the passengers not been packed so closely together, the movement of the ship would have sent them flying onto the floor.

Sometimes there was a pillow; sometimes a life preserver served that purpose instead. What blankets were provided were so thin that passengers inevitably fought the cold by sleeping in their clothes. The virtual complete lack of privacy prevented any of them from shedding too many clothes anyway. Any supplies brought by passengers were kept in the berth. They were not allowed to be kept on the floor, and there was no place on the ship to store them. The tiny portholes were kept shut to keep out the bad weather; this had the effect of keeping every smell inside. There were washing and lavatory rooms, few in number and filthy, usually with water several inches deep sloshing on the floor. No soap or towels were provided. The lines for the washrooms were so long that some passengers got up as early as 5 A.M. to be sure they would have time to get washed before breakfast, served two hours later.

Steerage was divided by gender, but this separation rarely prevented romantic encounters. These were so frequent—young people were in very confined spaces for weeks on end, after all—that the owners ordered strict regulations about intimacy on ships. There were notices on steerage cabin walls with a warning: "All couples making love too warmly would be married compulsorily at New York if the authorities deemed it fit, or should be fined or imprisoned." Despite such warnings, many romances bloomed on the ships.

Passengers tried to divert themselves in other ways as well. Some tried to read about America, but half of the immigrants could neither read nor write. Others talked or just stayed in their bunk or listened to another passenger's attempt at playing a whistle.

Sometimes first-class passengers would mock the passengers in steerage. In at least one instance, a passenger would stand on a deck above the poor travelers and throw down pennies, oranges, and candies just to see the crowd scrambling to get them. The author Robert Louis Stevenson once crossed the Atlantic, booking a second-class cabin so that he would have access to a writing table. He spent most of the actual voyage, though, with the steerage passengers. He wrote about attitudes toward these poor immigrants and why they were treated differently: "In the steerage there are males and females; in the second class ladies and gentlemen."

FOOD

Meals were often served from galleys in big pails, and depending on the ship, passengers ate at tables or in their berths. The food served to steerage passengers was of the lowest and cheapest possible quality. Breakfast typically consisted of watered-down coffee, ugly-looking potatoes, biscuits, and bread. Dinner, served at noon, usually started with soup—"a hot compound with a faint reminiscence of gravy and mutton bones, some grains of barley, and fragments of celery and cabbage; sometimes, instead, a thick mixture of ground peas"—and then included tough meat or nearly inedible salt fish or rice. At five, there was tea with hard biscuits and butter. Emma Beckerman recalled her mother grimacing as she gingerly cut green spots out of the bread and ate it with the soup, which to the young Emma appeared to be seawater. Benjamin Gordon couldn't eat the food, so he lived for his three-week voyage on bread, butter, cheese, and tea.

The ships, some of which had supposedly kosher areas, generally ignored all the rules of keeping kosher.

THE CREW

In the early years of steamship travel, the crew frequently thought of the steerage passengers as being in captivity. They flirted with young women and threatened any man seeking to protect the woman from their advances. Women took to staying below deck after dinner to avoid seeing the sailors. Still, the crew had access to the women's compartment and would enter whenever they wished.

The crew screamed obscenities at the passengers. Sometimes crew members resorted to violence or the destruction of the immigrant's belongings. The passengers were very reluctant to confront the crew because they were seen as authority

STEERAGE

In his memoir *A Dreamer's Journey*, the philosopher Morris Raphael Cohen recalled his own voyage:

> We were huddled together in the steerage literally like cattle—my mother, my sister and I sleeping in the middle tier, people being above us and below us as well as on the same level. Naturally, we could not eat the food of the ship, since it was not kosher. We only asked for hot water into which my mother used to put a little brandy and sugar to give it a taste. Towards the end of the trip when our bread was beginning to give out we applied to the ship's steward for bread, but the kind he gave us was unbearably soggy. The hardships of the trip began to tell on my mother, so that she took sick and developed a fever, but the ship's doctor did not think it was serious and prescribed some bouillon for her. As the law regulating kosher foods does not apply to medicines my mother took it, but I wouldn't touch it.

✦

figures and passengers feared that somehow such a response would hurt their chances of being admitted to the United States.

Unsurprisingly, crew members could be bribed. Luggage that had not been fumigated could be sneaked on board. Food from the upper-deck kitchens could be gotten.

ARRIVAL

Some ships sought to provide a final good memory of the voyage by handing out candy to women and a pipe and tobacco for men. But for the numbed, filthy passengers, the very idea of getting off the ship was reward enough.

FIRST GLIMPSE OF AMERICA

The great novelist Anzia Yezierska, author of such novels as *Bread Givers*, recalled her own reaction as she finally saw America:

> Land! Land! Came the joyous shout. America! We're in America! Cried my mother, almost smothering us in her rapture. All crowded and pushed on deck. They strained and stretched to get the first glimpse of the golden country, lifting their children on their shoulders so that they might see beyond them. Men fell on their knees to pray. Women hugged their babies and wept. Children danced. Strangers embraced and kissed like old friends in love. Age-old visions sang themselves to me—songs of freedom of an oppressed people. America—America.

It was always an exciting moment when land was finally spotted. Passengers saw Long Island first, though they probably weren't aware of it. Many passengers, overwhelmed with emotion, simply cried when they saw that their voyage had ended and there, right in front of them, was that magical Eden, the Golden Land.

People grabbed their belongings, tying up their sheets and blankets, combing their hair, washing as best they could, trying to make their appearance as pleasant as possible for their encounters with the inspectors who would have the fearsome power to reject them at the last minute after so arduous a journey buoyed by so much hope. The steerage passengers would go onto the deck, wanting to drink in their first impressions of their new home. George Gershwin's father leaned out so far his hat flew off in the breeze. He had tucked the name of the family's only contact in America inside the hat.

The ships would enter the Narrows, the harbor entrance between Staten Island and Brooklyn. Passengers were amazed at the enormous array of ships all around them.

A small cutter would then come alongside the ship. The steerage passengers might not have realized that the two men and the woman in uniform who were climbing the ladder were headed to the second-class area's saloon, where the inspector would ask a couple of questions. The other man was a doctor who looked at the eyes of each second-class passenger.

Because the passengers were barely examined at all, booking such a ticket became a way around the rules for steerage passengers who would be subjected to a much more rigorous examination. Indeed, it was not unheard of for a member of a family who had been deported back to Europe to save enough, with the assistance of those admitted to America, to buy a second-class ticket and thereby get through the cursory inspection. When the second-class passengers were done, the inspector looked at the ship's passenger list of names of first-class passengers. A quick look was enough; they were fine.

The ship continued to move as the inspections took place. The steerage passengers pushing toward the rail could see the magnificent Statue of Liberty on the left. Parents lifted their young children on their shoulders for a better view. It was a view that many of the children would carry in their minds for the rest of their lives. The impressive Manhattan skyline loomed a mere 2 miles away.

The ship then sailed past Ellis Island, just north of the Statue of Liberty, and into the Hudson River, where it finally docked. The steerage passengers were quickly pushed away from the rails; authorities feared that some of them would leap onto the dock. After the passengers in first and second class got off, the immigrants streamed onto the pier and, after about an hour, were herded onto a ferryboat until it filled. Barges were used to transport any remaining passengers.

The passengers knew they were on their way to an inspection that could end their dream and send them back to Europe or open the final gateway to freedom and rebirth. The inspection was their last test before entering America, and most were very scared as they approached the island where their fate would be sealed.

The Registry Hall on Ellis Island. *Source: Courtesy of Brown Brothers.*

TWO

LANDING AT ELLIS ISLAND

⤛⤜

THE JEWISH immigrants who fled Europe to start a new life in America didn't speak English. Many knew no one in their new homeland or knew only family members or people from their hometown. They had crossed a lot of space, but they had also crossed a lot of time. They went from what were often crude agricultural and trade economies to a bustling, modern industrialized nation. They went from a land of revered centuries-old traditions to a land that relished the shiny and new.

But somehow the Jewish immigrants felt at home in America, felt that America was different, that it would be a true safe haven, a land where no one would kill them just for being Jewish, a place where they could speak their minds without fear, where they would be judged on their skills and not their God.

Most of the new immigrants were destitute or very poor. Many arrived with no money at all. They averaged about $15.50 apiece, as opposed to $22.00 for non-Jewish immigrants. Between 1899 and 1910, 56.6 percent of the Jewish immigrants were male and only 43.4 percent female. During those same years, 24.9 percent were under the age of fourteen, 69.6 percent were between fourteen and forty-four, and only 5.5 percent were forty-five or older. It was indeed the young who made the journey. The Jewish immigrants who reported having a skilled occupation had a variety of jobs: 36.6 percent were tailors, 10.3 percent were carpenters, and 10.0 percent were dressmakers. There were also smaller percentages of shoemakers, clerks, painters, butchers, bakers, locksmiths, and blacksmiths, among others. Twenty-six percent of the Jewish immigrants over age fourteen were illiterate (about the same rate among all immigrants). For every hundred Jews admitted, eight were deported back to their home countries.

The boatloads of hopeful future Americans just kept on coming. And after surviving the wrenching experience of leaving their families, journeying across Europe evading Cossacks and thieves, crossing the Atlantic under the most trying of circumstances—they came face to face with the immigration inspectors.

CASTLE GARDEN

Castle Garden, adjacent to Battery Park in the southernmost part of Manhattan, was the first station the United States established to receive immigrants. The center operated from 1855 until 1889, and in that time 8,250,917 immigrants entered the country. It is worth remembering that it was Castle Garden that Emma Lazarus was referring to in her 1883 sonnet "The New Colossus" when she wrote, "Send these, the homeless, tempest-tost to me, I lift my lamp beside the Golden Door!"

Originally designed to be a fort protecting New York harbor, Castle Garden was a round stone building with a cupola. It was originally named Castle Clinton but was renamed Castle Garden in 1822 after becoming a concert hall where, among other distinctions, it became the site where Samuel F. B. Morse demonstrated the telegraph.

For Jewish immigrants, Castle Garden was very conveniently located because the newcomers could walk from there to the Lower East Side. That very proximity, however, carried its own dangers, for if immigrants could walk right into the New World, con men and other nefarious types could walk over and meet the sometimes naïve immigrants.

Before they could get to the Lower East Side, however, the immigrants had to pass the unpleasant inspection at Castle Garden. Under the aegis of New York State, a superintendent ran an increasingly harried staff of about one hundred people. Immigrants got off the barges or ferry, went into the building, and were herded into a baggage hall where they reclaimed any bags, which were then examined. Other exams followed; the inspectors didn't want to admit paupers, criminals, or people with serious diseases. After this examination, the immigrants went into the overcrowded, smelly rotunda, the main hall. There, crowded among three thousand

CASTLE GARDEN

A young Russian Jew named Isidore Kopeloff recalled Castle Garden:

> The main hall was huge and barren, and gave off an uncanny coldness,
> which produced in its inhabitants an involuntary oppression. One after
> another sighed and sighed. . . . [It] was often so crowded, so jammed, that
> there was simply nowhere to sit by day, or any place to lie down at night—
> not even on the bare floor.
>
> The filth was unendurable, so many packages, pillows, feather beds and
> foul clothing (often just plain rags) that each immigrant had dragged with
> him over the seas and clung to as if they were precious—all of this provided
> great opportunity for vermin, those filthy little beasts, that crawled about
> freely and openly over the clutter and made life disagreeable. The constant
> scratching and the distress of the little children touched one to the quick.

or so other immigrants, they perched on wooden benches or stood in line waiting to
go to the registration desk and state their name, age, nationality, destination, ship
on which they arrived, and date of arrival.

A lucky few immigrants had family members or friends who met them and so
could leave with a sense of where they were going. Many of these family members
had been the ones who had gone to the draft and passage office and exchanged
American money for 10 rubles that were sent back to pay for a steerage ticket.

Most immigrants, though, were unsure what to do. Many of them slept in the
rotunda for their first few days in America. People spilled out into adjoining streets
and sometimes just sat down and stayed there.

At the beginning of the 1880s, some of the Jewish poor were taken to the
Ward's Island Refuge, which was run by the Hebrew Emigrant Aid Society. Unfortunately, the quality of the aid was woefully inadequate. Food was dirty; worms

were found crawling around in it. On Jewish holidays, the HEAS workers offered *tsimmes,* a pudding made of carrots and potatoes. On one such occasion, a waiter refused to serve some of the tsimmes to an immigrant. A fight—later nicknamed the Tsimmes Revolt—broke out. Police, swinging clubs, arrived to restore order. The revolt did lead to some changes, but the refuge closed its doors in 1883.

People who lived near Castle Garden were also not happy about the immigrants. Cornelius Vanderbilt, ensconced in his mansion at 5 Bowling Green, complained that in the summer the wind would blow "pestilential and disagreeable odors" through his open windows. He and his neighbors feared declining property values. The *New York Daily Times* argued that Castle Garden should be demolished.

Castle Garden was eventually closed, but not because of the purported uncleanliness of the immigrants. The building was just too small to handle the masses of people streaming onto American shores. Several investigations also noted the scandalous behavior of some officials. Immigrants sometimes paid twice to have their baggage shipped. They were forced to pay bribes.

Young women found themselves the object of unwanted attention or outright sexual blackmail from officials who had the power to deny them entrance into America. The con men who prowled the Bowery looking for easy marks would cheat immigrants on changing European money into dollars.

OPPOSITION TO IMMIGRATION

Opposition to immigration had begun as early as the country's formation and spanned the centuries. Benjamin Franklin didn't much like the German immigrants in the eighteenth century. And a hundred years later, Samuel Morse was against "excessive" Catholic immigration. The anti-immigrant attitude began to spread in the 1890s when urban space to absorb the newcomers started to become scarce and native-born Americans, looking at the numbers of poor "peasants" arriving at America's shores, began to fear for their jobs. Moreover, the new immigrants were not primarily northern Europeans, like most Americans already here, but Eastern European Jews, along with many other groups. Longtime Americans combined their traditional anti-Jewish attitude with a concern that their own cultural values were being challenged.

This feeling soon found political expression. The Populists campaigned in 1896 in favor of immigration restriction. An immigration bill in 1897 that contained a

DEFENDING A BARRIER TO IMMIGRANTS

On March 16, 1896, Senator Henry Cabot Lodge spoke on behalf of the Immigration Bill of 1897, which included a literacy test for new immigrants. Here are some excerpts from that speech.

This bill is intended . . . to restrict still further immigration to the United States. . . .

The races most affected by the illiteracy test are those whose emigration to this country has begun within the last twenty years . . . races with which the English-speaking people have never hitherto assimilated, and who are most alien to the great body of the people of the United States. . . .

The immigrants excluded by the illiteracy test are those who remain for the most part in congested masses in our great cities. They furnish a large proportion of the population of the slums. . . . Illiteracy runs parallel with the slum population, with criminals, paupers, and juvenile delinquents of foreign birth or parentage, whose percentage is out of all proportion to their share of the total population. . . .

The exclusion of immigrants unable to read or write . . . will operate against the most undesirable and harmful part of our present immigration. . . .

More precious even than forms of government are the mental and moral qualities which make what we call our race. While these stand unimpaired all is safe. When those decline all is imperiled. They are exposed to but a single danger, and that is by changing the quality of our race and citizenship through the wholesale infusion of races whose traditions and inheritances, whose thoughts and whose beliefs are totally alien to ours and with whom we have never assimilated. . . .

In careless strength, with generous hand, we have kept our gates wide open to all the world. . . . The gates which admit men to the United States and to citizenship in the great Republic should no longer be left unguarded.

literacy test that Jewish immigrants would have found daunting passed both houses of Congress. Only President Grover Cleveland's veto prevented it from becoming law. It was to be a relatively short-lived victory, though, for a literacy test eventually did become law in 1917 and a quota system was established in 1921. It is staggering to consider the alternative course American Jewish history would have taken had both these measures passed in the 1890s.

Along with his veto of the bill, President Cleveland sent a stirring message to Congress on March 2, 1897, defending the immigrants.

ELLIS ISLAND

Ellis Island, on 27 acres not far from New York harbor, has become the symbol of immigrants arriving in America. Of course, Jews entered the United States in many other places, such as Boston or Baltimore or through Canada. But Ellis Island was the largest port of entry. Operating between 1892 and 1954, some twelve to sixteen million immigrants entered America after enduring the ordeal of inspection on Ellis Island. An average of five thousand people a day were processed on the island; on April 17, 1907, the busiest single day, 11,745 new immigrants arrived.

The United States had acquired the island from the children of Samuel Ellis, a New Jersey farmer, in 1808. The island itself had been used by the Dutch to hunt for oysters. Pirates and mutineers had been hanged on it. But the government was stuck trying to find an appropriate use for it. When they did decide to use it as an immigration station, they concluded that the island's 3 acres would be insufficient. The size of the island was doubled using landfill. A two-story wooden building was erected, but it burned down in 1897. A brick building replaced it and opened in 1900.

THE PROCEDURE

The immigrants on ferryboats or barges approached Ellis Island with a mixture of fear and high expectation. Often the boats couldn't dock because of the crowd of other vessels and everyone had to stay a little longer on the dreaded water.

Finally, they landed. Some of the immigrants, feeling earth beneath their feet for the first time in weeks and overwhelmed by actually being in the Golden Land, bent down and kissed the ground at Ellis Island, famous throughout Europe as either the Isle of Hope or the Isle of Tears.

Ellis Island in the early 1900s. *Source: Courtesy of Brown Brothers.*

The immigration officials who had come on the ships had pinned landing cards on the clothing of the newcomers. As they stepped off the ferries or barges, they were sorted into groups of about thirty. Hungry, tired, and confused, the new immigrants trudged along toward the red brick building. The guards tried to force them along with yelling and some pushing. An interpreter shouted directions in a series of languages, and the dazed immigrants went through the front door to the baggage room. After retrieving any wooden or wicker luggage they had brought, they went up the staircase to the second floor. There they stood in line as inspectors examined them.

Women went into a separate line where a nurse would examine them. Collars were unbuttoned so that doctors, in their crisp blue uniforms, could look for lumps on the neck, indicating goiter. The ears were checked and then the back. The worst part of the exam involved the eyes. Inspectors used a buttonhook to flip the eyelid up to search for signs of trachoma. The medical examiners looked for irregular breathing and, with long experience, sought out the mentally ill who made unusual facial expressions. If an immigrant was thought to need additional scrutiny, the inspector put a blue chalk mark on his or her lapel.

Immigrants arriving at Ellis Island. *Source: Courtesy of Brown Brothers.*

Such chalk marks didn't faze the boldest of the immigrants. They simply turned their coat inside out, and magically, there was no mark. Most of the immigrants were not as daring. Indeed, they were deeply embarrassed by the whole examination process. Most of the Jews had never gone to a doctor, and their cultural and religious upbringing made them uneasy about exposing any part of their flesh to a stranger and to the crowds around them.

The immigrants who had the check marks were pushed aside and put into pens surrounded by a wire screen. If a child under ten was sent into the pen, a parent had to be there as well to accompany the child in case a trip back to Europe was warranted. Children over ten were repatriated without a parent. This law forced many immigrants to decide whether to allow the marked to return alone or to go back to Europe as a family.

The people who passed the medical examination had papers without the dreaded LPN ("liable to become a public nuisance") stamp and were then sent to the Registry Hall. That room was 200 feet long and 100 feet wide, with a ceiling 56 feet high. It had arched windows and an observation gallery. There were rows of iron

ELLIS ISLAND CHALK MARKS

The chalk marks that the inspectors used to indicate potential problems included the following:

B	Back	L	Lameness
C	Conjunctivitis	N	Neck
CT	Trachoma	P	Physical condition and lungs
E	Eyes	Pg	Pregnancy
F	Face	Sc	Scalp
Ft	Feet	S	Senility
G	Goiter	X	Suspected mental illness
H	Heart	⊗	Definite signs of mental illness
K	Hernia		

railings delineating long aisles in which the immigrants lined up. While waiting for their names to be called, the immigrants sat on benches—for an average of five hours. Many used the time to try as best they could to rest. The hall was divided into sections based on the national origins of the immigrants.

Finally, the immigrant was called to see the official, usually an exhausted man who worked from 9 in the morning until after 7 at night, seven days a week. The immigrant had answered questions that were recorded on the ship's manifest—as many as twenty-nine of them—and the official now checked these answers.

The trickiest question the immigrants faced caused great confusion. The inspectors asked if the immigrants had a job waiting. Immigrants thought that the logical answer was to respond that they did have a job, assuming that such an answer would indicate that they were hard workers and could take care of themselves. But soon it was whispered that it was crucial to tell the inspector that there was no job because the officials assumed that those with employment already lined up were taking jobs away from Americans.

THE ANGEL OF ELLIS ISLAND

The following story appeared in a publication of the American Jewish Historical Society.

In 1907, the New York Section of the National Council of Jewish Women (NCJW) hired Celia Greenstone as assistant immigrant arrival agent at Ellis Island. . . . [The section] worried that thousands of single Jewish women must be "misled into immoral lives, and other girls [will be] subjected to great dangers because of the lack of some directing and protecting agency at Ellis Island.". . . Although only 20, Greenstone . . . worked six long days a week for months on end, ushering single women, mothers and children through the Ellis Island process. . . . She helped girls traveling alone to locate their families in other parts of the country, or to obtain work and respectable lodgings. Greenstone . . . arranged for kosher food to be delivered to inmates of the island hospital. She also established Shabbat and holiday services. . . . In 1962, looking back on her years helping Ellis Island's Jewish immigrants, Greenstone explained that she hoped "to show the immigrants that in all the hard sorrow of their lives, they did not stand alone, and that they did not have to succumb. [I wanted] to show them that if one person misused or betrayed them, another would not."

Young, single women were prevented from entering America until social workers could make sure they would have someone to take care of them. The fear of white slavers was very real.

The successful immigrants got their landing cards.

When they were finished in the Registry Hall, the immigrants descended the stairs—which they nicknamed the "stairs of separation." Once downstairs, they were separated, sent either to the detention room or the "kissing post," aptly named because from there they could see friends or family members who had come to get them. Finally, the immigrants went to the service center where they might exchange their money or send a letter at the post office. Those who were not going to New York were sent to the Railroad Room.

The many Jewish immigrants headed for New York worked their way through the dark corridor to the door with the clear and welcome sign inscribed "Push" and "To New York." Beyond the door, the immigrants met whoever had come to take them, and together they got on the ferry for the half-hour final journey to New York.

NAME CHANGING

Changing names has most frequently been ascribed to immigration officials. But immigration officials simply checked the immigrant's name against the names on the ship's passenger list and therefore had no need to write it down. When immigrants changed their names, it was typically long after they had left Ellis Island. Jewish immigrants themselves were often eager and willing to change their names, for a variety of reasons: They wanted to start a new life or they wanted to fit in more with America or they didn't trust authorities not to reveal their real names to the Russian military (who might demand that they return to the draft) or they weren't attached to their family name, which for some of them had come into existence only relatively recently. In 1787, the Austrian Empire had required Jews living within its borders to register surnames. Similar legislation—often with the goal of making tax collection more efficient—soon followed in other regions. In some cases, names were imposed on Jewish families.

When Jews themselves intentionally changed their names, they did the same or, as they had in Europe, chose to name themselves after a local area. Many simply adopted the street names from the Lower East Side. Suddenly there were Jews named Clinton and Ludlow.

THE DETAINED

Individuals who were detained usually stayed on Ellis Island for a week or two until a board of special inquiry determined their fate. Sometimes as many as 2,400 immigrants were squeezed into the detention area, which contained 1,800 beds. It sometimes happened that inspectors couldn't work their way through the crowds to find the person for whom they were looking. Meanwhile, the infections inherent in such

A ship's manifest from 1904 which includes the author's grandmother, uncle, and aunt. *Source: Courtesy of Lawrence J. Epstein.*

a situation worsened the plight of many stuck in the area as they waited to find out if they were to be sent back to Europe.

THE HEBREW IMMIGRANT AID SOCIETY

The Russian Emigrant Relief Society had been established after the pogroms in 1881. That developed into HEAS, the Hebrew Emigrant Aid Society, which, fearing that an influx of poor Russian Jews would adversely affect the status of the German Jews already living well in America, lobbied to restrict immigration. HEAS agents were notorious in their mistreatment of immigrants at Castle Garden. The group—not to be confused with HIAS, the Hebrew Immigrant Aid Society—ceased functioning in 1884. The work of HEAS was taken over by United Hebrew Charities, and they continued efforts to halt the immigration.

Eventually, the Hebrew Immigrant Aid Society was established in 1904. As efficient as its predecessor, HEAS, had been ineffective, HIAS established a bureau on Ellis Island. Its staff offered translators, helped the immigrants through the medical

A SPECIAL CASE

In 1905, President Theodore Roosevelt appointed Philip Cowen to be an immigration inspector on the board of special inquiry. In his book *Memories of an American Jew,* Cowen recalled his experiences, including the following:

> A Jewish woman from Russia came here to join her five children, all well-to-do. The family joined in sending for her as they wished their mother to spend her last days with them. The doctors certified her as physically defective because of her eyesight, and as of low mentality, because she had failed in the Binet-Simon [intelligence test] and other tests. It is a very serious matter when the doctors thus certify an alien, and nearly always results in exclusion and deportation. But the friends of an immigrant have the right to ask that medical specialists be called at their own expense to check up on the Government's medical examination. This was done. The woman admitted she could not see the time on the clock on the wall, but she stated she had brought up all her children and had done all the housework and cooking without medical attention. She could not play with the pictures the doctors had given her [alluding to the jigsaw puzzles given her to put together], but, if they would let her have some meat she would make a delicious soup for them, and if they gave her flour and the other ingredients she would bake a loaf of bread finer than they served on Ellis Island. She was admitted on appeal.

procedures, appeared before the boards at deportation hearings, lent money, got bonds to guarantee that the immigrants were employable, investigated the conditions in steerage on ships, and searched for relatives of immigrants who had been detained to show that such would-be Americans would not draw on public funds if admitted. In 1909, the Hebrew Immigrant Aid Society merged with the Hebrew Sheltering House Association and officially became known as HIAS.

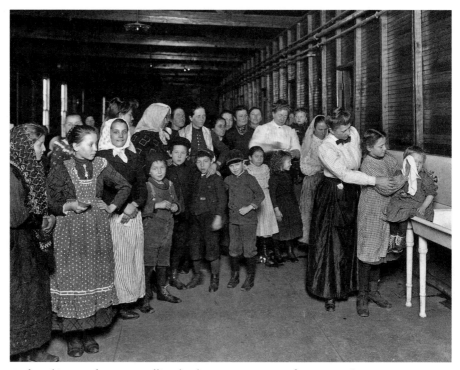
Gathered in a washroom on Ellis Island. *Source: Courtesy of Brown Brothers.*

In 1911, HIAS set up a kosher kitchen on Ellis Island. This was crucial because many of the new arrivals had chosen not to eat the nonkosher foods on the ships crossing the Atlantic. HIAS also offered religious services and concerts. It established an employment bureau and provided railway tickets at reduced prices and provided shelter for the new arrivals who had no other place to go. Thus HIAS was remarkably successful in improving the lives of hundreds of thousands of new immigrants, making their difficult passage into America smoother than it otherwise would have been.

LEAVING ELLIS ISLAND

The ordeal of working through the labyrinth of Ellis Island took most immigrants somewhere between four hours and one full day. Once they were cleared for entry, they went off with friends and relatives or by themselves. The relatives weren't always happy with the way the immigrants appeared. Their distinctly European dress would make them stand out as foreigners new to the country and as such both a potential embarrassment to their families and an easy mark for the multitude of thieves and con men eager to take advantage of their confusion and ignorance of American ways.

To prevent such reactions, many newcomers were almost immediately led into a nearby washroom or even pushed behind a large tree. More traditional American garments quickly replaced the caps and peasant skirts, kerchiefs and trousers from the Old Country. It was common to see discarded clothing littering the sidewalks of the island and on the dressing room floor. Sometimes the clothing was tossed only after the immigrants got off Ellis Island and reached Manhattan.

When the immigrants looked presentable, they boarded a ferry for the half-hour ride to the Battery.

They had made it. The long journey was over. They were in the Golden Land. Some, like the comedian Henny Youngman's father, who had no place to go because they had no families to greet them, went to the Lower East Side and found their way to the Mills Hotel, which charged 25 cents a night. Other newcomers without family searched for a corner of a room where they could board. Once the entertainer Eddie Cantor needed money for a dentist and arranged with several people who had space to rent to bring boarders to them. Cantor met immigrants as they came off the ferry and offered to help them find a room. The immigrants were happy for the assistance, and Cantor got a little money for providing the service.

With families or not, the new immigrants almost invariably ended their physical journey in that center of Jewish immigrant family life, the tenement. There they were about to embark on another kind of journey, that of adaptation to American life, a journey that taxed their souls as much as the physical journey had taxed their bodies.

They were about to discover America.

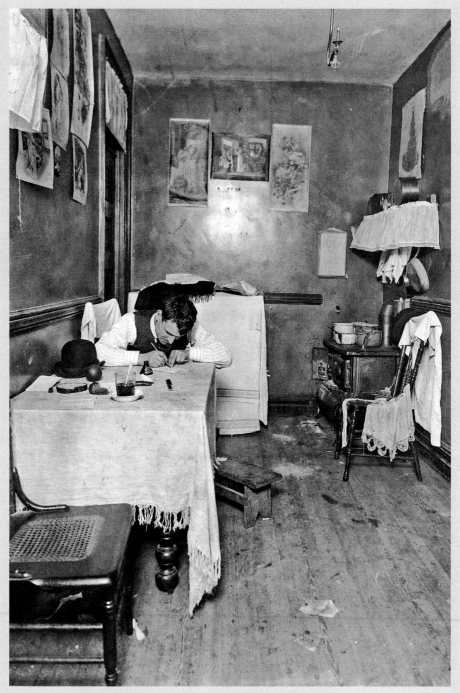

A Jewish Immigrant studying in a tenement parlor by day. *Source: Courtesy of Brown Brothers.*

THREE

LIFE IN THE TENEMENTS

>†×†<

T HE FIRST sights for the new immigrants were overwhelming. They made
their way tentatively through incredibly crowded streets traveling to a new
home, probably the home of a relative or someone from their hometown.
The sights on the city streets were odd to them. They saw inventions they didn't
know about and smelled strange and not always pleasant odors.

Some saw a black person for the first time in their lives. Indeed, Jews who came
to the Lower East Side might have been surprised that there were Irish, Italians,
Germans, Poles, and others living in the area.

Maybe they saw the members of a family sitting, dejected, out on a sidewalk
with their household goods beside them because a landlord had evicted them.
Sometimes a plate rested near the tired-looking mother to collect money for the rent.
The family hoped the pennies would accumulate so that by sunset they could get
back into their flat.

When the immigrants made it to their destination, their eyes looked up at the
odd fire escapes clinging to the facade of the tenement, a six- to eight-story
building with many apartments inside. The British novelist Arnold Bennett,
observing tenements on Rivington Street, observed that "the architecture seemed
to sweat humanity at every window and door." The tenements were numerous; in
1881, there were twenty-two thousand tenements holding half a million people;
in 1895, there were forty thousand tenements housing 1.3 million people.

THE STORY OF TENEMENTS

It was as early as 1833 that builders concluded that the Lower East Side was a perfect place to build inexpensive housing for new immigrants. Irish immigrants fleeing the famine and German immigrants escaping political turmoil settled in the area. The section north of Division Street was called Kleindeutschland, Little Germany. In the 1880s, Jews and Italians started moving in, and many of the Germans, including German Jews, having gained some prosperity, moved out, leaving more tenement space for arriving Jews to occupy. By 1900, the burgeoning Jewish population had formed loose neighborhoods on the Lower East Side. Hungarian Jews lived in the northern part, above Houston Street, where the German Jews had lived before moving uptown. Jews from Galicia lived between Houston and Broome and east of Clinton Street. Romanian Jews lived directly west of them, and Russian Jews lived from Grand Street south to Monroe Street.

It is crucial to remember that although the Lower East Side is most frequently associated with Eastern European Jewish immigrants, Jews from other parts of the world came to that neighborhood as well as other parts of New York City. German Jews continued to arrive, along with other Jews from Western Europe.

Sephardic Jews (the descendants of Jews who had been forced to flee Spain in 1492 and Portugal in 1497) had arrived not only as the first Jews in America as early as 1654 but also as later immigrants. Indeed, thirty thousand Sephardic Jews, mostly from Turkey, the Balkans, Bulgaria, and Greece, arrived in New York City between 1890 and 1924. They faced special problems. Many Eastern European Jews did not understand Ladino, the Sephardic Jews' Judeo-Spanish language, and found their customs, dress, and foods to be foreign to what they thought of as Jewish. Compounding this sense of being a minority within a minority, Sephardic Jews already settled in the United States felt that these new "Oriental" Jews were different from them. The new Sephardic immigrants responded to these challenges by establishing their own communal organizations, synagogues, and schools.

The tenements that the Jewish immigrants lived in were built on small rectangular lots 25 feet wide and 100 feet long. After the Tenement House Act of 1879, it became common for tenements to be shaped like a squared-off dumbbell or letter H, with two apartments at the front of the building and two at the back, connected by a narrow hallway. Front apartments had three or four rooms; rear apartments, measuring just 325 square feet, generally had three. Landlords charged between $10 and

Large immigrant family in a tenement apartment. *Source: Courtesy of Brown Brothers.*

$20 a month for the apartments. Renters commonly had two weeks' free rent; for some families, that meant moving every few weeks. One immigrant, Martha Dolinko, recalled, "When I used to come from school or work, sometimes I didn't know where we lived. The neighbors had to tell me."

In the backyard were the privies (toilets) used by the tenement dwellers. These privies were commonplace until the 1901 Tenement House Act mandated that outhouses be removed and replaced by indoor toilets.

Privies were originally preferred because indoor toilets took up space that could be made part of the rental area and thus be income-producing. For the comedian George Burns, whose family moved to 259 Rivington Street when Burns was five, it was a family adventure to get to the outdoor toilet:

The upstairs halls were dark. So if you had to go to the bathroom at night in the wintertime, my sisters were scared stiff.

We weren't very brave either. So my mother used to talk them down to the bathroom downstairs. She'd open up the window and shout down to them. So when my sisters went to the toilet they knew it in Altoona.

There were also cellar apartments—if possible, even worse than the apartments above. Without adequate sewage and with horses providing much of the city's transportation, Manhattan's streets threw off a terrible smell aimed right at those apartments. When Eddie Cantor's parents died, his grandmother took him in, and they were forced to move to a basement apartment at 47 Henry Street. When songwriter Irving Berlin and his family arrived in New York, they were forced to spend their first few weeks in a basement apartment on Monroe Street until they fled to a slightly better place at 330 Cherry Street.

As the new immigrants climbed the stoop and walked inside a tenement, they would first step into the hallway. Hallways were typically dark, but the 1901 Tenement House Act mandated that the hallways be illuminated. The immigrants felt along until they got to the rickety stairs and from there started up. The first landing might have two toilets—if the tenement had them—and a couple of apartments. The poorest immigrants lived on the top floors. The immigrants made their way into one of these apartments. They were small and stifling.

Each apartment in tenements such as the one at 97 Orchard Street—the site is currently the Lower East Side Tenement Museum—consisted of three rooms: a small, windowless bedroom; a kitchen; and a front room with windows. (The windowless bedroom was outlawed by the 1901 Tenement House Act.) There might be a window through which tenants could see an air shaft that separated the tenement buildings from each other. The airshafts built in response to the 1901 law were to provide ventilation for the toilets, not to provide tenants with more fresh air and light. These were widely used to dump garbage and so were riddled with filth and bacteria.

The front room was a parlor. It was often used as a workplace by day, where activities such as sewing clothing, gluing labels on cigar boxes, making artificial flowers, or rolling cigars took place. Eddie Cantor's grandmother was once arrested for rolling cigars without a license.

The parlor turned into a bedroom at night. The space was so small that people slept in shifts on whatever was used as a bed. Children might sleep on a thick rug or on orange crates.

The kitchen was central to the apartment. Sabbath prayers were said in the kitchen. It was the place where decisions were made and where guests were greeted.

A tenement parlor at night. *Source: Courtesy of Brown Brothers.*

A tenement kitchen. *Source: Courtesy of the Lower East Side Tenement Museum.*

Card games were played around the kitchen table. The children did their home-work there.

Clotheslines were strung between tenements. The lines were of course used to hang clothes out to dry, but they also served to send messages or packages between buildings. The comedian Bert Lahr's mother once saved a child's life by sending money across the clothesline so that her neighbor could pay a doctor.

IN THE TENEMENT

The people who lived in the tenements retained vivid memories of their experiences throughout their lives. For those who grew up in such living conditions, tenement life shaped their values and their experiences.

Emma Beckerman, a new immigrant, described the inside of a tenement when she first entered as follows: "The furnishings were worn and shabby. Four rickety chairs, a scarred wooden table, a leaky icebox, and a rusty coal stove greeted us. The bedroom contained a sagging double bed and a broken-down bureau." In other apartments, there was a sofa in the parlor that would sleep four at night.

There were cast-iron coal stoves, with soot fires frequently flaring in the pipes. Children got burns.

The stove was not the only danger to children. They had to face vermin: rats running all around and lice in their beds at night. Such a reality made it crucial for parents and teachers to stress the importance of cleanliness. The rats had long been part of the Lower East Side's life. In the mid-nineteenth century, there were rat fights organized in saloons with patrons betting on the outcome.

The typical Jewish apartment also included various items that weren't just for everyday survival. The pushke was one prominent example. The pushke was a can in which family members dropped extra change. The money was collected on behalf of some charity. The most famous was a blue-and-white can for the Jewish National Fund. The monies were for property purchases in the Land of Israel. Pushkes also existed for such various charities as a yeshiva, an old-age home, and Jewish children.

By 1904, many tenement homes had acquired a piano for the parlor. Children were given music lessons, and the whole family could use it for entertainment.

Victrolas (early phonographs) were another common item. They began to appear everywhere, in homes, candy stores, restaurants, and other places where people gathered. Most immigrants loved the new invention. Abraham Hyman recalls

RUTH J. ABRAM: A MUSEUM GREW IN HER

Ruth J. Abram is the president of the Lower East Side Tenement Museum. It was her experiences and vision that gave shape to an institution that seeks to "promote tolerance and historical perspective through the presentation and interpretation of the variety of immigrant and migrant experiences on Manhattan's Lower East Side, a gateway to America."

Ruth grew up in Atlanta, Georgia. One vivid childhood memory involves a bus trip she took with the family maid, Rosa May Maddox, who was African American. The two boarded the bus, and Rosa found a seat for the child. Then Rosa took her own seat in the back in the so-called colored section. Worried that Rosa might get off the bus without her, Ruth went to sit with her. The maid brought Ruth back to the white section in the front. Looking back, recalling a society that didn't allow an adult to protect a child, Ruth believes that the seeds of the museum were planted that day.

After her family moved to New York, Ruth went to college and became a social worker and reformer seeking to redress the social ills of discrimination and poverty and eventually to get involved in the revived movement for women's equality.

Ruth began searching for a way to promote tolerance. Eventually, all her ideas formed a unique vision: create a tenement museum, a place to remember the common ground of immigrants from all over the world. Working out of the Eldridge Street Synagogue with Anita Jacobson, Ruth began looking for the building that would bring that vision to life. It took several years, but in January 1988, the two women found 97 Orchard Street, the museum's flagship tenement building. The tenement had been sealed since 1935, but between its opening in 1863 and its closure in 1935, about seven thousand immigrants from more than twenty nations had called it home. Within months, the museum began when the two women moved into one of the building's storefronts. The museum itself officially opened on November 17, 1988.

THE LEVINE FAMILY APARTMENT

The Lower East Side Tenement Museum has carefully restored apartments to interpret the lives of actual residents from different historical periods. The museum describes the Levine family and its efforts to explain their experience as follows:

In 1890, Harris and Jennie Levine came to the United States from Plonsk, in what is today Poland, approximately 35 miles northwest of Warsaw. Family lore reported that the couple arrived on their honeymoon. Harris Levine listed himself as a dressmaker and living in 97 Orchard Street in the City Directory from 1892 to 1904. According to the Annual Reports of the Factory Inspectors of the State of New York, Levine's contracting shop was investigated first in 1892 and again in 1895, when he was ordered to post the Factory Inspection law in his shop, an order with which he complied.

According to the 1900 census, Harris and Jennie had their first child in 1892, a girl named Pauline. Museum researchers have yet to find her birth certificate. Hyman (known as Herman) was born three years later in 1895, and his brother Solie (known as Max) was born on November 30, 1897. It is right after this birth that the Museum has chosen to re-create the Levine apartment.

Just before moving out of 97 Orchard Street, Harris Levine declared his intention to become a citizen in 1904. The two witnesses to the naturalization were Jacob Vogelman and Gedalia Scheinbaum. According to the naturalization, the Levines immigrated to the United States in 1890; however we have found no ship manifest to verify their entry date. Harris Levine's naturalization petition confirms that he was born in Plonsk, Poland, and Jennie Levine's death certificate indicates the same. Both are buried in Washington Cemetery in Brooklyn. Cemetery records show that a benevolent association named the Wisdom of Man Society paid for both Levine burials. Harris Levine died in 1929 while living in the Bensonhurst section of Brooklyn.

WELCOME TO THE NEIGHBORHOOD

Samuel Chotzinoff recalled moving into his first apartment on the Lower East Side in his extraordinary memoir *A Lost Paradise:*

> My mother journeyed to New York and rented a suitable apartment on Stanton Street, . . . one block from the Bowery. Into this we moved one very hot morning in late August. Right in front of our house a large black horse lay dead in the gutter. He must have been there for some time, for the stench was dreadful, and flies, large and small, covered every inch of the carcass and hovered in swarms over it. Later in the day I looked out the window and saw several small boys astride the animal, engaged in skinning it with their pocketknives.

his family's enthrallment with recordings of the great singer Enrico Caruso: "We listened to those records over and over again. We would put the records with the speaker to the yard and let the neighbors enjoy it." But not everyone was happy with the new contribution to the noises and problems of immigrant life. As the *Jewish Daily Forward* noted, "God sent us the Victrola, and you can't get away from them unless you run to the park. . . . You lock your door at night and are safe from burglars, but not from the Victrola."

The Victrola became a symbol to immigrants, a step on the path to becoming a true American and a step away from the dreaded label given to newcomers: greenhorn or green one, *griner* in Yiddish. The aim of every greenhorn was to become American as quickly as possible. This desire was reflected in dress, language, the abandonment of traditional religious rites, and the furnishing of the home. Having a piano or Victrola or other goods was crucial, for it was a mark of respectability, a sense that the newcomers were adapting to American life and to the material abundance embodied in such a life.

In the Old Country, money wasn't very important because no one had much. Great learning gave a person status, and families took pride in their learned children. In America, money became a yardstick for success and respectability, and families soon ached for both, for they were signs that one had truly left Europe behind, had put the status of greenhorn permanently away, and had the right to feel truly part of the Golden Land.

FOOD AND DRINK

Poor immigrants didn't have much money for food, and maybe because of that, food occupied a central place in their thoughts. As Blanche Lasky recalled, "Schmaltz is chicken fat. My mother used to render the fat from the chicken. We'd get this corn bread and toast it on top of the coal stove, and we'd rub it with garlic, put chicken fat on it. That was a meal." The immigrants ate pickled herring, pickles, potatoes (a lot of potatoes), smoked fish, lokshen kugel (a pudding made with noodles and raisins), red cabbage soup, fruit in season, tsimmes from grated carrots, and potato latkes with applesauce. On the Sabbath perhaps a chicken, if it could be afforded, or matzoh brei, made by soaking pieces of matzoh in eggs and then frying them. The immigrants ate bialys, black or rye bread with butter, and, of course, bagels (the name possibly derived from a German word for "ring"). Bagels originated in Europe, perhaps in Poland. There is a document from Krakow describing "beygls" that were gifts given to women at childbirth. An alternative possible origin is that the bagel was born after a Jewish baker made one as a gift for a Polish king. The Jewish immigrants coming from Eastern Europe took the bagels with them across the Atlantic. Starting from the Lower East Side, the bagels began their journey as an ethnic food that non-Jewish Americans came to love.

However, a mass-produced cream cheese to put on the bagel was not available until 1920, when Breakstone's introduced it. The immigrants also enjoyed knishes, pastries filled with cheese, mashed potatoes, buckwheat groats, or chopped liver. Yonah Shimmel's, which opened on Houston Street in 1910, was and remains the unofficial headquarters for knishes.

They washed down their foods with a variety of drinks. The immigrants loved seltzer. This carbonated water soon became known as "Jewish champagne." It was particularly prized after a fat-filled meal because of its desirable ability to produce a *greps*, or belch. Seltzer was extremely useful for kosher households because it could be served with meat, whereas milk could not.

MAMA FEEDS A CROWD

The humorist Sam Levenson used to tell this story about his "Mama." She prided herself on her ability to feed unexpected company. To accomplish this, she kept a pot full of chicken legs always available on the stove. The cost of whole chickens was beyond the family's budget, but the legs were cheap.

One day, Uncle Louis and Aunt Lena showed up unannounced with their eleven children. Mama Levenson had never faced a greater challenge. She was anxious because there were not enough chicken legs to feed everyone. She quickly called her own children into the tiny bedroom and pleaded with them, "Children, do me a favor. Say you don't like chicken."

The children sympathized with their mother and readily agreed. They returned and dutifully turned down the offer when the relatives volunteered to share their chicken legs.

After the meal, it was time for dessert. Mama Levenson faced the same problem, but this time she didn't need to consult with her children. Instead she announced to one and all at the table, "Now, all the children who wouldn't eat the chicken don't get any dessert."

A driver with a horse and cart came once a week to deliver seltzer and remove the empty bottles. Seltzer could also be found in candy stores, where a 6-ounce glass of it without flavoring added cost 2 cents (the famed "two cents plain"), and it became a key ingredient of egg creams, along with milk and chocolate syrup. Since neither eggs nor cream were used in this delight, it is unclear how the name was chosen. Dr. Brown's Cel-Ray tonic, a celery-flavored carbonated drink, was also popular. For ceremonial occasions such as a Sabbath dinner, many immigrants purchased "wine so thick you can almost cut it with a knife." This slogan from Schapiro's Wine appealed to the immigrants who made their purchases from Schapiro's House of Kosher and Sacramental Wines on Rivington Street. This oldest kosher wine company in the United States boasted that only Orthodox Jews touched the grapes that made its wine.

Despite the lack of food, immigrants, especially traditional women, tied their identity to their ability to provide nourishment not only for their families but also for family members and friends who might suddenly show up.

Indeed, women were often the center of the household. Some Jewish fathers found their traditional religion belittled by their own children and unhelpful in gaining jobs from employers. George Burns recalled that his father wanted to sing in synagogues as a prayer leader, a *ba'al tefillah*. But the old man's voice was not good, and though he struggled with other jobs, he never had much money. Characteristically, Burns joked about his father's would-be religious career: "After he sang in one little synagogue, the following synagogue, instead of hiring him, they kept it closed during Rosh Hashanah and Yom Kippur."

Immigrant Jewish fathers struggled with the English language as well as employment. In some cases, husbands and fathers abandoned mothers and children.

If too many fathers were failures in the Golden Land, mothers were not. They had to be strong, industrious, and clever to help their families survive.

BOARDERS

Many families had to take in boarders for simple economic reasons. Similarly, as large numbers of male Jewish immigrants—either unmarried or alone because they had left their family in Europe—streamed into New York, they needed a cheap place to stay. The boarder did not have an easy time of it. Space was extremely limited.

In her blistering novel *Bread Givers,* Anzia Yezierska has a character explain a boarder's possible lodgings: "Put the spring over four empty herring barrels and you'll have a bed fit for the president. Now put a board over the potato barrel and a clean newspaper over that and you'll have a table. All you need yet is a soapbox for a chair and you'll have a furnished room complete."

When boarders shared a family apartment, it was not unusual to have nine or ten men sleeping on the floor.

Boarders became mythic characters on the Lower East Side, famous for romantic entanglements with their landladies or the wives or daughters of the families from whom they rented. Sometimes boys stood on the corners making up obscene songs about such supposed relationships. But boarders also became known for their com-

MOTHER OR SAINT?

The journalist Zalmen Yoffeh recalled his mother's heroic efforts:

With . . . one dollar a day [our mother] fed and clothed an ever-growing family. She took in boarders. Sometimes this helped; at other times it added to the burdens. Boarders were often out of work and penniless; how could one turn a hungry man out? She made all our clothes. She walked blocks to reach a place where meat was a penny cheaper, where bread was a half-cent less. She collected boxes and old wood to burn in the stove instead of costly coal. Her hands became hardened and the lines so begrimed that for years she never had perfectly clean hands. One by one she lost her teeth—there was no money for dentists—and her cheeks caved in. Yet we children always had clean and wholesome clothing. There was always bread and butter in the house, and, wonder of wonders, there was usually a penny apiece for us to buy candy.

plete involvement in family life—which included being able to care for and discipline the children.

HEALTH ISSUES

It was very difficult to stay clean in the tenements. As George Burns noted, "We took baths in the kitchen tub. There was only enough hot water for one tubful, so the oldest got the first bath and the rest of us took turns, according to age, in the same water. You can imagine what it was like when it got to me. I was cleaner when I got in."

Burns also joked about the lack of light: "We had gaslight but very little of it, because about once a week when the gas ran out you had to put a quarter in the meter. My mother always kept the flame turned down very low to make the quarter last as long as possible. . . . I was eight years old before I knew what my sisters looked like. Then one night my mother turned up the light. I got a look at my sisters and blew it out." Burns's humor was typical of the strategy that some people on the Lower East Side were able to use to get through the tough times. They defended themselves with humor, or they simply blocked out the troubles as if they weren't there.

Many children were born in the tenements. The songwriter Ira Gershwin, for example, was born at 60 Eldridge Street, a bit north of 19 Eldridge, where Eddie Cantor had been born. George Burns was born at 95 Pitt Street and Fanny Brice at 102 Forsyth Street.

Summer was the worst season in the tenements. The sun combined with the heat of the stove, steam boilers, and lamps. Four hundred and twenty people died from heat in New York, for example, between August 5 and 13, 1896. During the most insufferable summer heat, many children slept on the fire escapes or on "tar beach," the roof of the tenement. Many roofs were also home to pigeons, large numbers of which could commonly be seen flying above the tenements. Many people—selling goods, collecting rents, helping the families—used the roofs as their walkways, avoiding the crowds on the sidewalks below.

Despite precautions tenement dwellers took, there were epidemics in the late nineteenth and early twentieth centuries. Visiting nurses sometimes had to force the immigrants to go to hospitals; most Americans believed that people only went to the hospital to die. Quarantines were also used in tenements, as they had been in steerage. Anyone suspected of illness was removed from the tenements. The tenements themselves were barricaded, preventing the immigrants from going to work, shopping, or playing outside.

Jews were sometimes blamed for diseases in New York. This was particularly true of tuberculosis. In 1912, the death rate from this disease was 215 for every 100,000 inhabitants. By 1918, there were 50,000 cases of tuberculosis in New York. Tuberculosis was widely considered a "Jewish disease" despite the fact that Jews had a lower mortality rate from it than some other ethnic groups, such as the Irish or Finns.

Jews were considered unhygienic, but a bigger reason was that tuberculosis was somehow associated with clothing; it was sometimes even referred to as the "tailor's disease." It is unclear exactly why that was. Presumably, the belief was because clothing was frequently made in sweatshops and other unsanitary environments, the clothing bred the disease in its workers, who then passed it on to others.

Because Jews were associated so fully with the industry, they were accused of being such carriers. Jews were hardly the only victims of such prejudice. Italians were thought to cause polio and the Irish to cause cholera.

OUTSIDE THE TENEMENT

It was inevitable that with the complete lack of privacy, the inevitable squabbling among family members, the sense of being trapped, and the summer heat, the immigrants felt an urgent need to get outside.

In this way, along with tenements, the lives of the immigrants were played out in the streets, in libraries, in small Yiddish theaters and movie theaters, in houses of worship, around fountains, and in many other places where they might learn or relax. But most male immigrants spent most of their time outside the tenements working.

It was the immigrants' work that fed their children but also challenged their sense of self. The difficult economic conditions in which work put them led many of them to challenge the economic system, which to their minds was brutally unfair. Others turned inward and found in American values a profound challenge to their Jewishness, their religious rites or diet, or their faith in their parents' beliefs.

Every morning for most of them meant rising early to face another insufferable day of labor for low wages. And every day, as they went off, they must inevitably have thought about the long, difficult hours that lay ahead and perhaps the more philosophical even pondered why fate had given them such jobs.

Tailors at work in a sweatshop around 1890. *Source: Photograph by Jacob Riis © Hulton-Deutsch Collection/CORBIS.*

FOUR

WORKING ON
THE LOWER EAST SIDE

><><

A FTER FINDING an apartment or a corner of an apartment, the new immigrants
had an immediate problem: finding a job. Studying Talmud and praying, so
valued in the Old Country, were more problematic on the Lower East Side,
where Sabbath observers had greater difficulty finding jobs and where respect for
religious tradition was gradually being replaced by respect for material success,
worldly achievement, and social status. In the Old World, if Jews didn't have a job,
they might have had a garden or a cow or hens to fall back on. It was socially per-
missible to borrow from one's neighbors. Being unemployed in Europe didn't necessarily mean going hungry, but it did in America, as the immigrants quickly
learned.

This New World was immensely confusing to many immigrants. They, their
families, or their neighbors abandoned traditions to fit the cultural and vocational
requirements of urban American life.

FINDING WORK

The most pressing concern was for the new immigrants to find a way to make a living. The search for the first job was always memorable.

A FIRST JOB

The labor lawyer Louis Waldman recalled in his autobiography the search for his first job:

> Finally I stumbled across a chandelier factory on Canal Street which proclaimed on a crudely painted sign—but in three languages—that a "hand" was wanted inside. I walked up several flights of stairs and finally spoke to the foreman. He looked me over, and made careful note of my husky appearance, and told me I could start working. My salary was to be two dollars a week, but he added: "Don't worry, there's room for advancement." Five months later when I quit I was still getting two dollars a week.

Many immigrant workers had to start at the bottom.

PEDDLERS AND PUSHCARTS

Peddling had long been part of Jewish life. It was an easy business for even the poorest of new immigrants to enter. All they had to find were a few rags or some goods somewhere and start selling them. The very ease of starting such a business guaranteed that as the surge of new penniless immigrants arrived, there would be an ever-increasing number of competitors and an ever more difficult struggle to make a living.

Some peddlers could not afford the pushcart rental fee of 8 to 10 cents a day, so they created their own contraptions, often adapting a baby buggy that had been discarded. There was also the $25-a-year pushcart license and various bribes to police officers to consider.

Peddlers also somehow had to obtain wholesale goods. They might get them in various places, such as on Canal Street. For some immigrants, peddling marked a profound loss of status from their station in European life. The writer Marcus Ravage recalled his shock at seeing a man "who had been the chairman of the hospital

Street peddler on the Lower East Side. *Source: Picture Collection, The Branch Libraries, The New York Public Library, Astor, Lenox, and Tilden Foundations.*

committee in Vaslui and a prominent grain merchant . . . dispensing soda-water and selling lollypops on the corner of Essex Street." Another man was a scholar, but "in America he had attained to a basket of shoe-strings and matches and candles."

Men who could not afford the costs of peddling simply carried the wares. The peddlers were often in the buying-and-selling business. They would wander around yelling, "I cash clothes!" looking to buy some piece of clothing that they judged could be sold at a higher price to another customer.

Peddlers specialized in certain locations. Sellers of wedding dresses went to Grand Street. Those selling coats and furs congregated on Division Street. If customers wanted a chicken, they headed to Hester Street. More than fifteen hundred peddlers plied their wares each day just in the area around Hester Street and along parts of Norfolk and Essex.

Customers were always eager to save a penny, so they searched carefully for the *metsieh*, the bargain; whether such a bargain was real or imaginary, customers wanted to believe they had spent wisely. Of course, no bargain-hunting customer was willing to accept the stated price. A ritual bargaining session developed. It might include a plea or even a threat. Sam Levenson's mother taught him how such a system worked. She would find what she wanted, and the dialogue would proceed:

"How much are these cucumbers?" she'd ask.
"Two for five."
"And how much is this one?"
"Three cents."
"Okay. I'll take the other one."

The Jews from Eastern Europe had come to the United States with experience both with pushcarts and bargaining. They knew that they should start walking away if their price has not been agreed to, whereupon almost inevitably the peddler would stop them and only then would an agreement be reached. After all, there was simply no place to store the goods. Whatever was on the cart in the morning had to be gone in the evening. Both buyers and sellers came to enjoy this process, at least to some extent.

Unsurprisingly, pushcart peddlers rarely made much of a profit. They averaged about $5 a week, so it became a common practice for such peddlers to buy additional pushcarts so that their wives and children could operate them too.

The pushcart trade declined only when Mayor Fiorello La Guardia formed the Municipal Enclosed Retail Market, which forced the street peddlers indoors.

Another kind of peddler also made the rounds. This was the customer peddler who went from house to house taking orders.

The next-highest level of peddling involved saving enough to rent or own a store, living in the back part of it and selling goods in the front. New and subtle skills were required to open such a store. The immigrants had to learn, sometimes the hard way, about the many ways in which they could be cheated. They faced very long hours, opening early and closing late. They endured the pleadings of women and children who literally begged for food or goods and promised to pay the shopkeeper eventually. Sometimes the payment was made, and sometimes it wasn't.

Sometimes customers paid in other ways. The great American film producer William Fox was brought up on the Lower East Side. One day, his mother sent him to the local butcher. Fox's father was not working, and the family had reached the end of its food supply. Fox asked if he could "borrow" a pound of meat. The butcher, smiling, inquired about when the meat would be returned.

Fox replied, "Some day I'm going to be wealthy. You'll be old and won't be able to work, and I'll take care of you."

Evidently, the butcher liked the boy's spirit and gave him the meat.

Years later, after his success, Fox remembered the butcher and brought him to Hollywood where the man worked at Fox's studio for fifteen years.

Finally, the successful Jewish peddlers or shop owners who had enough drive and vision might save the relatively small amount it took to become manufacturers, almost inevitably of clothing.

THE GARMENT INDUSTRY

German Jews had begun work in the garment trade in the 1850s. The arrival of Eastern European Jews in the 1880s coincided with technological inventions and economic circumstances that propelled these new immigrants to enter the "needle trade" or "rag business" or "shmattes," as the industry was variously known.

The sewing machine and the cutting knife (able to slice several pieces of fabric simultaneously) made the mass production of clothing profitable. The spurt of population growth brought about not least by the arrival of millions of new immigrants made for an enormous potential pool of customers. Workers who were desperate for work were needed, which meant that the new Jewish immigrants were actually needed. In 1890, fully 60 percent of the Jewish immigrants who were employed worked in the garment industry.

About 11 percent of the immigrants were tailors when they arrived; the rest took up the trade when they reached America's shores, and because of that they were dubbed "Columbus tailors."

SWEATSHOPS

The need for sweatshops arose due to the 1890s boom in clothing. The term *sweatshop* itself is contentious. Invented by reformers on the Lower East Side to describe a tenement apartment where garments were being made, the word soon took on the connotation of a dangerous and terrible place.

A lot of different types of work went into the making of clothing. A manufacturer cut the materials and bunched them according to the article of clothing to be produced, relying completely on others to sew the garment together. Manufacturers were also known as jobbers.

The shlepper was a man who took bundles of fabric from the jobber to the contractors and from there to the wholesaler. (*Shlep* means "drag" or "carry." The term *shlepper* was also used along Canal Street to refer to people who dragged passersby into a store. This shlepper was also called a puller. Waiters were sometimes also called shleppers because of their tray-carrying skills.)

Contractors, called "sweaters," received large shipments of clothes, depending on their specialty, such as making pants or coats. Some of the contractors put the pieces together themselves or hired help. Others subcontracted to another sweater who worked at home. The people who received the subcontracts were called sweaters because of the cramped conditions and often intense heat, unbearable in the summer, in which they worked. The sweatshops were either in factories or tenements.

In a typical tenement that was transformed into a sweatshop by day, the boss, who lived with his family in the tenement, would transform the parlor—the larger front room—and the kitchen, which was between the parlor and the tiny bedroom, into work areas. The air was stale. The sewing machines, with their incessant whirring, were put by the windows in the front of the parlor. Workers were positioned in various spots. The pressers, for example, typically stood, keeping their irons hot for the pressing and using gaslight to see as they worked.

The "sweating" system worked because of the pool of cheap laborers, the enormous need for ready-made clothing, and the division of labor requiring different activities. Some workers cut the fabrics while another stitched and still another made buttonholes. The workers all had to buy their own cutting knives, needles, or thread. It was commonplace for the contractor to sell the workers the tools of the trade—for a 500 percent profit. Workers typically got paid every three or four weeks. The full amount owed was not always given; more commonly workers got "part payments."

The workers began at dawn and worked through the day and into the night. There were no clocks in sweatshops. Many who didn't work in their homes took work home with them. They desperately needed the extra pay. After all, for

A TENEMENT SWEATSHOP

Jacob Riis was a reporter, and in his book *How the Other Half Lives*, he described a sweatshop in a tenement on Ludlow Street:

> Five men and a woman, two young girls, not fifteen, and a boy who says unasked that he is fifteen, and lies in saying it, are at the machines sewing knickerbockers [short pants]. . . . The floor is littered ankle-deep with half-sewn garments. In the alcove, on a couch of many dozens of "pants" ready for the finisher, a bare-legged baby with pinched face is asleep. A fence of piled-up clothing keeps him from rolling off on the floor. The faces, hands, and arms to the elbows of everyone in the room are black with the color of the cloth on which they are working. The boy and the woman alone look up at our entrance. The girls shoot sidelong glances, but at a warning look from the man with the bundle they tread their machines more energetically than ever. . . . [The shop] turns out one hundred and twenty "knee-pants" a week, for which the manufacturer pays seventy cents a dozen.

instance, the person who sewed boys' jackets got 8 cents, while the person who ironed them got 3 cents.

Workers had to have skills, but they also had to endure the tiresome repetition of their labors. Boredom and sweating from limited or nonexistent ventilation, crowding, and warm weather, though, were not the only problems. Workers were restricted in the number of bathroom visits they could make. There were constant charges of sexual harassment. Obviously, bosses could threaten to hold back pay or even to fire a woman worker who commonly needed the job to survive.

Under such conditions, women sometimes felt forced to overlook leers, touches, or tickles, although some bosses went further, demanding that the women workers provide sexual favors. There were very few defenses against such harassment, which is why husbands were reluctant to have their wives or daughters work in sweatshops and why women were sometimes desperate to find husbands so they could leave the trade.

In one rare case, women did fight back, undertaking an "orphan strike." The name derived from a boss who argued that he pinched the women in his shop "as a father would." In response, Rose Schneiderman, a labor leader, replied, "We would rather be orphans." More generally, women quit or pretended they didn't hear suggestive remarks or sought some assistance from coworkers.

Bosses were sometimes cruel in other ways as well. In his book *Tales of a Tailor*, Samuel Liptzin recalled his boss catching an operator smoking a cigarette at a sewing machine. The boss sneaked up beside the worker, grabbed the cigarette from his hand, and crushed it out against his arm.

By 1900, about two hundred thousand Jews were in the garment industry on the Lower East Side. Pressers earned $500 a year for their sixty-hour workweek. Cutters, highly valued for their skills, earned $900 a year. Women were paid less. A woman in 1900 might be paid between $3 and $6 a week; the workweek for many was 108 hours.

A child in the system averaged $2.94 a week. A 1907 investigation revealed that there were sixty thousand children working in sweatshops at home. In Europe, Jewish parents had mastered the skill of faking a child's age to deal with such matters as the military draft. That skill was used in reverse on the Lower East Side. Youngsters from twelve to fourteen were "accelerated" so that they were of supposedly legal working age. Some of the immigrants openly wished for more children so that they could open up their own shop.

Factories enabled workers to be together in much higher numbers than in the complex web of smaller sweatshops. Once workers were together in large groups, they were able to gather strength from common suffering and talk over their grievances with sympathetic peers. In such an environment, unions emerged to protect the rights of the workers, and these labor unions made life far easier for those who produced garments for the rag trade.

OTHER OCCUPATIONS

Jews were in a wide variety of occupations besides the garment industry. Some were illegal. And some were borderline legal. For example, "Professor Dora Meltzer," a palm reader, once resided at 97 Orchard Street, the current home of the Lower East Side Tenement Museum. There were many fortune-tellers on the Lower East Side

SIXTY THOUSAND CHILDREN IN SWEATSHOPS

The poet Edwin Markham wrote about young people in a sweatshop in this article, excerpted from the January 1907 issue of *Cosmopolitan Magazine:*

> Nearly any hour on the East Side of New York you can see them—pallid boy or spindling girl—their faces dulled, their backs bent under a heavy load of garments piled on head and shoulders, the muscles of the whole frame in a long strain. The boy always has bowlegs and walks with feet wide apart and wobbling. . . . Once at home with the sewing, the little worker sits close to the inadequate window, struggling with the snarls of thread or shoving the needle through unyielding cloth. Even if by happy chance the small worker goes to school, the sewing which he puts down at the last moment in the morning waits for his return.
>
> Never again should one complain of buttons hanging by a thread, for tiny, tortured fingers have doubtless done their little ineffectual best. And for his lifting of burdens, this giving of youth and strength, this sacrifice of all that should make childhood radiant, a child may add to the family purse from 50 cents to $1.50 a week. . . .
>
> Besides work at sewing, there is another industry for little girls in the grim tenements. The mother must be busy at her sewing. . . . A little daughter, therefore, must assume the work and care of the family . . . washing, scrubbing, cooking. In New York City alone, 60,000 children are shut up in the home sweatshops. . . . Is it not a cruel civilization that allows little hearts and little shoulders to strain under these grown-up responsibilities . . . ?

who, for a fee, would foretell what usually happy events lay in the future for the customer. Most of the fortune-tellers were simply housewives seeking to raise a few dollars. They sometimes went through a person's belongings searching for clues to provide verification of their talents.

Buying pretzels from a street vendor. *Source: Photograph by Robert L. Bracklow © Photo Collection, Alexander Alland, Sr., CORBIS.*

While the occupation was of dubious actual help, it did have its place in the immigrant economy. Housewives who had no other income could raise some funds, be relieved of the tenement's isolation, and develop social relationships with others. Some of the fortune-tellers ended up in the advice business, giving suggestions to the greenhorns about how to adapt to American ways and painting reasonably accurate portraits of what they might expect in the next year or two of their lives as they ventured further into American life. Unconvinced of the value of such advice, in 1911 the New York State Assembly outlawed fortune-telling for profit. That, of course, did not completely eradicate the profession.

Immigrant parents may not have wanted their children to grow up to read palms, but they did want to keep their daughters out of the factories. Some of the younger immigrant women became servants until they got married. Many parents struggled to do without a daughter's wages so that she might, for example, stay in school studying business in order to get a job as a bookkeeper in an office or maybe even as a teacher.

Men who didn't work as peddlers or shopkeepers or in the garment industry struggled to find suitable jobs. A few obtained higher education and became professionals, such as physicians, pharmacists, dentists, lawyers, or professors.

Most immigrant Jews, though, were workers. They might be photographers or barbers or bakers. Indeed, hundreds of "bakeries" opened up in refuse- and vermin-filled basements. Bakers had a very difficult life, working eighteen to twenty hours a day in 1885, often in overheated conditions. While waiting for their dough to rise, bakers gathered in local saloons, where they drank and wrestled for beers.

The saloons also functioned as employment bureaus. Jewish bakers might be approached by bakeries in the city or by representatives from Jewish communities across the country who hired the bakers to come to their community for several weeks and prepare a large amount of kosher goods when they got there. The saloons did well with such an arrangement. Bakers in search of jobs were forced to spend some of their money on the beer or else the saloons wouldn't let them stay; this arrangement came to be known as the vampire system.

The brutal working conditions were profoundly important in shaping the attitudes of the Jewish immigrants. Work formed such an overwhelming part of their life that such an influence was inevitable.

Living in crowded tenements and working either there or in packed factories led inevitably to a sense of being trapped and to a need to get out. For that, the immigrants turned to the streets.

Children on the street outside the New York Rescue Band. *Source: Courtesy of Brown Brothers.*

FIVE

LIFE ON THESE MEAN STREETS

THE STREETS, like the tenements and the factories, were overflowing with streams of people, noisy with a cacophony of languages, screams, whistles, and cries. As the novelist Michael Gold wrote in his novel *Jews Without Money*, "Excitement, dirt, fighting, chaos! The sound of my street lifted like the blast of a great carnival or catastrophe. The noise was always in my ears. Even in my sleep I could hear it; I can hear it now."

The streets produced a sort of culture shock for many of the brand-new immigrants. They were often disappointed—after all, wasn't America the land of perpetual sunshine?

STREET SIGHTS AND SOUNDS

The immigrants were overwhelmed and surprised at the filth, at the variety of hats the men and women wore on the streets, at the laundry hanging out, at the young people who would stare at them or make mocking noises, at the dirty water running in the street gutters, into which children for fun sometimes would place a baby in a basket, Moses-like, and let it float down the street. Of course, compared to the overt violence of the anti-Semites in Europe, this was easily bearable, but it did feel strange, as did various American mannerisms such as chewing gum.

Similarly, most of the immigrants had come from relatively small towns, so it took time to adjust to the sights of New York City skyscrapers or mailboxes or people of color. The tall policemen swinging clubs instead of sabers seemed strange, and those swaying billy clubs seemed very frightening to the newcomers until they realized that the clubs were not about to be used on them.

The pullers who "encouraged" them to shop in a particular store were unusually assertive. The pullers tried not to grab a potential customer too hard because doing so might tear his clothes, but the grip had to be firm enough so that he could not escape the grip. If the customer complained about a lack of time, the puller promised on the honor of his ancestors that the customer would be finished in two seconds. If the customer revealed a lack of money to buy any goods, the puller assured him the goods were practically free.

But as crowded as they were, the streets were in the open, and that fact gave them an expansiveness, a sense of unending possibilities, not available in the cramped tenements where people were squeezed like herring in a very crowded barrel or the filthy factories or unendurable sweatshops in which they toiled. The streets were a refuge. The sidewalks, corners, stoops, fire escapes, and basement stairs were natural centers for gossip and flirting. People also socialized as they rode the el, the elevated railroad.

The stories of the streets were many, and the peddlers, such as those selling frankfurters, joined the boys and girls playing and the women shopping. Most women, married women especially, wore skirts that reached the ground, and they wore them not just on the street but also, for example, when scrubbing a floor.

Women learned early how to take a handful of their skirt and push it off to one side as they crossed the street, ever mindful, in an era still marked by Victorian morality, not to show even an ankle for males to see. Of course, the American idea of getting up when a woman approached or allowing "ladies first" was entirely new to the immigrants.

Not all the women were demure. The incredible lack of privacy sometimes provided an education of sorts to the young men of the Lower East Side. These men saw a lot of nursing babies not only at home but in the streets as well. The act of breast-feeding was considered perfectly natural and was done without embarrassment.

The streets were filled with young lovers and young people searching for lovers. They were filled with young George Burnses and Eddie Cantors, *comikers* always ready with a *vitz*, some philosophical piece of wit, or a smaller joke or a pun, appropriately called a *vitzl*.

Street scene. *Source: Courtesy of Brown Brothers.*

There were also a variety of street entertainers, especially organ-grinders. George Burns recalled that his love of being an entertainer began as a response to such a man:

> At five I was getting the scent of show business. We had an organ-grinder on our street—with a strictly second-class organ, very flat. The men who owned the good ones worked Second Avenue. We only got the organ-grinders that were breaking in, and why they bothered to come around I'll never know. Nobody had any pennies to throw them. Anyway, it was music of a sort, and all the little girls in the block would dance around him. I did too. I had a Spanish number I did, and, if I say so myself, I was very graceful. The people clapped for me and I got my first feel of an audience.

Men who made a living weighing people were another diversion, especially on Saturday nights. The machine, on wheels, stood above 5 feet tall. It cost 2 cents to get weighed, although some enterprising men charged 5 cents, but there would be no charge if he couldn't guess the correct weight within 3 pounds. The most successful of these scalemen were handsome young men who gathered a group of young women to take turns paying.

As Harry Golden recalled one of the tricks to keep onlookers amused:

When the customer was a male, the scaleman would feel the biceps, and then reach down and have a feel of the fellow's thighs and sort of pat him all around. He went out of his way in thoroughly feeling the fellow, which heightened the tension when a woman was the next one to step up to the scales. The spectators would ooh and aah and maybe even scream for joy; the girls would giggle all over the place as the fellow made various motions as if to go through the same feeling operation. But it was all acting. The spectators "dared" him and shouted encouragement but, of course, in the end the fellow did no such thing. . . . He was amazingly accurate. . . . We have a relative who financed himself through law school pushing a scale on the East Side. His fees are much more than two cents today.

There was a lot to stare at on the streets. If people became boring or annoying, like the beggars, the residents could always look at the horses. They wore straw hats and sometimes had flowers or bells over their necks. They were watered usually at a corner trough. Despite warnings of being bitten, the children patted the horses and gave them a lick of lollipops, which then went back into the child's mouth.

At night, the streets were more dangerous, not simply because of the possibility of being robbed but also because the darkness hid oncoming dangers from above. Walking along the streets, pedestrians had to be careful not to be hit by falling garbage or dirty water tossed from a tenement window.

STREET NAMES

Many of the names of the streets on the Lower East Side have become familiar, such as Delancey. Here are the names of some of the famous streets and a little bit about the name, such as how it originated.

Allen Street was named after Captain William Henry Allen, the youngest naval captain during the War of 1812. He died fighting at the age of twenty-nine. The el, or elevated railroad line, roared above Allen Street beginning in 1878. Along with Chrystie and Forsythe Streets, Allen Street under the el was infamous for its prostitutes.

Attorney Street received its name from the variety of lawyers who set up offices there.

Baruch Place and Baruch Drive were both named after Dr. Simon Baruch, a Jewish immigrant from Germany who was a surgeon for the South during the Civil War before moving to New York. He became well known as a doctor on the Lower East Side. Bernard Baruch, a financial genius and presidential adviser, was his son. The street names, however, were not given until 1933. Baruch Place had previously been Goerck Street, named in memory of Casimir Goerck, a surveyor who in 1803 provided a map of the city.

Bialystoker Place was named for the Bialystoker Synagogue and was formerly known as Willett Street, named after Marinus Willett, a sheriff of New York from 1784 to 1788.

Broome Street was named after John Broome, a merchant and the lieutenant governor of New York in 1804. He initiated trade with China.

Canal Street was named for the canal, 40 feet wide, that was dug in 1905 in order to drain a pond into the Hudson River. After being in use for a decade, the canal was filled in and made into a street.

Cherry Street had a 7-acre cherry orchard owned by a wealthy Dutch merchant. George Washington moved to a four-story mansion on Cherry Street in 1789 just after being elected president. The house, then, became the first executive mansion.

Chrystie Street was named after Lieutenant Colonel John Chrystie, who died after being captured during the War of 1812.

Clinton Street bears the name of General George Clinton, who fought in the Revolutionary War. He was also the first governor of New York after American independence. In 1804, he became vice-president of the United States.

Columbia Street was named after the explorer Christopher Columbus. Columbus did not always have a good name among the immigrants. "*A klug ʒu Columbus'n*," which meant "A curse on Columbus," was a common expression on the Lower East Side, meant in jest as a reaction to yet another supposed indignity suffered in the Golden Land, such as a child getting into a fight or water that wasn't hot enough in the steam bath. There was even an ironic admiration intended in the curse.

Delancey Street was named after James de Lancey, who was chief justice of the New York Supreme Court. The family's estate was bordered on the north by what is now Delancey Street.

Division Street separated farms owned by James de Lancey and Henry Rutgers.

East Broadway was originally supposed to relieve the traffic on Broadway.

East Houston Street was once a part of the northern boundary of New York City and was known then, appropriately, as North Street.

Eldridge Street, once part of James de Lancey's farm and named Third Street, underwent a name change in 1813 and was named for Lieutenant Joseph Eldridge, who was ambushed and killed in the War of 1812.

Essex Street was named after Essex County in England.

Forsyth Street was named after Lieutenant Colonel Benjamin Forsyth of North Carolina, who was killed in upstate New York during the War of 1812.

Gouverneur Street, Gouverneur Lane, and Gouverneur Slip were named after Abrahm Gouverneur, a New York merchant.

Grand Street received its name for its width.

Henry Street was one of two streets named after Henry Rutgers because he gave two lots to New York on which to build a school.

Hester Street was named for Hester Rynders, the daughter of Jacob Leisler, a lieutenant governor of the state unjustly convicted of treason and hanged in 1691. The street became immortalized in Joan Micklin Silver's 1975 film *Hester Street*, which tells the story of immigrant life. The great author Anzia Yezierska wrote about her tenement at 59 Hester Street.

Houston Street was not named after Sam Houston of Texas but for William Houstoun, who was a member of the Georgia delegation to the Continental Congress. That is why the street's name is pronounced "Howston" and not "Hewston." Houstoun's wife, Mary, was the daughter of Nicholas Bayard III, who owned land in New York.

Jefferson Street, originally Washington Street, was renamed after the third president.

Ludlow Street was named after Lieutenant Augustus Ludlow, who had served in the Navy during the War of 1812. Captain James Lawrence was addressing Ludlow when he uttered the famous words, "Don't give up the ship."

Montgomery Street is named after General Richard Montgomery, who tried to attack Quebec on December 31, 1775. He was killed in the attempt.

Norfolk Street was named after a county in England.

Orchard Street received its name from the orchards on James de Lancey's farm. The street later became famous as a shopper's paradise. Pushcarts lined both sides of the street and were there from 10 in the morning until midnight. In winter, the vendors had little kerosene stoves to keep warm. To sell eyeglasses, the vendors on Orchard Street would let customers read a newspaper until the correct pair of glasses was found. Today, the Lower East Side Tenement Museum is located on Orchard Street.

Pike Street was named after Zebulon Pike, a soldier who has a more famous location named after him—Pikes Peak in Colorado.

Pitt Street was named after William Pitt, the earl of Chatham.

Ridge Street received its name from a ridge on some land James de Lancey owned.

Rivington Street was named after James Rivington, who published the *Royal Gazette*, a newspaper that supported the British during the Revolutionary War. After the war, he repented, and the street's name was retained in part because of a widely held belief that Rivington had aided George Washington's local spies.

Rutgers Street was named after Henry Rutgers, a patriot during the Revolutionary War.

Stanton Street was named after a foreman on the James de Lancey family estate, but Stanton's first name and achievements are unknown.

Suffolk Street was named after the county in England.

SHOPPING

Jewish immigrants were expert shoppers. They could look a carp in the eye and tell how long it had been dead. They knew that a cloudy eye meant that it wasn't fresh. They had to be careful with fruit. If it was piled very high—in double or triple tiers—and was artistically arranged, that meant the price would be higher. Disorganized fruit would more likely lead to a good price.

Katz's "Famous" Deli. *Source: Courtesy of Yura Dashevsky.*

Shoppers and vendors on Hester Street. *Source: Hulton Archive/Getty Images.*

THE GHETTO MARKET, HESTER STREET

The *New York Times* described the market on November 14, 1897. Here is an excerpt.

> The pavements along both sides of Hester Street are lined by a continuous double row of pushcarts filled with eatables of every kind agreeable to the palate of the Russian Jew. The latecomers among the vendors, no longer able to secure a place for their carts along the main avenue of the market, form an overflow market along the pavements of the side streets—Ludlow, Essex, Norfolk, and Suffolk. Here is a cart laden with grapes and pears, and the fruit merchant, a short, dark-complexioned, bearded fellow, clad as to outer garments in an old cap, a dark-blue sweater, and a nondescript pair of dirty-hued trousers, is shrieking at the top of his voice: "*Gutes frucht! Gutes frucht! Metziehs! Drei pennies die whole lot.*" [Good fruit! Good fruit! Bargains! Three pennies a whole lot!] . . . Instead of heeding the hoarse, guttural cries of the fruit merchant . . . women and market baskets swarm and push and jostle around some pushcarts at the lower end of the street. . . . Another organ of sense besides the eye informs one that it is fish—big fish and little fish, light fish and dark fish, bluefish and whitefish, fresh fish and fish not quite so fresh. . . . These people love fish.

These skills were tested every Thursday night and Friday morning in what was ironically called the Chazzer-Mark, the so-called Pig Market on the corner of Hester Street and Ludlow. The market's name derived from the fact that virtually any item could be bought there—except a pig. On Thursday nights, each pushcart had a torch, making for an extraordinary sight of people darting in and out of the light.

There were chickens and geese as well as fish, soda water, and all kinds of clothing and related items such as suspenders. People could buy bread or eyeglasses or shoes or peaches. They could have fun haggling, get a bargain, and shop for the Sabbath all at the same time. Naturally, the Pig Market was always packed with people.

Some were there for bargains. In 1898, a *New York Times* reporter noted that lace curtains that would have cost $75 in an expensive uptown store cost 50 cents on Hester Street.

GANGS

Every street on the Lower East Side had its gang. Although street gangs may be thought of as the incubator of criminals, that is not an entirely accurate picture. The gangs often congregated in candy stores when they weren't roaming the streets. Some gangs were just social organizations that got together to play games, especially sports. Another kind of gang gathered each evening either in the store or on a street corner where the gang members flirted with the young women who walked by and tried their best to annoy the passing males. Sometimes they shot craps while a younger boy was on the lookout for the police and given the strict instruction to yell a password when a cop was approaching. It was the third kind of gang that caused trouble. These gangs stole money from passing children, gambled, engaged in fights with other gangs, and tried out a variety of criminal behaviors, usually starting with picking pockets.

This gang of young toughs typically ranged in age from six to twenty, with the older ones schooling the youngest recruits in the ways of crime as they hung out in a poolroom. The older boys might move on to become professional criminals, and the gang would continue with the younger ones taking their place. Not all of the members of these tough gangs continued in crime. Eddie Cantor, for example, had been a member of "Pork-Faced Sam's" gang. The gang had its own criminal specialty: members would steal from a shop and then sell the same goods back to the owner; they would also work as scabs during a strike, filling in for striking workers. Cantor soon got out of the life.

GAMES

The streets of the Lower East Side were paved with stones until the 1890s. The children still played games outside, but the stones made it difficult to do so because of their jagged edges and the fact that they collected mud and were slippery because they retained rain for a long while. But then the stones began to be paved over with asphalt, and the new surface, easier for the city to clean, coincidentally made it far easier to play games.

Among young people, there was a strict gender distinction. Boys played games with boys, and girls with girls.

Marbles rolled along smoothly on the new surface. Hoops could be rolled with ease. Prisoner's base was a popular game. For this, the players divided into two equal teams. A chalk line was drawn between the two groups. Depending on how much room was available, a large chalk square—the prison—was drawn about 20 feet behind each group. One fleet-footed member of each team was the prisoner, and the point of the game was to free the prisoner by sending a team member through the other team without being captured and bring the prisoner back. If the team member made it to the prison, he didn't have to return immediately but could pick an opportune moment. If, however, the team member was caught, he also became a prisoner. Therefore, each team simultaneously tried to rescue its own prisoner and protect the prisoner it had. The winning team was the one with the most prisoners.

Of course, there were all kinds of ball games such as stickball and stoopball and a variant of baseball called "one o' cat." In this game, a piece of wood was used instead of a ball. The wood was whittled so that it had points at each end and was about 4 inches long and an inch across. Sides were chosen, and then each batter would come up with a stick and lightly hit the wood, which was on the ground; there was no pitcher in the game. The wood would rise a few feet off the ground from such a tap, and then the batter would swing to hit it as hard as possible and then run around the bases until the "ball" could be caught or the runner tagged or thrown out at a base.

CRIME

There were relatively few Jewish "holdupniks" or burglars, although some Jewish burglars, such as Michael Kurtz, were famous at the time for their "skills."

Before the 1880s, there had been only a single murder case involving Jews. (In 1876, a certain Pesach Rubinstein was given the death penalty for murdering a female cousin. Rubinstein starved himself to death before the penalty could be exacted; he claimed that the jail would not provide kosher food.)

IMMIGRANT CRIMINAL SLANG

Jewish criminals prior to World War I had their own lingo.

Booster—a woman who specialized in stealing from department stores

Cadet, Smicha, Mack—a pimp

Chaneleh—a warm-hearted prostitute

Doorman—a lookout spotting trouble for gamblers or for madams in brothels

Gun—a pickpocket or general thief (probably derived from *gonif*, Yiddish for "thief")

Gun-mol—a woman pickpocket

Kishkes—the friendly owner of a seedy bar

Nafka bes—a house of prostitution

Pipe fiend—someone who smoked opium

Rabbi—a gang boss

Shlamme, Shtarke—an enforcer or strong-arm man (the notion of the "strong arm" derived from the act of hitting someone with a piece of lead pipe wrapped in a newspaper)

Shammes—a detective

Trombenik—a loser

But there was plenty of Jewish crime. In a single square mile on the Lower East Side, it was estimated that there were 200 houses of prostitution, 336 places where gangs congregated, and 200 pool halls, a traditional center for placing bets. Pimps and others in the prostitution trade more traditionally hung out in dance halls, which popped up every two or three blocks around the neighborhood.

Beyond the Lower East Side, Jewish criminals established ties with the Mafia. Although Jewish criminal activity generally lasted only one generation and Jews after World War I were much less involved, individual Jewish criminals became famous across the country.

Individuals in the early years on the Lower East Side also attracted attention. Monk Eastman was short, perpetually sneering, and bullet-headed. Using a pet shop on Broome Street as his headquarters, Eastman ran extortion, prostitution, and gambling rings. After being sent to prison, his criminal enterprise was taken over by Big Jack Zelig, a murderer who is credited with organized racketeering in New York City.

Louis "Lepke" Buchalter, born on the Lower East Side in 1897 and an honor student at the renowned Jacob Joseph Yeshiva, organized Murder, Inc., the killers who enforced the rules for the Syndicate, a national confederation of criminal groups. Arnold Rothstein, a man the colorful writer Damon Runyon had nick-named "The Brain," was a gambler and criminal organizer. He became most famous for fixing the 1919 World Series; F. Scott Fitzgerald used him as the basis for the character Meyer Wolfsheim in *The Great Gatsby*.

Meyer Lansky, whose family settled on the Lower East Side in 1911, was a major criminal mastermind of the underworld, partially responsible for the expansion of the Mafia in the United States. He was an astute but violent leader who specialized in gambling (he invested in the development of Las Vegas) and money laundering; he later expanded into other illegal activities.

Jews also entered into picking pockets. Schools to train potential thieves were mockingly called *cheders* (schoolrooms), and a teacher was called a *melamed*, just like a schoolroom teacher. The pickpockets worked in teams. Typically, two would start a fight on a street. As a crowd gathered, a third member of the team would pick the pockets of those in the crowd.

Jewish criminals engaged in a wide variety of illegal activities. Joseph Toblinsky acquired the nickname "King of the Horse Poisoners" after his specialty, done when someone wouldn't pay the required protection money.

Some of the criminals lived by their own ethical standards. For example, Dopey Benny Fein—who had gotten his nickname not from his lack of intelligence but from his droopy-looking eyes that were the result of an adenoid condition—was a thief and a murderer. But he would join garment workers on picket lines, and he was not above breaking the legs of an uncooperative manager. When approached by the management at a factory to attack the pickets, Fein grew irate, though for the right amount of dough, his scruples became more malleable: he charged $60 to shoot a scab in the leg and $500 to leave someone dead.

Not all of the Jewish criminals were men. Frederika Mandelbaum, known as "Marm," was by 1890 a nationally famous "fence" for stolen goods. Monk Eastman had been part of her gang. By day, she ran a dry goods store on the corner of Clinton and Rivington Streets and seemed to be a struggling widow raising her four children. In the lavish apartment above the store, she and her gang planned bank robberies and other crimes. When she was finally indicted, Marm Mandelbaum jumped bail and moved to Canada, where she remained until her death in 1933.

"Stiff Rivka" became infamous because of where she engaged in her illegal efforts. During a High Holiday service, Rivka, who was intimately familiar with the prayers and rituals of the *shul* (synagogue), would enter religious services as just another worshiper. She would sit in the front row and look for a woman wearing expensive jewelry and then "accidentally" bump into the woman on their way out of services and steal the jewelry.

Tillie Taub was a famed Jewish prostitute on Allen Street, but she refused to work on Rosh Hashanah and Yom Kippur, because then, as she told a reporter, "I go to shul."

Prostitutes like Taub could be found in various places on the Lower East Side, but nowhere more so than on Allen Street. Some of the prostitutes put red lamps in their apartment windows to indicate the nature of their business. These immigrant Jewish women had Jewish pimps who were called "lighthouses" because they controlled all those red lights. The prostitutes also stood on the street inviting customers. As Judge Jonah Goldstein recalled, "If a woman called out to you as you walked down Allen Street, you knew she wasn't calling you to a *minyan* [prayer gathering]."

Harry Golden recalled his relationship with the prostitutes on Allen Street: "They always gave me an extra nickel for delivering the paper and another nickel for running to the grocery store or the soft-drink stand. These brothels were $1 whorehouses, and on my way home in the evening I often saw the girls standing on the stoop, opening their robes to induce the passersby upstairs. There was a strip of oilcloth at the bottom of every bed so that the customer didn't have to take his shoes off."

Some of the prostitutes who didn't stay in the house to service customers had to have an alternative to red lights as they walked. These women used handkerchiefs;

the women were known as the "handkerchief girls." They would walk along the streets holding a handkerchief. When the woman saw a man who might be a possible customer and who looked at her, the woman dropped the handkerchief. If he returned it, a deal had been silently made. She then led the man to a room—or, just as likely, an alley or rooftop.

"Mother" Rosie Hertz was the most infamous madam. She started work as a prostitute in 1882, specializing in frequenting coal cellars and basements. By 1909, she had so successful a brothel that a judge noted that she was "as much a fixture of the Lower East Side as the Brooklyn Bridge."

Not all of the prostitutes had chosen the profession willingly. White slavery—originally an offensive term used to describe the abduction of white young women and forcing them into a life of prostitution—was an ever-present danger for young immigrant women.

The existence of Jewish prostitutes and the participation of Jews in the white slave trade was a source of profound embarrassment for the Jewish community, and there were powerful efforts to end these practices.

Allen Street was home to other vices besides prostitution and attracted more than Jewish customers. There was, for example, a well-known drug house at 123 Allen Street. Patrons, including Chinese, climbed up three flights, went down the left hallway to the rear, and came to room 11. There they found a hangout run by Abe Greenberg, who had previously run such an establishment on Twenty-Fifth Street. The kitchen in Greenberg's apartment had two beds. The bedroom had a bunk on which six people could sit and smoke narcotics. The walls bore signs inscribed "Home Sweet Home" and "Call Again."

Happily for the more morally strict members of the community, drug use and prostitution were limited in scope and duration. Jewish men and women were by far more interested in becoming good breadwinners and fine wives and mothers. Indeed, the vast majority of married male immigrants focused first on finding a place to live and a job and only then on bringing their wives and families from the Old Country—or abandoning them and starting life over with a new partner—and only once they had become established could the single ones entertain thoughts of starting a family. For family had always been the central institution of Jewish life.

The Lower East Side, though, was going to add its own curious twist to the search for a spouse, for in America, love—a daring new concept to most European Jews—was the true marriage broker.

A young Jewish couple's wedding portrait. *Source: Courtesy of the Lower East Side Tenement Museum.*

SIX

ROMANCE IN THE NEW WORLD

〜〜〜

THE JEWISH emphasis on marriage and family, the longing and loneliness the unmarried adult immigrants endured, and the search for some help in confronting the challenges of the Golden Land all made many newcomers eager to get married.

As in the Old Country, the immigrants most often relied on family members and friends to introduce them to potential marriage partners. But America offered some new ideas: romantic love was more important than old traditions, and individuals were expected to find mates on their own by searching for that love. These ideas, combined with a loosening of religious ties and the lack of communal pressures to control individual actions, produced happiness in some and confusion in many others.

There were those who considered marriage a practical venture, as for example, young men seeking so-called college marriages. In such marriages, a young man who desired to attend college but could not afford to do so arranged with a woman—typically a woman who worked in a sweatshop—to get married. She agreed to support him while he got a higher education. The educated husband, sometimes then embarrassed by his uneducated wife and sometimes because of contact with wealthier single women, did not always make the best marriage partner.

Others went in search of a woman with whom to start a family. These seekers after love looked in more traditional places and adhered to the rules of that tradition. In such a traditional environment, if a man and a woman were seen together for more than a few weeks and there was no mention of marriage, the community considered the situation a moral disgrace. Sometimes this disgrace resulted in the brothers of the young woman having an unfriendly chat with the male who was going out with her.

For most of the Jewish community, the search for a partner had the elements of a ritual dance. A couple would go out once or perhaps even a second time before the young woman invited the man to meet her family and have dinner, almost always a Sabbath dinner on Friday evening. His acceptance was crucial; it was tantamount to an expression of serious marriage interest.

Men who did not find a partner through family and friends had to find another way.

MATCHMAKERS

The Jewish matchmaker, a *shadchen,* was much prized in Eastern Europe, but in America, the matchmaker didn't have such an easy time. Every young man in search of a bride, though, usually came in contact with one, and fairly soon after his arrival.

Harry Golden observed that there was an order concerning the people the new immigrants met: first came relatives and then a man who would sell the new immigrant a gold watch and chain, which, he claimed, meant that the newcomer was now a real American. He was followed by a worker from Tammany Hall trying to convince the new immigrant to go to night school and study for citizenship. This concern for education did have a motive; the new citizen could vote. Finally, Golden observed, each newcomer would meet a matchmaker.

The *shadchen* usually dealt with the young person's parents or, if the parents were still in Europe or deceased, with an aunt or uncle. A young woman's parents would inform their daughter of this previously hushed discussion, and a meeting with the young man the *shadchen* thought suitable was arranged. Of course, the reactions of young women varied greatly. Some resented the intrusion of their families; others were grateful for it.

The community ethos, reflecting in part the limited roles women were allowed to have, was to marry young, a fact that yielded a Lower East Side joke about a young woman's reaction: At eighteen, the woman asks, "What does he look like?" At twenty-five, she wants to know, "What does he do for a living?" And at thirty, she asks, "Where is he?" Indeed, daughters were supposed to be married in order of

BAD BUSINESS
FOR MATCHMAKERS

The matchmaker's difficult lot was described in the *New York Tribune* on September 30, 1900:

> This has been a hard year for the Cupids of the Ghetto, as the matrimonial agent of the Jewish quarter might be called. To the Jews he is known as the *shadchen,* but unless the marriage business picks up, the broker is going to drop out of sight. Already, he is branching out into other ways of making a living. He writes letters for the illiterate, acts as interpreter in business transactions, or does odd jobs around the synagogues. . . . The Jews . . . had always been accustomed to having a professional matchmaker arrange their marriages, and at that time they did not know how to get along without it. The young men were bashful and were more than willing to give up 10 percent of the girl's dowry if some one else would put the question. Besides, they made sure of getting a wife in this way. They would go to the broker . . . and outline their ideal of a wife, not forgetting to mention the amount of dowry they expected. The *shadchen* would take note of all the young man's advantages—personal appearance, education, and moneymaking ability. Then he would go among the young women of his extended acquaintance and speedily find someone who was willing to wed on the terms which the broker had to offer. . . . Sometimes the *shadchen* had trouble collecting his fee; in those cases he evened things up by breaking off the match. There were many ways of doing this. If the man were at fault, the *shadchen* would get the girl a more desirable match. As love had not entered into the first engagement, it was speedily broken, leaving the man sadder but wiser. If the *shadchen* discovered that the girl objected to paying the fee he found a prettier girl for the man.

their birth because to do otherwise was thought to bring bad luck. Many parents worried as the eldest daughter passed one more year without being married. There was a deep concern that she would be "left," the euphemism used on the Lower East Side for women who didn't get married.

The matchmaker usually charged between 5 and 10 percent of the bride's dowry for finding a suitable match, although sometimes, if the bride was too poor for a dowry, the matchmaker agreed on a set fee. Also, if the bride was particularly beautiful, the matchmaker accepted the set fee because it would be so easy to find a match for such a bride. The male matchmakers soon developed what became a sort of uniform. They had a beard. They wore a derby hat. And to appear to have become a success in America, they always carried an umbrella.

The *shadchonim* considered themselves professionals, with an expert eye and shrewd judgment about joining couples who would enjoy a long relationship. The matchmakers therefore deeply resented ordinary people who simply couldn't resist trying to make a match of their own. Housewives were rumored to be always on the lookout for someone for their child or niece or nephew or even boarder.

With all this competition and with many young people yearning to find someone to love themselves, the *shadchonim* had a tough time making a living. Most had another profession, such as rabbi, cantor, or business owner. For people like rabbis, the match was more than a business; it was the fulfillment of a mitzvah, a religious commandment.

After locating a young man, the *shadchen*'s work continued with a visit to the prospective bride's house. Her mother would start by mentioning the young woman's range of talents. The obvious domestic talents were mentioned: cooking, sewing, and the ability to take care of children. If there was even a hint of musical ability, such as a skill at playing the piano, that was also loudly proclaimed. Business skills were important to the young man. It was common on the Lower East Side for families to talk about their daughter's having *alle drei,* "all three," meaning she was a skilled stenographer, bookkeeper, and typist. In the eyes of many a *shadchen,* there was a familiar subtext to this extended résumé: the more skills the young woman had, the less physically attractive she was. So parents didn't brag too much; they wanted to suggest subtly that they thought their daughter beautiful.

Then it came time for the heart of the discussion—the *nadan,* or dowry. The dowry was not meant to be a commercial transaction—a monetary gift in exchange for the man taking a bride. Instead, the dowry was a source of pride for the woman's

למזל טוב.   למזל טוב.   למזל טוב.

למזל טוב!

קול ששון וקול שמחה! קול חתן וקול כלה!

בשבת .... ב .... לחודש .... שנת חמשת
אלפים ושש מאות .... לבריאת עולם למנין שאנו
מנין כאן ק"ק .... במדינת אמעריקא צפון איך
החתן .... אמר לה להדא ....
.... הוי לי לאנתו כדת משה וישראל ואנא אפלח
ואוקיר ואיזון ואפרנס יתיכי ליכי כהלכות גוברין יהודאין דפלחין
ומוקרין זנין ומפרנסין לנשיהון בקושטא ויהיבנא ליכי ....
.... כסף זוזי .... דחזי ליכי .... ומזוניכי וכסותיכי
וסיפוקיכי ומיעל לותיכי כאורח כל ארעא וצביאת מרת ....
.... דא והות ליה לאנתו ודין נדוניא דהנעלת ליה
מבי .... בין בכסף בין בזהב בין בתכשיטין במאני דלבושא
בשימושי דירה ובשימושי דערסא ארת הכל קבל עליו ר' ....
.... זקוקים כסף צרוף וצבי ר' ....
חרת .... והוסיף לה מן דיליה .... זקוקים כסף צרוף
אחרים כנגדן סך הכל .... זקוקים כסף צרוף וכך
אמר ר' .... חתן דנן אחריות שטר
כתובתא דא נדוניא דין ותוספתא דא קבילת עלי ועל ירתי בתראי
להתפרע מכל שפר ארג נכסין וקנינין דאית לי תחות כל שמיא
דקנאי ודעתיד אנא למקניא נכסין ראית להון אחריות ודלית להון
אחריות כלהון יהון אחראין וערבאין לפרוע מנהון שטר כתובתא דא
נדוניא דין ותוספתא דא ואפילו מן גלימא דעל כתפאי בחיים ובמות
מן יומא דנן ולעלם ואחריות שטר כתובתא דא נדוניא דין ותוספתא
דא קבל עליו ר' .... חתן דנן כחומר כל
שטרי כתובות ותוספתא דנהגין בבנות ישראל העשוין כתיקון חז"ל
דלא כאסמכתא ודלא כטופסי דשטרי וקנינא מן ר' ....
.... חתן דנן למרת ....
.... דא בכל מה דכתוב ומפורש לעיל במנא דכשר למקניא
ביה הכל שריר וקים
נאום ....
ונאום ....
.... החתן
.... מסדר הקדושין

Published by J. KATZENELENBOGEN,
35 Ludlow Street, N.Y.

צו פֿערקויפֿען ביא י. קאטצענעלענבאָגען מוכר ספרים
35 לודלאו סטריט, נויאָרק

A *katuba*, or wedding contract. *Source: Courtesy of the Lower East Side Tenement Museum.*

A WEDDING ON LUDLOW STREET

I. Raboy, a Yiddish novelist, described the wedding of a relatively well-to-do couple that took place on Ludlow Street:

> From the butcher they ordered two hundred chickens and fifty calves' livers, two hundred pounds of beef. From the baker on Essex Street white rolls and cakes; and they told him to bake sugar and honey cakes, fruitcakes, and tortes topped with nuts. They went to the saloon on Suffolk Street and ordered twenty casks of beer, twenty gallons of wine and countless bottles of slivovitz.
>
> A phaeton with two horses bedecked with ornamental trappings raced down the length of Ludlow Street bearing the groom to the house of the bride. . . .
>
> When the bride and groom entered the dimly lit hall, the electric lights came up with great brilliance. The bride and groom were seated at the head table and received the blessings of guests and relatives amid much kissing and happiness.

family. In Eastern Europe, the dowry allowed the young man to continue his religious studies; in America, it was to help the young man start a business.

Of course, the young woman's family wanted to know all about the young man—his family, his ability to support their daughter and any children, and, for some, the nature of his religious devotion.

The *shadchen* would frequently accompany the proposed bridegroom on his first visit to the intended bride. The other children in the house were their own source of problems. They knew that the occasion was a perfect opportunity to seek some sort of bribe from their family. And there was another problem—at least in the stories Jews told each other. That problem was the pretty younger sister, the one the intended bridegroom liked a lot more than the proposed bride. Of course, parents were aware of such a potential problem, so they "suggested" that the younger sister be somewhere else during the dinner.

With the preparations all carefully made, the best food obtained and lovingly cooked, the apartment made to look its cleanest, perhaps with some borrowed pieces, the potential bride and the potential groom met. Both had a lot at stake in the meeting. Both knew how awkward it would be if either or both found the other distasteful. But those were the moments of anticipation and excitement that were the stuff of dreams and the stories of legend.

Finally, the young man and young woman met.

Happily, many of the immigrants who searched found such a partner and celebrated the union with a joyous Jewish wedding.

Sadly, not all marriages worked out as they had in the couple's dreams or their parents' plans.

DEATH, DESERTION, AND DIVORCE

The dangerous, unsanitary, and crowded working conditions in the factories and sweatshops led to diseases and accidents and sometimes even to death. Widows and young children without fathers were a common sight on the Lower East Side.

Jewish families also faced another problem: desertion. By 1910, there were an ever-increasing number of reports of men abandoning their wives and children. As early as 1905, more than 14 percent of the relief funds provided by the United Hebrew Charities went to deserted women.

The horrified women who had been abandoned began to write letters to the newspapers. In some cases, they wrote to find their husband, ironically hoping he had been the victim of some accident rather than having voluntarily left. In other cases, the letters were simply cries from the heart, anguished screams at their husbands. The *Jewish Daily Forward* got so many of these letters that they offered a "Gallery of Missing Husbands" with photographs of the husbands who were gone.

ECONOMIC COMPETITION

Desertion became a problem because of the economics of immigration—husbands generally had to set off for America ahead of the family, work to save the money needed to pay for travel, and then send for the family. Originally, it was widely

ABANDONED!

Here is an excerpt from a letter sent by a distraught woman in 1908 to the *Jewish Daily Forward:*

Max: The children and I now say farewell to you. You left us in such a terrible state. You had no compassion for us. . . . Have you ever asked yourself why you left us? Max, where is your conscience; you used to have sympathy for the forsaken women and used to say their terrible plight was due to the men who left them in dire need. And how did you act? I was a young, educated decent girl when you took me. You lived with me for six years, during which time I bore you four children. And then you left me. Of the four children only two remain, but you have made them living orphans. Who will bring them up? Who will support us? Have you no pity for your own flesh and blood? Consider what you are doing. My tears choke me and I cannot write any more.

✕✕✕✕

believed that such a process would take only a brief time because, surely, money was so easy to come by in the Golden Land that even the lowliest of the immigrants would quickly have pockets overflowing with money.

The reality was that it was common to have a lengthy separation. In most cases, families were happy to be reunited. But in some instances, the husbands could not bear the time alone and found other women companions. In other cases, the men became so Americanized that when their wives arrived, the women seemed like strangers from a strange world. This situation is the basis for Abraham Cahan's novel *Yekl* and the movie based on it, *Hester Street.*

The male immigrants who came to America assumed they would find freedom and money, that they would be safe from discrimination and attack, and that they

Family portrait. *Source: Courtesy of the Lower East Side Tenement Museum.*

would be able to practice their religion in peace. These things were true to some extent, but American life had overt and subtle effects on them.

The competitive nature of American economic life and the emphasis on individual achievement and individual responsibility were at odds with the economic interdependence that Jews had in Eastern Europe. In Europe, relatively few people had been wealthy, so there was no point in competing with one's neighbors. The center of life was the wider family and the still wider community, not the individual. Furthermore, the individualism of American life was spurred in the immigrants by living in a city where there were more lures and attractions and greater moral latitude than in the rural areas they had left behind. And a shift in their moral compass was the result not just of the availability of prostitution but also of the crowding, with its lack of privacy, and the placing of large numbers of young, attractive people near each other. The shtetl had lacked privacy as much as the tenements, but a shtetl life was marked by religious controls over the individual that were simply missing in America.

SEXUAL COMPETITION

Economic competition was mirrored in sexual competition. In popular immigrant lore, this competition was most directly played out between a husband and a family's boarders. This relationship blossoms, for example, in *Hester Street* and results in happiness. But in real life, that was not always the case. For example, in the Yiddish play *Minna*, a woman falls in love with the boarder but ends up killing herself.

But sexual and other kinds of attraction to another person were not the only reason for desertion. Simple economic hardship was a major cause. Some immigrants simply could not find jobs or could find only seasonal jobs or jobs that provided inadequate wages. These financial pressures inevitably worked their way into the family, leading to arguments and eventual separation.

THE IMPACT OF DESERTION

The results of desertion were devastating. Abandoned women simply had no means of support. Some of them turned to prostitution. Others were forced to surrender their children to an asylum for orphans or to another family.

The Jewish community reacted to the situation by creating the National Desertion Bureau in 1911. The bureau, which handled about twenty-five hundred cases annually, sought to trace the husband who had deserted, to effect a reconciliation, to provide financial aid, and if necessary, to prosecute uncooperative husbands.

In many ways, desertion became a sort of divorce proceeding for the poor. Unsurprisingly, then, as Jewish immigrants grew slightly more prosperous, the rate of desertion declined and the rate of divorce increased. The rate was still low in this country. The ratio of marriages to divorces in the Gentile population was 9.4 to 1 at the turn of the twentieth century; the Jewish ratio was 24 to 1. It took several decades for the Jewish ratio to equal the Gentile.

INTERMARRIAGE

Marriages between immigrant Jews and Christians were relatively rare but of intense communal interest when they did occur. According to Julius Drachsler, who in 1920 wrote *Democracy and Assimilation: The Blending of Immigrant Heritages in America,* the first careful study of the phenomenon, only 1.17 percent of American Jews intermarried between 1908 and 1912. This compared to 16.73 percent among Italian Americans and fully a third of German Americans. The rarity of Jewish intermarriage resulted from the fact that social interactions for the immigrants were mostly limited to other Jews, that religious and family and cultural disapproval still affected the young, and that Jews, whether religious or not, still felt a strong identity as part of the Jewish people. Early contacts with non-Jewish Russians and Italians in the garment industry led to a small number of intermarriages.

But imbibing the freedom of individual choice, some immigrants, loosed from the communal bonds that had so restricted their ancestors and increasingly coming in contact with attractive people from other backgrounds, were willing to risk the sometimes intense criticism that might result from an interfaith relationship.

For most Jews, "intermarriage" was between an Orthodox Jew and a secular one or between a *yekke*, a German Jew, and an *Ostjuden*, an Eastern European Jew, or between a Galitzianer and a Litvak.

Increasingly, younger Jews, especially those born in America, felt a strain between the tradition they had been taught and the tugging of their own heart. This inner struggle was given voice in various pieces of literature.

The most famous work of popular culture reflecting this conflict in the immigrant era was *The Melting Pot* by the British author Israel Zangwill, a four-act play that appeared in 1908. The play's vision, perhaps reflecting Zangwill's own marriage to a Christian, was that America produced a new breed of people. Immigrants may have come from different lands, spoken different languages, and practiced different religions, but in America, all that foreignness simply melted away, and what was left was a new entity, the American.

Although the play had some famous supporters—Theodore Roosevelt and Jane Addams among them—most critics thought the plot thin and the whole enterprise melodramatic. Whatever its literary merits, Zangwill gave voice to what would, over time, come to be the view of an ever-increasing segment of the Jewish community.

Other literary works also reflected the communal struggle over intermarriage. For example, Anzia Yezierska's novel *Salome of the Tenements* portrayed intermarriage as the very definition of freedom and personal liberty in America. In the 1926 novel *I Am a Woman—and a Jew,* written by Leah Morton, the protagonist described her feelings about wanting to marry a Gentile: "I wanted a new thing—happiness. I am not a girl representing a race. I was not a Jewish maiden responsible to a race. . . . I was no Biblical Rebecca sorrowfully pleading for her race. I was an American, now, just as he was."

ON INTERMARRIAGE

Here is a letter to the *Jewish Daily Forward* from 1906. It reflects the paper's general position that intermarriage creates special problems.

Dear Editor,

For a long time I worked in a shop with a Gentile girl, and we began to go out together and fell in love. We agreed that I would remain a Jew and she a Christian. But after we had been married for a year, I realized that it would not work.

I began to notice that whenever one of my Jewish friends comes to the house, she is displeased. Worse yet, when she sees me reading a Jewish newspaper her face changes color. She says nothing, but I can see that she has changed. I feel that she is very unhappy with me, though I know she loves me. She will soon become a mother, and she is more dependent on me than ever.

She used to be quite liberal, but lately she is being drawn back to the Christian religion. She gets up early Sunday mornings, runs to church and comes home with eyes swollen from crying. When we pass a church now and then, she trembles.

Dear Editor, advise me what to do now. I could never convert, and there's no hope for me to keep her from going to church. What can we do now?

Thankfully,

A Reader

Unfortunately, we often hear of such tragedies, which stem from marriages between people of different worlds. It's possible that if this couple were to move to a Jewish neighborhood, the young man might have more influence on his wife.

Sometimes, the literary efforts came from the Gentile side. The most famous example of that was the Broadway comedy *Abie's Irish Rose,* written by Anne Nichols. The play described the lives of Nancy Carroll, an Irish Catholic young woman, who married Abie Levy over the objections of his Jewish family and her Catholic one. Like *The Melting Pot, Abie's Irish Rose* received poor reviews. It ran, however, for five and a half years.

In addition to the literary efforts of some to support the idea that romantic love was more important than adherence to tradition, American Jews saw some of the entertainers who had risen from their ranks intermarry as well. From George Burns and Irving Berlin to Al Jolson and Sophie Tucker, many of the entertainers, who had money, fame, and access to large numbers of potential partners, married out of the faith. These people were often wildly admired in the Jewish community, and they served as early models equating success and intermarriage.

The personal desires and relationships among immigrant Jews were also reflected in the Jewish press. The *Jewish Daily Forward* published many letters from anguished Jewish parents, struggling mightily and seeking advice about how to understand or stop an interfaith relationship or an impending intermarriage. In general, the *Forward*'s advice tended to be what the editors considered practical. As socialists, the editors didn't make a religious argument but instead focused on how any interfaith marriage would add another layer of difficulty onto an institution such as marriage that was already difficult enough.

These literary efforts and personal cries might be seen as sensationalized, except for another statistic in Drachsler's study. The intermarriage rate, he discovered, virtually tripled for immigrants between the first and second generation of Americans. This general statistic would very quickly be reflected in the Jewish community.

For the overwhelming number of Jews, though, getting married continued to mean marrying another Jew. And marriage also meant the raising of children, children who would grow up to provide not only the usual challenges that raising children usually did but also specific challenges to immigrant parents.

Children around a bonfire. *Source: Courtesy of Brown Brothers.*

SEVEN

CHILDREN AND FAMILIES

><><

THE IMMIGRANTS faced many daunting challenges—debilitating poverty, haunting hunger, culture shock, and resentment by some native-born Americans, among others—but they thought they could rely on the cornerstone of communal life, the Jewish family, which had always served as a haven and shield against external threats. Unfortunately, the overwhelming realities of immigrant life in America, which overturned centuries-old values and practices, undermined the family as they did so much else in Jewish life.

The pressures of acquiring housing, a job, a language, and a new culture were emotionally overwhelming for some newcomers. The work, so far beneath what the immigrants had hoped to find in the Golden Land, combined with the grinding poverty; the radical departure from the old ways, especially religious and cultural traditions; and the feelings of wanting desperately to be American for some—and the more mixed feelings of wanting to be American but stay Jewish for others—was nearly more than they could take.

Becoming American was itself a full-time job, and different people, including husbands and wives, adjusted in different ways and at different rates. Women, especially, prized the independence the city provided that the shtetl had not. Some of their husbands resented this newfound freedom for their wives; the husbands had lost status and the wives had gained it, and this was tumultuous for many couples.

Besides the travails of making their way in their strange new world, many immigrants strongly desired—or felt strong pressure to desire—to become citizens of the United States. District courts would be especially crowded in late July or early August in election years because election day was always the Tuesday following the first Monday in November, and people had to be citizens for ninety days before they could vote. For many an immigrant, becoming a U.S. citizen was akin to a complete rebirth. For their children, born in America or living here for most of their lives, adaptation was far more natural.

CHILDREN

A proverb popular among Jewish immigrants held that "in America, the children bring up the parents." The children went to school, where they were immersed in English. When their parents spoke Yiddish to them, they responded in English. They were young enough to absorb the culture and the language, and they had tremendous incentives—peer approval, teacher approval, potential success—to adapt quickly to American life. After all, they were the ones who got "greenhorn" yelled at them by street gangs, classmates, and young neighbors, and the name-calling was usually accompanied by a shove. This sort of physical confrontation provided early lessons in survival. Children quickly learned to walk home from school in groups. But mostly they acquired extraordinary incentives to adapt.

DEALING WITH AMERICAN CULTURE

Jewish immigrant children didn't resent their poverty because it was all they knew. They didn't mind selling newspapers or being a bootblack. It is telling that the great musician Samuel Chotzinoff chose to title his exemplary memoir of growing up on the Lower East Side *A Lost Paradise*. It is virtually impossible to imagine that any adults living there thought they were living in a paradise. Children, though, loved the excitement. What was poverty to an adult was adventure to a child. George Burns fondly recalled the rolls he would buy and how far they would go: "You'd buy six rolls and then you'd buy a can of tomato herrings, and there'd be six tomato herrings in a can, and six rolls would be six cents and a can of tomato herrings would be about six or seven cents, and for fifteen cents you could feed eight or nine kids."

The younger Jewish immigrant children carried either no experience or no vivid memories of living elsewhere or hearing Yiddish from everyone. They didn't live in a world bounded by Jewish law. And they were dazzled and confused by the lures of American life.

One prominent example of this was Christmas, when Jewish children, according to the *Jewish Daily Forward,* kept their heads down and didn't look at the glittering holiday lights in the store windows. The separation from the rest of America became clear and acute during such moments. The defenses adults had were not available to the younger generation.

And not all Jewish adults could or did explain what being Jewish meant. After all, many of them had left tradition behind or realized that American survival meant being more adaptable. It was the traditional Jews who had the toughest time, so Jewish children did not hear clear messages about being Jewish even at home.

The children loved to pitch pennies or play other games. This sometimes completely befuddled their parents. In 1903, a very confused father wrote a letter to the *Jewish Daily Forward* seeking advice about how to deal with his son's keen interest in baseball. The father wrote, "What is the point of this crazy game? It makes sense to teach a child to play dominoes or chess. . . . [But when playing baseball] the children can get crippled. . . . I want my boy to grow up to be a mensh, not a wild American runner." The father wasn't alone. Eddie Cantor remembered that as an insult, his grandmother, who raised him, used to call him a baseball player when she was angry. Cantor noted, "To the pious people of the ghetto, a baseball player was the king of loafers."

LEARNING TO PLAY BASEBALL
AND OTHER AMERICAN PASTIMES

For his part, Abraham Cahan, who edited the *Forward,* tried his best to calm the befuddled father and to make sense of the game for his adult readers. Cahan counseled that parents should allow children to play baseball "as long as it does not interfere with their education." After all, "the body needs to develop also. Baseball is played in the fresh air. The really wild game is football. . . . Accidents and fights occur in football, but baseball is not dangerous."

There was a deeper confusion underneath the parents' fear and anxiety. Baseball had no purpose except fun. It didn't help the mind develop as, presumably, chess did. It wasn't a quiet indoor game that wouldn't disturb anyone. It was raucous and without a single shred of value beyond the sheer enjoyment of the game. It was, to the Eastern European Jewish mind, a waste of time.

The Jews had very little time to waste. When they weren't working, the traditional among them were studying Torah. Those with a social conscience struggled to see how spending time frivolously could be justified when there was so much suffering both in the Jewish community and in the wider world. Many Jews felt guilty about enjoying themselves when there was no moral purpose to the activity, no religious lesson, no social good advanced. The hedonism practiced by those who gambled, visited brothels, became drunks, or engaged in crime was a foreign drive for most Jews. They therefore couldn't really understand their children.

RELIGIOUS PRACTICES

The children also were a transition generation in terms of religious practices. The immigrant parents, most of them not very religious themselves and sometimes proudly hostile to traditional Judaism, did not give their children a Jewish education, sometimes did not give the boys a bar mitzvah ceremony, and did not keep kosher homes. Even in homes where the Sabbath or the dietary rules were followed, however, parents would frequently be lenient when it came to their children. Some parents understood that in America, holding a job often meant working on Saturdays. It was relatively easy to keep kosher outside the home on the Lower East Side but not easy at all in the wider American society. Some parents compromised and said children could eat what they wished outside the home, as long as they kept kosher at home.

THE ABSENT OR WEAK FATHER

Most of those children came from homes where the father was, in theory, the central authority. But in reality, that was not always the case.

Some families, of course, did have the traditional stern father. Some children adapted or even thrived in this environment. Others struggled. The best literary expression of such a struggle is in Anzia Yezierska's great novel *Bread Givers*.

The book is a thinly veiled self-portrait centering on the protagonist's fiery relationship with her father. Indeed, from her first book, *Hungry Hearts*, which Samuel Goldwyn eventually turned into a movie, Yezierska had tried to describe her paternal relationship.

The closeness she eventually hoped for was not to be. After the first book was published, she went to face her father, who was as unyielding as ever: "What is it I

A FATHER'S ROLE

Harry Golden explained the role of his father—and the subtler role of his mother—in their immigrant household:

> No one sat down to the dinner table until he came home from work and . . . we did not speak until he spoke first or until he had asked us a question. . . . Mother made all the decisions. . . . Alone, she would tell my father, "I found an apartment on Ludlow Street. I paid a deposit and I've asked the moving van to come Monday." That evening at the dinner table during a lull she would say, "Children, pay attention. Papa has something very important to say to you." Father would proceed to describe the move next Monday and Mother would listen through the whole process as though hearing it for the first time, even congratulating him afterward on his excellent judgment."

hear? You wrote a book about me? How could you write about someone you don't know?"

Other immigrant children were profoundly affected by the absence of their fathers, whether through death, divorce, desertion, or simply working long hours. This was compounded by the loss of status for Jewish fathers in America. The father had been indisputably in charge in Europe. That was no longer the case in America. Moreover, father substitutes were fewer because there were fewer extended families.

The absent or weak father had important influences on many young Jews, especially males. The lack of a powerful authority gave permission of sorts for some to skip school or take risks that would not have been taken if a strong father figure had been in the picture. The negative effects of this situation led some to petty or serious crime. It made most of the boys assertive, comfortable assuming the vacant leadership role in the family, and willing to take risks. Of course, these were children whose parents had taken the enormous risk of traveling to a new world. It is therefore unsurprising that great risk takers emerged from the Jewish community. The first generation of filmmakers consisted mostly of Jewish males. The comedians who rose in vaudeville were disproportionately Jewish. Numerous business entrepreneurs emerged from the Jewish community. All of these motivated men were fueled to a great extent by this assertiveness developed as a result of conditions at home.

The absent or weak father had a second effect as well. The sons and daughters of the immigrants wanted to feel that they were worthy Americans. If their parents had fallen short, they absolutely would not. They had to prove themselves—not just to their new country but also to their mothers and, not least, to themselves.

Some of the people who would become famous entertainers absorbed these attitudes and became young thieves. George Burns even stole his name. He took it from the Burns Brothers coal yard—from which he also stole coal. Fanny Brice was a shoplifter, even from her own mother's store. Bert Lahr stole a pumpkin—from a police officer. Eddie Cantor stole from pushcarts.

But entertainers weren't the only thieves. Ordinary children nurtured in the environment of the Lower East Side saw stealing as natural. Sometimes the thievery had a profound effect. Sura Katz, for example, was an eight-year-old immigrant whose five-year-old brother languished in a hospital on Ellis Island. Sura desperately wanted to get a toy for her brother, but she had no money. Enlisting the aid of her six-year-old sister Raisel, she concocted a plan. Raisel distracted a pushcart vendor, and Sura stole the toy. Her parents were outraged at her behavior, but when they rushed downstairs to return the toy, the vendor had vanished. Sura never forgot the incident, and it made donating to charity a central moral obligation she honored for the rest of her life.

HOW SOME FAMOUS JEWISH ENTERTAINERS GOT STARTED

All the future entertainers showed their skills at an early age. Fanny Brice, born Fanny Borach, worked in her father's saloon on Forsyth Street. The young girl heard all the accents and began copying them. When she tried show business, she attempted to disguise her Jewishness at first, but in 1910, Irving Berlin told her to sing his song "Sadie Salome" employing a Yiddish accent. That made her a star.

Berlin himself used to assert later in life that "everyone should have a Lower East Side in their lives," although his life there had not been the least bit pleasant. Berlin used to make money by selling the *Evening Journal*, a newspaper. He was once reading a copy on a pier overlooking the East River when a crane unloading coal knocked him into the river by mistake. A bystander jumped in and pulled the boy to shore. Berlin, who had swallowed a lot of water, was taken by ambulance to the hospital. Whenever he recounted the story, he would proudly mention that through it all, he had held on to the five pennies he had earned, so crucial were they to his family.

Many youngsters like Berlin tried to sing to make a few pennies. George Burns, for example, joined a group called the Peewee Quartet when he was seven. The boys, who had met while working in a candy store, sang on street corners or wherever else they could. Burns always claimed they were most successful on the Staten Island Ferry because the only way passengers could avoid them "was by jumping overboard."

Older boys, like Berlin, would go to the saloons on the Bowery. These singers, called buskers, played to a tougher audience than they were used to among their families and friends. But if the laborers and sailors and prostitutes who were the mainstay of the saloon's customers liked the singers, they would pitch pennies, and the youngsters would pocket their take and move on to the next saloon.

Ira Gershwin, the lyricist partner of his brother George, wrote in his diary of the adventures of a bright young boy on the Lower East Side. Ira was given to studying and reading, unlike his brother and most young boys. Ira would go to a laundry on Broome Street "where the bosses ran a nickel novel library as a sideline. For the return of a novel plus two cents, one was privileged to ransack until some novel attracted or appealed. Soon I was reading four of them a day." Ira also recalled visiting Hubert's Museum on Fourteenth Street, a museum that was especially entrancing for its trained fleas and magic acts; the Eden Musée on Twenty-Third Street, which specialized in waxworks; and various racetracks and other places. He listed as his favorite "Epicurean Delights . . . 1) Chinese Nuts 2) Polly Seeds [sunflower seeds] 3) Hot Arbis 4) Sweet Potatoes 5) Lolly Pops 6) Candy Floss 7) Half Sour Pickles."

George Gershwin, unlike his brother, was often in trouble. He recalled one terrible incident when, on his usual roller skates, he was trapped by a rival gang. Seeking to escape, he wandered into an apartment building then under construction and fell into the open elevator shaft, a fall that resulted in a concussion. George was nicknamed "Cheesecake" by the other boys because his father ran a bakery at the time.

More traditional Jewish children than these boys who would grow up to be famous were less antiauthoritarian, less willing to stand outside the society. They found a very American way to succeed: the schoolroom.

SCHOOL

The job of the schools was to turn immigrants into Americans within a single generation. With Jews, at least, they were extraordinarily successful. Public School 20, at 45 Rivington Street, for example, produced such students as the actors Paul Muni and Edward G. Robinson, the writer Harry Golden, Senator Jacob Javits, and the songwriters Irving Caesar and George Gershwin. Many of the immigrants who later wrote about their experiences had vivid recollections of their life in an American school.

The schools centered on studying English. Whatever was done always had a language component. Speaking properly was emphasized through singing or participating in assemblies. Students were drilled and drilled again. They learned how to stand in front of an audience, how to make their voice rhythmic, how to pronounce the difficult sounds English required.

Besides language, the teachers stressed cleanliness. The teachers mandated that students come to class with clean hands and washed faces. The teachers wanted students also to comb their hair and shine their footwear. There were monitors in front of assembly doors to inspect students as they entered. Students were generally subject to tight discipline in the schools.

LEARNING CITIZENSHIP

To teach citizenship, the schools focused on civics lessons and on American history. Students memorized poems and speeches, such as the following bit of doggerel:

> I love the name of Washington.
> I love my country, too.
> I love the flag, the dear old flag,
> The red, the white, the blue.

The students saluted the flag daily. National holidays were special occasions. Sometimes the schools would bring in a Civil War general to recount episodes of that conflict.

The normal class size was forty-five to fifty pupils in each class. Indeed, P.S. 188 on the Lower East Side was the largest public school in the world: five thousand students sat in its ninety-six classrooms.

TEACHERS

In his fascinating autobiography *A Lost Paradise,* the musician Samuel Chotzinoff recalled his early schooldays. He began school in America in the second grade. He recalled his mother shopping for a pencil box that cost a dime; four writing pads, which each cost a penny; and some colored blotters for a nickel. His teacher, Miss Murphy, a middle-aged, graying woman, was in charge of fifty boys in her class. As Chotzinoff wrote about her:

> She was severely distant, and her impersonal attitude, added to the formality of being called by our last names, cast a chill on the classroom. Soon one began to long for the sound of one's first name as for an endearment that would, at a stroke, establish a human relationship between oneself and Miss Murphy. But it was not to be.

Not all of Chotzinoff's teachers were so formal. Indeed, there was another teacher who inspired the young student both intellectually and musically:

> Mr. Strassmeir was the young and talented teacher of my class at No. 2. A man of seemingly immeasurable learning, he was also an amateur pianist of such proficiency as to make his passing into the professional category contingent only on his pleasure. It is true that we never heard him play anything but *The Mosquito Parade* at morning assembly. Even on the morning when the entire school was summoned by Mr. Denscher, the principal, to mourn the death of President McKinley, we marched in to the strains of *The Mosquito Parade.*

Students were under additional pressure because until 1903, they were placed in classes not according to their age but according to their language skills. Of course, this provided tremendous incentives for students to improve rapidly so that they

SCHOOL DISCIPLINE

In his autobiography *The Time That Was Then*, Harry Roskolenko recalled the strictness of his school's rules:

> Schooling in my time at P.S. 31 was very stern. The teacher, though not a cop, was nevertheless a ruler-wielding teacher. We knew the ruler because it was often applied . . . by both teacher and principal. We would get slapped, and they were right. I was never right at any time—said my parents, who were immediately told of each incident by a note from the teachers or the principal. They sided with the teachers, and my report card proved that I was sleeping when I should have been studying. I was *left back*—a phrase that became quite familiar around our house. . . .
> Nevertheless, all of us learned quickly.

>✧✧✧<

would no longer be sitting with younger children but would be in the same class as their chronological peers.

Seeing the humiliation many immigrant children felt, the board of education changed this system and set up specific classes for students who were older or smarter than their mastery of English would otherwise indicate. The classes were smaller than the regular ones, consisting of thirty to thirty-five students. Ordinarily, students stayed in these classes for a relatively brief time—four or five months— and then were integrated into regular classes.

TROUBLES WITH LEARNING

The effort to accomplish the task of teaching language quickly and completely came at a cost. First of all, school was difficult for many students. They didn't come from English-speaking homes, so rarely could parents help with homework.

Teachers became additional authorities for students who didn't much like authority. To even out the power relationship between themselves and teachers, students often resorted to coming up with nicknames for the teachers, usually based on appearance. An unattractive teacher might be dubbed "Bulldog" because of a bulky face or "Cockeye" because of an eye problem. Of course, this presented a potential problem for students. When pressed to come up with a direct answer to a question, they first had to remember not to address the teacher inadvertently by the nickname.

There were other problems for students as well. Learning difficulties were rarely spotted. George Burns, for example, had dyslexia, but it went undiagnosed. Knowing he was smart but frustrated by the words he was supposed to read, he left school early. Some creative students didn't pay much attention either. As one teacher commented about Irving Berlin, "He just dreams and sings to himself."

Of course, schools could not always successfully compete with the excitement of a game, hanging out with friends, making a few cents, or getting on with life.

THE LANGUAGE PROBLEM

Viewing English as a key to their students' progress, teachers made children ashamed of the foreign languages their parents spoke and even of their un-American backgrounds. The schools therefore came into direct competition with the home for the hearts, minds, and general loyalty of the children. The father or mother as the authority faced a formidable alternative authority in the teacher. Parents were judged on a scale of successful adaptation. Could they speak English well? Were they economically successful? If not, a gap grew larger and larger between parent and child as the child grew.

Forced to choose, children all made their own compromises. Some simply went along one way at home and another at school, though the tension between the two selves couldn't have been easy. Other children made clearer choices, but whichever choice they made created difficulties either at home or at school.

Parents had their own mixed feelings. They felt awkward as they relied on their children to translate for them, but they were incredibly proud of their children's achievements in school. The parents encouraged learning as a sacred undertaking. One immigrant, Robert Leslie, remembered his mother telling him, "America is a land of gold. There is no gold in the streets. The gold is in your head. When you are educated, you obtain the gold."

The philosopher Morris Raphael Cohen recalled that his mother cried when he won a gold medal for having the highest score on a college entrance examination. The tears came not from the award itself but from its meaning: her son could now go to college. When an aunt told her that a college education was beyond her financial means, she said that if she had to, she would scrub floors so that her son could go to college.

DROPPING OUT

Despite this widespread admiration for learning, many Jewish children left school early, primarily because they needed to work. In 1910, only six thousand Jewish students were attending high school. One-third of the students in New York City were Jewish, but only one out of four high school students was.

The Jewish students who were intellectual stars were thus a talented minority, not an abundant majority. And the average parents may have prized education, but they prized survival more. As George Burns noted in describing his reasons for entering show business, "We weren't hungry for recognition. We were hungry for food."

An additional problem for the Jewish students on the Lower East Side was that many of their mothers feared even going into the school because they thought that teachers would ridicule their lack of English skills or that they themselves would be punished for a child's scholarly failures. Sometimes even a child's deficiencies, vision or hearing problems, for example, were kept from the teacher, who had to discover them independently, sometimes long after a child was classified as backward or recalcitrant.

THE ADENOID RIOT

Beyond disputes and praise, children were always at the center of the Jewish home; indeed, they were considered the greatest blessings of life. The *New York Times* on August 28, 1905, ran a story about a Lower East Side artist named Jacob Malkin who had disappeared. His wife believed he had drowned himself because the couple had remained childless.

This love of children sometimes led to a conflict between home and school, especially when the safety of the child was involved. The most prominent case began in 1906 with an effort by Julia Richman, a Jewish school district superintendent, to introduce smallpox vaccinations to children in the school. During the vaccinations at P.S. 100, the physicians saw children with swollen lymph nodes in the throat—adenoids—and thought these should be removed. The principal sent a letter home suggesting that the family physician perform the simple procedure, or else physicians from the Board of Health would do the surgery if parents signed the form. Many parents, whose command of English was not enviable, signed without understanding the implications of what they were signing.

The operations began, but then so did the rumors. Soon word spread that doctors were murdering young children in the school, slashing their throats and then burying them in the schoolyard.

The rumors reached fever pitch early in the summer of 1906. Crowds of women and children marched on various schools on the Lower East Side, beginning what would eventually be called the Adenoid Riot. From Rivington to Grand and from the Bowery to the East River, the crowd swept along and, when the protesters reached a school, they began to bombard it with stones. Windows shattered. The police arrived, armed with nightsticks, and put down the riot.

DISCRIMINATION

Despite that outburst, teachers generally admired the intellectual skills of their Jewish students, though their classroom manners were not always as deeply cherished. The immigrant Jewish boys, especially, tended to have less respect than their Gentile counterparts, at least according to reports in the Jewish newspapers.

The Jewish students were essentially segregated even though they went to public schools. For example, in 1905, there were sixty-five thousand students in thirty-eight elementary schools on the Lower East Side. Ninety-five percent of those students (sixty-one thousand) were Jewish. The immigrant parents found no objection to this because classmates came from the same general background and therefore could translate both language and culture for the new students. Of course, religious separation was very familiar to them from the Old Country as well.

For their part, the teachers preferred the homogeneity of their classes. Translations from English had to be done in only one language, and although the teachers refused to accept bilingualism in the classroom, they needed to communicate with new students during emergencies or to get them started on the path to learning English.

There were objections to such arrangements. Social workers complained that having Jewish students study more or less exclusively with other Jewish students would retard their complete entrance into American society. There were complaints in the Yiddish press as well, mostly couched as objections to the coarseness of the American culture that the students were so thoroughly absorbing.

It is difficult, though, not to interpret such objections to include the idea that it was secular Yiddish culture that was under attack rather than just traditional Jewish culture. There was also an economic consideration. If American students studied English exclusively, who would be around in the next generation to buy Yiddish papers? As it turned out, that concern was extremely well founded.

JEWISH IMMIGRANT WOMEN

Unmarried Jewish immigrant women worked interminably long hours in sweat-shops or elsewhere in the clothing industry. Some were servants, although the number of Jewish women in America who were servants was much lower than the number who held such positions in Europe. In America, these servant women sometimes worked in homes of well-to-do families who treated them well and sometimes served families that didn't.

Women who were without families and living on their own might have a corner in some small room to sleep in. In some extreme cases, these women were driven by loneliness and a seeming poverty without end to either accept a loveless marriage or take their own lives. The Yiddish papers ran accounts of these suicides with the headlines that the women had *genumen di gez* ("taken the gas").

Jewish immigrant women, living in a Jewish world with defined roles and an American world that was struggling with its Puritan heritage, did not have the political or social structures to define themselves apart from their families or their religious or cultural traditions. There were exceptions, usually political rebels, but the overwhelming majority of Jewish women had to find their emotional resources not in social activism but in the privacy of their own imaginations. In particular, they found their souls stirred by reading Russian and English novels. Some women were inspired by a women's movement in Russia and others by the various radical movements in America.

WORKING WOMEN

A remarkable number of married women worked. The general ethic of the immigrant family, in fact, was that everyone worked because every penny was needed. It was rare for married women to leave the household to be employed, say, in a factory, but it was common to be employed at home as, for example, a tailor's assistant.

IDEALS LEARNED FROM BOOKS

Rose Schneiderman, an early labor organizer, recalled the effects of reading books on her youth:

> My adolescence was a far from happy one. All the romantic novels I consumed made me a most romantic young woman, and when I looked at myself in a full-length mirror I was very unhappy. Then I would despair. I wanted to be tall, and I thought I had several other counts against me. First of all, I was a redhead with curly hair, and neither the color nor the texture was stylish at the time. . . .
>
> From the books I read I had also developed a special taste in men. Among other traits, I wanted them well-read and cultured. I never dreamed of marrying a rich man. . . . My idea of what a man should be didn't quite match up with the boys Ann Cypress and I were meeting at the Saturday-night dances in the neighborhood. Most of them were loud and dull and suffered when compared with the heroes in my books.

Married women also worked to help their husbands, aiding their man's career in any way they could.

With all the work, it remains crucial to understand that for most Jewish women, the family—their husband and their children—were the centers of their world. The most emblematic stories about Jewish immigrant women are domestic—fights with children, sharing secrets with daughters, subtly asserting power within the family, fiercely defending their children, tenderhearted self-sacrifice, hardheaded practicality, and all the rest.

Women were responsible for an incredible amount of work. This was a tradition inherited from shtetl life. Women had to clean their tenements, do the cooking and the laundry, shop, and be responsible for raising the children. Beyond that, they often ran a business either in the home or outside it.

Women also played a central role in Americanizing the family. Some of the ways were obvious, such as stressing success in school or making sure their children got a library card. But because women did the shopping, they were the ones who brought American goods into the home and taught the family about them.

WRITERS AND THE CHANGING FAMILY

The dramatic circumstances of the immigrant family—the poverty, the crowds, the residue of confusion from dislocation, the hunger, the confusion in family roles, the desire to hold on to memories mixed with the desire to break free for the future, the need for children to explain America and English to their parents, the normal conflicts of generations, adapting to the individualistic, material ethos of American life—all made for potentially explosive material for writers.

Writers wrote about these subjects, the ones the immigrants dealt with in their everyday lives. Since some of the writers were socialists, they flavored their prose with pungent critiques of capitalism.

Writers also wrote about the New World's erosion of traditional Jewish religious practices. It was a common theme to proclaim not just that such practices were eroding but that persisting in them actually made it more difficult for people to enter and embrace American life. Given the emotional distance or literal physical absence of the father in many immigrant homes, it is unsurprising that another common theme in immigrant fiction is the search for a father.

The Jewish family individually and collectively was radically transformed by the immigrant experience, an experience that involved leaving one way of life and adopting another. The second one, the American one, was much more fragmented, much less tied to cultural or religious or family traditions. But it was simultaneously freer. If it deprived the immigrants of a safe identity haven and tossed them into a maelstrom of noise and unceasing labor, it gave them the extraordinary opportunity to be judged as individuals rather than as members of a group, opened the doors to self-expression, and made them heirs to the boundless optimism and spirit that the American dream offered.

For the traditionalists, this freedom too often came at the highest of prices— the erosion of a Jewish identity, alienation from the Jewish community, an inability to speak Yiddish or Hebrew and to understand—or even care about—Torah or

In the snow. *Source: Courtesy of Brown Brothers.*

Strolling on the sidewalk. *Source: Courtesy of Brown Brothers.*

Swimming in the street. *Source: Courtesy of Brown Brothers.*

Earnest students in a classroom. *Source: Courtesy of Brown Brothers.*

Girls with bread. *Source: Bettmann/CORBIS.*

Talmud, and ultimately, separation from God. This acculturation—this mixing of Jewish and American culture—more and more favored the New World over the Old. The traditionalists saw in the immigrant success story what their more religious families in Europe had warned: America was embracing Judaism to death.

As some of the young immigrants slowly or quickly separated themselves from being Jewish, they sought other identities. Many found one by entering the business world, while others entered the arts or academic life. Still others, especially the intellectual elite, found a new identity in a very practical political life that sought to improve their conditions and, ultimately, to do nothing less than transform the world.

A union protest for better working conditions. *Source: Courtesy of Brown Brothers.*

EIGHT

POLITICS AND STRIFE

><><

A S JEWISH immigrants entered the United States, they brought with them certain indisputable talents. They had an extended and extraordinary intellectual heritage. They were adventurous, at least in part because they knew precisely from what and whom they were escaping. They had vivid language skills, which, although in Yiddish, would eventually fit well in urban settings. They had drive, business skills, and a keen sense of injustice and the need to correct social inequalities.

However, they didn't bring highly developed political skills. By and large, Jews had been forbidden to enter politics in Eastern Europe, so their sense of being outsiders made it more difficult to adapt to the rowdy politics of America in general and New York in particular. After all, for Jews, the government was historically the enemy, and political leaders and their agents, the police, wielded power unfairly and unjustly and were to be feared, avoided, and bribed when necessary because the Jewish community had no military, political, or economic power to resist them.

Because the Russian government in particular was so oppressive, many Jews there became interested in revolutionary parties and socialism, but they didn't get much chance to organize or put those beliefs into effective organized action.

Nevertheless, no matter how politically inept they may have been when they arrived, the Jewish immigrants soon found their political voices.

NEW YORK CITY POLITICS

The Jewish immigrants' initial reluctance to trust local politicians must have been baffling to the leaders of Tammany Hall, the political machine established by the Democratic Party in the city. (It took its name from its headquarters, Tammany Hall, which was named for a Native American leader.) The ward bosses worked diligently to get the support of the community, primarily to win their votes at election time. But they did provide many useful services: they gave clothing and food to impoverished immigrants, took care of business infractions, and found some of the newcomers jobs.

It was common for a Tammany district captain to appear at a Jewish event—a bar mitzvah, a wedding, or a funeral, for example—with a gift. Being good Tammany workers, they also sometimes sought to purchase the immigrants' votes. The Jewish community, forced by countries in Europe not to depend on governmental help, had developed a long-standing tradition of self-help. Their distrust of government authorities made them less inclined, at least initially, to turn to Tammany the way other immigrant groups did. They thought politics was a rough and tumble sport for Gentiles.

It was only after a larger number of immigrants had arrived that Jews in America began to see the need to assert themselves politically. After all, they were living in unbearable tenements, sweating in dangerous and unpleasant jobs, and crowded into a relatively small neighborhood.

The vast Jewish community of workers soon found itself organizing to fight injustice and dangerous working conditions. The most famous symbol of those conditions was the Triangle Fire.

THE TRIANGLE FIRE

March 25, 1911, was a typical sunny Saturday, with a hint of spring in the air. At the time, it cost 2 cents to mail a letter. The average salary was $750 a year, although a Ziegfeld Girl earned $75 in just a single week. Life expectancy was 48.4 years for men and 51.8 years for women. There were seventy-six lynchings that year, thirty million people went to the movies, and one couple in a thousand divorced. Book buyers could take advantage of a sale at the Simpson Crawford Company: a twenty-volume set of Balzac for only $17.50. And two weeks earlier, the police had cap-

VOTES FOR SALE

In his memoir *The Education of Abraham Cahan,* the great journalist recorded his experience as an election took place and Tammany politicians sought to affect the outcome to retain their power:

> I spent almost my entire first presidential election day walking the streets and watching the politicians operating and the people voting. There was as yet no secret ballot. The names of candidates were listed on printed sheets that were distributed not by officials sitting at the ballot boxes but by politicians who had posted themselves outside the polling places.
>
> Each party printed its ballots or listed its candidates, and then friends of the candidates descended on citizens on their way to the voting places. With the same vigor that "pullers" of clothing stores on Canal Street show toward passing customers they persuaded them to vote for their candidates.
>
> Votes were bought and sold in the streets. There was haggling in open view, as if it were fish and not votes that were being sold. Politicians posted themselves at the street corners and flashed bundles of dollars. I had seen this happening on a small scale during the 1882 and 1883 election days. Now the stakes were much greater and so too was the haggling.
>
> I was pained by the ease with which corrupt politicians were able to persuade our uneducated Jews to sell their votes. There were no elections in the country from which we had fled. The ballot box and all it represented was the sacred hope for which many of our socialist comrades in Russia had martyred their lives.

tured the "Pickles" Berg gang, a notorious group of burglars. It was in all the papers. But there would be a much bigger story for the newspapers the next day. For everyone alive on the Lower East Side, March 25, 1911, would be a day they would never forget.

The day began normally enough at 174 Attorney Street, a typical tenement building housing many immigrant families. Two men in the building were up early. Josef Scheinert, age forty-four, liked to dress up for the Sabbath. He went each week with his son Julius to the synagogue, where they always sat on the aisle. Josef was a presser, working fifty-six hours a week with the heavy machine that ironed suit pants.

Loeb Rosen, age thirty-eight, had no choice that Saturday. It was payday at his job. He had to go to work. At least on Saturday, the hours were shorter and they didn't start until 9:00 A.M. Rosen journeyed over to the corner of Washington Place and Greene Street. He was a block from Washington Square Park. Classes at New York University were in session. Children were already playing in the park.

There were about five hundred people, mostly very young Italian and Jewish women, waiting to go in to the ten-story Asch Building. They stood on the sidewalk by the freight entrance waiting for the two elevators to take them up to the Triangle Waist Company, the largest blouse-making establishment in New York, on the top three floors. Only the managers and customers could use the regular elevators.

Rose Rosenfeld was among those waiting to go to work. She planned to celebrate her eighteenth birthday in two days. She had immigrated to the United States from a small town near Vienna only two years earlier. Her job was to operate a machine and stitch buttons onto the shirtwaists. She worked six days a week and earned $3 for the week. Her father had enough of an income that she wasn't required to work, but she wanted to feel like a true American.

The elevators came, and Loeb Rosen and Rose Rosenfeld joined the crowds going to work.

Josef Scheinert, meanwhile, was praying. He finished after the long Sabbath service and went back home. At some time around 4:45 P.M., Josef gathered his family for the Havdallah prayer that closed the Sabbath and separated it from the rest of the week.

FIRE!

Closing time on Saturdays at the shirtwaist company was 4:45 in the afternoon, so at 4:30, the workers began cleaning up for the day. Employees in the rest of the Asch Building had left at noon. As the bells sounded, some workers went to get their weekly pay and others stayed for a few minutes, preparing to leave. A worker recently engaged received a cake from other employees on the ninth floor.

Down on the eighth floor, someone tossed a match or an unextinguished cigarette into a trash bin filled with fabric scraps. Israel Abrowitz, a cutter, grabbed a red fire pail and emptied its water onto the flame, but the burning cotton fabrics refused to go out. Calls rang out and others charged to the area to deal with the fire. Two men grabbed a fire hose, but it didn't work properly. Others of the 180 people working on the eighth floor heard the call "Fire!" and scattered in panic, unable to find any other pails of water to throw on the fire. They fled to the small opening leading to the stairway down and out to Greene Street. The narrow stairs forced people to go down in single file. Seeing the way blocked by such a long line of people, others headed to the elevators or the fire escapes. It took five or six minutes for the flames to engulf the entire floor.

The flames spread rapidly in a factory filled with flammable materials. Up on the ninth floor, the 350 workers were engulfed in heat and smoke that were as bad as the flames. The wooden floors, soaked with oil, fed the fire. The staircases became impossible to enter. The workers heading toward the elevators found themselves blocked by iron doors. There was a fire escape, but the shuttered windows that led to it were locked. Workers forced the windows open. So many went out onto the rickety structure that it bent and then tore itself from the side of the building, carrying its occupants down with it.

The two passenger elevators were working, but they measured only 6 square feet each. A maximum of fifteen people at a time could fit. The operators, Gaspar Mortillalo and Joseph Zito, decided to take a chance. They doubled the allowed number of passengers on their final trips. One worker, Sarah Cammerstein, saw the elevator going down, assumed it would not return, and leaped to land on its roof. She blacked out. When she regained consciousness, she saw the elevator moving up again. She pounded the top of the elevator and screamed. It was lowered and she was taken off safely.

Flames shot out the windows. The young workers, desperate now, some on fire themselves, leaped out the windows to their death. Down below, horrified onlookers saw the bodies, trailed by smoke, falling down. Some of the workers held a friend or two and jumped together. One man, seeing the horror of a death by flames, took several young women to the window and helped them out. An onlooker from the sidewalk saw him take a final young woman, kiss her, and help her out. And then he jumped himself. By 4:57, the last of the people had jumped.

The sixty workers on the tenth floor, including management, had received a phone call from the eighth floor when the fire began. They headed for the roof.

Fire Department Company 72 arrived at 4:46. The ladders reached only to the seventh floor, and so some of the workers jumped toward them and missed. The water from the engine hoses could not reach the top floors either. Instead, the firefighters used the hoses on the burning bodies as they hit the sidewalk. Others, along with police, had fought the fire on the staircase and had reached the floors. By 5:05, they had the fire under control. It would only take ten more minutes before it was out. An hour later, they were able to make their way through the factory, where they found the burned bodies. At 8:15 that night, they found a man stuck in water in an elevator shaft. He had survived.

THE RESCUERS

By the time the Triangle Fire was over, 146 people had died. Many more would have had it not been for some very brave people who helped the workers.

Professor Frank Sommer was teaching his students at New York University's law school. Suddenly, he saw the frantic workers on the roof of the Asch Building. Two of his students, Charles Kremer and Elias Kanter, led other students to the law school's roof, which was one story—about 15 feet—higher than the Asch Building. They had two small ladders that painters had left and dragged the ladders over to the edge of the building. Kremer went down to the roof of the Asch Building, set up a line, and helped people up the ladder to the law school. One hundred and fifty people were saved in this way.

When there were no more workers in line, Kremer went into the tenth floor of the burning building. Only one young woman was there. Her hair was on fire as she screamed and ran toward him. She fainted as she reached his arms. Quickly, he used his hands to smother the sparks in her hair. He took strands of her long hair, wrapped them around his hand, and dragged her to the ladder. Kanter, waiting, helped him get the woman safely onto the law school roof. Only one worker from the tenth floor had died.

Rose Rosenfeld was one of those who had been saved from the tenth floor. Working on the ninth floor, she had decided that her fate would be best served if she did whatever the executives on the top floor did, so she went up instead of down. She was among those led across to safety.

Meanwhile, the police and firefighters struggled mightily to rescue the workers. The firefighters, contending with their inadequate equipment, heroically worked to put the fire out.

Sheet music for "Mameniu," written to honor the victims of the Triangle Fire, 1911. *Source: Courtesy the Archives of the YIVO Institute for Jewish Research, New York*

Jimmy Meehan, a police officer, had been the first on the scene. He jumped off his horse, ignored the fire, and charged up six smoke-filled flights of stairs. He found the door blocked. Bracing his shoulder against the door, he pushed it in. He found about twenty young women waiting, but they didn't want to leave because of the smoke. Meehan ordered them to leave, but they wouldn't. He began physically forcing them to go down the stairs. All of them survived.

The police on the sidewalk did their best to catch falling bodies. One boy landed in the arms of a police officer. Both fell as the officer caught the falling youngster. Then the boy stood up, uninjured.

THE AFTERMATH

Josef Scheinert heard that one of the tenants at 174 Attorney Street was missing in the fire. Relatives were anxiously searching for Loeb Rosen.

As if the poverty, crowds, sweatshops, and tenements weren't enough, the Triangle Fire was a final reminder of the misery of the Lower East Side.

The results of the investigation into the fire shocked residents of the Lower East Side. There had never been any fire drills in the factory. The doors leading to the staircase had been locked to prevent thievery. The tragedy galvanized the labor movement. The owners of the factory were acquitted of building code violations. Ironically, that verdict allowed insurance companies to pay surviving family members.

On March 27, two days after the fire, Loeb Rosen's sister and cousin identified his body. He had died of asphyxiation and burns. They feared telling his wife or bringing the body home because his wife was so ill.

Rose Rosenfeld Freedman would be the last survivor of the Triangle Fire. She died on February 22, 2001, at the age of 107.

It was tragedies such as the Triangle Fire, which might have been averted through greater forethought and action by the officials in charge, that compelled immigrant Jews to enter politics through a variety of leftist ideologies, considered quite radical at the time.

RADICAL IDEOLOGIES

There was considerable animosity among the various leftist political movements. All of them sought to improve the conditions of Jewish workers, but they had wildly different methodologies and often fought vigorously, even among their own groups, about ideological positions and political actions.

ANARCHISM

Anarchists believed that any government had to be subordinate to the individuals who lived under that government. In its extreme forms, anarchists believed in the elimination of government. Anarchists became known for forceful action. Much of their infamy came from violent acts, but they acted out their views in other ways as well. On the Lower East Side, they became infamous for holding Yom Kippur balls,

AN ANARCHIST SPEAKS

Abraham Cahan was present when Emma Goldman, under an assumed name, briefly left the United States in November 1899. He recorded her comments on leaving:

> I have spent years in an honest and conscientious effort to enlighten the American workingman as to the real causes of his misery and to show him the remedy for it. What is the result? My very name makes him shiver; the newspapers have invented thousands of malicious lies about me, the parsons have denounced me from their pulpits, and the fakirs who prey upon the workingmen, the so-called labor leaders, have pictured me as a sort of a grandmother to the devil himself. From reading all those ghost stories you would believe that I am in the habit of murdering a dozen people before breakfast, burning down a couple of blocks for lunch, and perhaps blowing up a whole county before I get my dinner. And the American workingman swallows all these lies and takes them for gospel truths. There is no hope nor help for him. He will not think, and he has always stabbed his best friend in the back and worshipped the man who makes a slave of him.

dances held on the most holy of Jewish days. Prior to such dances, the anarchists and their supporters held parades. The anarchists wanted to replace a day of atonement with an evening of fun and mockery of Judaism. They would therefore eat ham sandwiches and drink a cup of tea—with milk, violating kosher laws as much as possible. As it turned out, not all the anarchists had completely eliminated their Jewishness. Some of the celebrants gagged on the ham.

Perhaps the two most famous American anarchists were Emma Goldman and Alexander Berkman. "Red Emma" Goldman, "the high priestess of anarchy," emigrated from Russia to Rochester, New York, when she was seventeen. She moved to New York City, where, on the day of her arrival, she met Alexander Berkman. They

A woman delivers a political speech. *Source: Courtesy of Brown Brothers.*

became companions until his death. In 1893, she was imprisoned for causing a riot in Union Square. Released, she was arrested again when in 1901, President McKinley's assassin specifically cited her writings and speeches as inspiration for his act. After her release, Goldman became an editor for various publications, including *Mother Earth*, where she provided space for the first American publication of such European authors as Henrik Ibsen and August Strindberg. Her one-room flat at 210 East Thirteenth Street became famous as "the home for lost dogs" because of her hospitality to itinerant and poverty-stricken rebels and anarchists. She found such people in Sach's Café on Suffolk Street, the headquarters of the anarchists on the Lower East Side.

Rutgers Square (now Straus Square), the triangle where East Broadway and Essex, Canal, and Rutgers Streets meet, was the place radicals like Goldman went to whip up support. All sorts of speakers would gather there to promote a variety of economically, socially, or politically radical causes.

Alexander Berkman acted on his anarchist beliefs by both shooting and stabbing Henry Clay Frick, who worked for Carnegie Steel. Frick survived, but Berkman spent fourteen years in prison for his crime. When he left prison, he resumed his relationship with Goldman. In 1919, they were both deported to Russia. Once there,

Goldman became dissatisfied with the slow pace at which the Soviet Union was providing freedom for its citizens. By 1921, she and Berkman had left for Berlin. Berkman killed himself in 1936. Goldman, who continued to be an anarchist and also to oppose the Soviets, died four years later.

COMMUNISM

The various revolutionaries who came to America migrated to different movements that were under the general banner of socialism and were separate from anarchism. They might well have simply remained scattered among groups on the socialist left had it not been for the 1917 Bolshevik Revolution in Russia. That upheaval pitted the "Red" Bolsheviks against the "Whites," a virulently anti-Semitic faction. The split left only one choice for American Jewish Marxists to support, and so American communism began to organize. By 1919, the Jewish Federation of the Communist Party came into existence, and the *Freiheit*, a communist daily newspaper, began publishing in 1922.

Some noncommunist socialists also supported the Bolsheviks, believing that their support would allow Yiddish culture to thrive in the Soviet Union. The poor, young political radicals on the Lower East Side found a congenial home in communism. By the 1920s, according to one estimate, 15 percent of American communists spoke Yiddish. And the communists were somewhat successful among the immigrants. One important goal for the communists was to gain control over unions, and they did gain victories among the cigarmakers and the furriers. They were also, for a time at least, powerful in the International Ladies Garment Workers Union.

Like the socialists, the communists sought a broader appeal among the masses than simply a political one. They began Camp Kinderland, a children's camp—where bunks were dubbed "the Thirty-Six Soviet Republics." They also established adult camps, which received a wide but not always accurate reputation. One camper, a New Jersey teacher named Mel Lasky, recalled, "I went there because I heard everyone believed in free love. This, I must say, proved to be untrue." The communists also had an orchestra and a singing society.

The decline of communism among Jews began in 1929 when the Communist Party supported an Arab attack on Jews in the Land of Israel. The Stalinist purges of the 1930s and the Hitler-Stalin pact signed on August 23, 1939, further decimated Jewish communist ranks.

LABOR ZIONISM

Nachman Syrkin, who immigrated to the United States in 1907, spearheaded Labor Zionism, or Socialist Zionism. Like others on the left, Syrkin believed that Jews needed a national home, and he also believed in the ideals of socialism. Concerned that there was often a rift between the two (symbolically, both the founding of the Jewish secular socialist party, the Bund, and the First Zionist Congress, took place in 1897), Syrkin sought to find a meeting ground. In America, these Labor Zionists published various magazines and supported Hebrew day schools and Yiddish cultural institutions. The movement's deepest influences were not in the United States but in the nascent state of Israel—at the time a remnant area of the Ottoman Empire that had been placed under British control by the League of Nations—where David Ben-Gurion and Golda Meir were among the key leaders who subscribed to Labor Zionism's political and economic philosophy.

SOCIALISM

Socialism on the Lower East Side was a political philosophy, a political movement, and a way of life.

Socialism, broadly defined, is the belief that the means of the production and distribution of goods and services in a society should be owned collectively. The socialists believed that various forms of inequality in society stemmed directly from capitalism. For communists, the belief included the notion that a central government should plan and control the economy. Most communists believed that socialism was a stop on the way from capitalism to communism when the people had not yet achieved full control over the economy. Such a definition, however, fails to capture the utopian nature of socialism as Lower East Side Jews saw it.

Socialism, for them, represented an ideal society, freed from tyranny and the exploitation of workers, situations they understood all too well. This utopian society was marked by a shared popular culture and widespread harmony. It was the secular version of the more religious longing for the Messiah. It was a projection of a world in which Jews would be physically and psychologically released from a painful present.

In the shorter run and more practically, socialism was a political plan for the immigrant Jews to escape the tenements and the sweatshops or at the very least improve conditions there.

It is commonly believed that the Lower East Side Jews brought socialism with them when they immigrated to America. And indeed, there was a long-standing radical movement in Europe, and there were Jewish radicals who came to the United States. But in the Old Country, there were no labor unions, the organizations Jews on the Lower East Side used to propel socialism. The labor movements arose in the United States around 1887, when there were already two Jewish groups associated with the Socialist Labor Party.

These emerging Jewish labor unions grew because of the large number of Jews in the working class, the exploitation they suffered and the miserable conditions under which they worked, the socialist intellectuals in their midst, and the lessons they were taught by German American socialists who had come to America a generation earlier after having been driven out of Europe by the political turmoil of the 1840s. It was these Germans who had developed the necessary socialist ideology and already had vast experience in organizing that allowed the Jewish unions to be born.

THE COURSE OF SOCIALISM

Why did most Jewish immigrants gravitate to political movements on the left? One reason is that those movements sought them out. Another is the realistic nature of their condition. But there is a third reason: for most Jews, there was simply no available alternative on the political right. The right was generally anti-immigrant and sometimes explicitly anti-Semitic. The right opposed granting the very rights that immigrant Jews regarded as vital for their well-being.

The socialists, in addition to their political appeal to Jews, offered a secular alternative to traditional religion; they ultimately sought nothing less than to develop entirely new forms of association to replace the traditional forms such as synagogues. They wanted to provide Jews with a way of understanding how the world really worked, which the socialists believed was not provided by religion. The young Jewish immigrants, broadly speaking, were less religious than those who stayed behind and less familiar with the sacred texts of Judaism. They were most receptive to the notion that the heart of Judaism lay in social justice. They were therefore least able to pass on a Jewish religious heritage and most anxious to adapt an American way of life and engage in political efforts that sought to help working people and their families.

The socialists set up day schools, debate societies, reading rooms, newspapers, and many other institutions—including synagogues for those not yet ready to leave traditional religion. There were alternatives to traditional synagogues as well, the most famous of which was the Labor Temple. Charles Stelzle, a Presbyterian minister, set up the temple in 1910 at the corner of Second Avenue and Fourteenth Street. The Jewish socialists who formed the bulk of the congregation found it a center for attacks on organized religion and intellectual lectures by such speakers as John Dewey and Thorstein Veblen.

Unsurprisingly, the socialist vanguard among the Jews on the Lower East Side very quickly saw the need to enter American politics. In 1915, Meyer London became the first member of the Socialist Party to be elected to the U.S. House of Representatives. London, a renowned labor lawyer, was more moderate in the Congress than some of his radical supporters would have liked.

THE WORKMEN'S CIRCLE

Because immigrants had founded various benevolent societies, the socialists sought to establish one as well, and so the Workmen's Circle (*Arbeter Ring*) was established in 1892 at 151 Essex Street in the tenement of Sam Greenberg. Six workers were present at the founding; it became a national order on September 4, 1900, and by 1917, it had nearly sixty thousand members.

The Workmen's Circle sought to help those in need and to promote socialism. It established schools (which stayed open on Jewish holidays and closed on May 1, a socialist holiday). Eventually the communists within the Workmen's Circle ranks split because of ideological differences and established their own benevolent society, the International Workers' Order. Over time, the Workmen's Circle itself became increasingly concerned with maintaining a Yiddish culture. It sponsored day schools, the Folksbiene Yiddish theater group, and other cultural organizations. Its influence can be seen in the fact that two giants of Yiddish culture, Sholem Aleichem and Abraham Cahan, were buried in the Workmen Circle's section at Mount Carmel Cemetery.

Indeed, it was the Workmen's Circle that provided the single grave in which the 146 young women who died in the Triangle Fire were buried. The fire had provided a major rallying point for workers, especially because of what happened later. In the aftermath of that fire, angry workers and other citizens sought answers as to why the fire had begun and generally wanted to improve the conditions in other workshops to prevent similar tragedies.

The angry protesters also demanded that the owners of the Triangle Factory, Isaac Harris and Max Blanck, be put on trial. On April 11, 1911, the co-owners were indicted for manslaughter. A trial was held later that year. Its outcome depended on whether the jury believed the owners knew that the doors that could have provided escape were locked. In December 1911, the jury, after less than two hours of deliberation, concluded that there remained sufficient doubt as to the owners' knowledge and rendered a verdict of not guilty. The cries of "Where is justice?" filled the courthouse.

Eventually, civil suits were filed against the owners. On March 11, 1913, the suits were settled. The owners paid $75 for each life lost.

Some of the early socialists opposed the use of Yiddish because it was too particularist a language, but most later adopted it as the most efficient means to reach the Jewish masses.

THE DECLINE OF SOCIALISM

Enthusiasm for socialism among the Jews eventually dissipated for a number of reasons. For one thing, Jews slowly left the working class and would ultimately end up in suburbia, where it was harder to have the population density needed for a successful Jewish union. For another thing, the Socialist Party made some political miscalculations. It vigorously opposed America's entry into World War I, and many Jews feared that ordinary Americans would perceive Jews as unpatriotic. Finally, with the campaign and election of Franklin Roosevelt as president, most of the socialists became political Democrats. The militancy soon weakened.

OTHER POLITICAL POINTS OF VIEW

It would be inaccurate to conclude that all Jewish immigrants were associated with the political left. Wealthier Jews were sometimes Republicans, and individual Republicans, especially Theodore Roosevelt, received great support from Jews. Roosevelt, who had gained fame fighting in the Spanish-American War, campaigned in 1899 for governor of New York by reminding Jews of the Spanish Inquisition. Perhaps because of his progressive politics, Theodore Roosevelt became the last Republican to receive significant Jewish support in his race for the presidency. Indeed, when he ran unsuccessfully in 1912 on the Progressive Party ticket, no less a Jewish writer than Mary Antin campaigned for him.

Indeed, American Jewish immigrants so admired Teddy Roosevelt that they followed news reports of his travels. On one trip, Roosevelt, renowned as a hunter, refused to kill a small bear cub. A cartoonist drew the bear, and a Jewish immigrant named Morris Michtom was impressed. He and his wife Rose owned a candy store in Brooklyn. Morris asked Rose to sew a toy bear that looked like the one Roosevelt had let live. Morris labeled the product "Teddy's Bear." After many customers asked for the bear, Morris sent one to the White House for the president's children and requested permission to use the name "Teddy" for the bear. Roosevelt doubted that the name had commercial value, but he agreed. So popular was the Teddy bear that eventually Roosevelt adopted it as an election symbol. And it has remained the standard designation for cuddly stuffed bears ever since.

UNIONS

The bosses at Tammany Hall didn't like the leftist ideologies because they directed political passion away from traditional electoral politics and reduced the ranks of Democratic voters. Socialist politicians like Meyer London were, however, mostly ineffective. There were very few people in Congress interested in how socialism was going to transform the United States. But the Jewish community, especially in the garment industry, didn't rely on ideology. The Jews founded institutional structures through which to exercise their political power: the labor unions.

Jewish immigrant women were crucial to the rise of unions. The women, shedding traditional roles, sometimes having to take charge when especially religious men seemed baffled by the new culture, and bearing the pain of sweatshops the most along with children, were motivated and able to organize. They were the *farbrente*, the ones "on fire," the ones most eager to get to the task at hand.

THE INTERNATIONAL LADIES' GARMENT WORKERS' UNION

The "International" or ILGWU began in 1900 when seven smaller unions of people in the garment industry in New York, Newark, Baltimore, and Philadelphia joined together. The union started with a mere two thousand members and grew slowly. But as labor troubles increased on the Lower East Side, the union was there.

ORGANIZING A UNION

In her book *All for One*, union organizer Rose Schneiderman recalled her efforts to start a union in the garment industry:

> We formed a committee composed of my friend Bessie Mannis, who worked with me, myself, and a third girl. Bravely we ventured into the office of the United Cloth Hat and Cap Makers Union and told the man in charge that we would like to be organized. . . .
>
> We were told that we would have to have at least 25 women from a number of factories before we could acquire a charter. Novices that we were, we used the simplest methods. We waited at the doors of factories and, as the girls were leaving for the day, we would approach them and speak our piece. We had blank pledges of membership ready in case some could be persuaded to join us. Within days we had the necessary number, and in January 1903 we were chartered as Local 23, and I was elected secretary.
>
> It was such an exciting time. A new life opened for me. All of a sudden I was not lonely anymore. I had shop and executive board meetings to attend. . . . The only cloud in the picture was mother's attitude toward my becoming a trade unionist. She kept saying I'd never get married because I was so busy—a prophecy which came true. Of course, what she resented most of all was my being out of the house almost every evening. But for me it was the beginning of a period that molded all my subsequent life and opened wide many doors that might have remained closed to me.

The year 1909 was a turning point. A year earlier, the union needed to borrow $25 to rent an office. But in 1909, leaders of the still weak International demanded that shirtwaist factory workers strike. Workers met at Cooper Union to hear the strike call, and in a famously rousing speech, an eighteen-year-old worker named

BUSTING A STRIKE

McAlister Coleman described the 1909 strike by shirtwaist factory workers in the *New York Sun:*

> The girls, headed by teen-age Clara Lemlich, described by union organizers as a "pint of trouble for the bosses," began singing Italian and Russian working-class songs as they paced in twos in front of the factory door. All of a sudden, around the corner came a dozen tough-looking customers, for whom the union label "gorillas" seemed well-chosen.
>
> "Stand fast, girls," called Clara, and then the thugs rushed the line, knocking Clara to her knees, striking at the pickets, opening the way for a group of frightened scabs to slip through the broken line. Fancy ladies from the Allen Street red-light district climbed out of cabs to cheer on the gorillas. There was a confused melee of scratching, screaming girls and fist-swinging men and then a patrol wagon arrived. The thugs ran off as the cops pushed Clara and two other badly beaten girls into the wagon.
>
> I followed the rest of the retreating pickets to the union hall, a few blocks away. There a relief station had been set up where one bottle of milk and a loaf of bread were given to strikers with small children in their families. There, for the first time in my comfortably sheltered, upper West Side life, I saw real hunger on the faces of my fellow Americans in the richest city in the world.

Clara Lemlich rose and declared (in Yiddish), "I am a working girl, one of those striking against intolerable conditions. I am tired of listening to speakers who talk in generalities. What we are here for is to decide whether or not to strike. I offer a resolution that a general strike be declared—now! If I turn traitor to the cause I now pledge, may this hand wither from the arm I now raise." (It is not known whether she was aware that this language echoed Psalm 137, with its lines, "If I forget thee, O Jerusalem, may my right hand wither.")

The crowd jumped up screaming. People started waving their fists. They then marched out to the street and began singing and shouting. The next morning, more than twenty thousand shirtwaist factory workers went on strike. Only one in one hundred of these immigrant young women had previously belonged to a union, but at the end of the three-month effort, virtually all of them joined the ILGWU.

The International, eager to continue the momentum, called for a rally in Madison Square Garden on June 30, 1910. Sixty thousand workers attended and sparked the Cloakmakers' Strike. Louis Brandeis, then a lawyer, was brought in to arbitrate the dispute and did so effectively, primarily by having the clothing industry recognize "the preferential union shop."

In the 1920s, the ILGWU faced a series of crises, from dealing with a communist insurgency in their ranks to bad agreements and inept leadership to criminal indictments of some leaders. Slowly, its huge membership withered away. In 1995, the ILGWU merged with the Amalgamated Clothing and Textile Workers Union and in 2004 that united union merged with the Hotel Employees and Restaurant Workers to form UNITE HERE.

AMALGAMATED CLOTHING WORKERS OF AMERICA

The Amalgamated was founded in 1914. From its inception, the Amalgamated expanded the vision of a union from a focus solely on the workplace to include a worker's entire life. Toward that end, for example, the union opened the Amalgamated Bank to grant loans at an advantageous rate for workers and established the Workers Cooperative Colony in the Bronx to provide housing for needy workers.

FUR WORKERS UNION

The Fur Workers Union was the longest-lasting communist union in the garment industry. The union's leader, Ben Gold, was, at fourteen, already an assistant leader of his union shop. The furriers primarily worked between Twenty-Sixth and Thirtieth Streets along Seventh Avenue. Their union was in constant battle with anticommunist unions, the police, fur manufacturers, and various gangsters hired to make life miserable for them.

UNITED HEBREW TRADES

The UHT was designed to give birth to new unions rather than have its own membership. The dynamic Morris Hillquit led the union. Hillquit had worked in a shirt factory before becoming a socialist. He finally went to law school and was a key figure during a number of strikes. Hillquit ran for mayor of New York as a member of the Socialist Party.

Thanks to their association with all these various unions, with their reputation for radical politics, their alien religion or atheism, their supposed participation in crime, and much else, the Jewish immigrants who were members of such unions and would contribute so much to America were not welcomed by a great many other Americans.

POLITICAL LEGACY

It is easy to understand the attractions of the political left for the immigrants. However, given the fact that political activism was new in Jewish life, it is less obvious why the next generation of American Jews continued to find the left an appealing home.

Tony Michels, author of the groundbreaking study of Yiddish socialists *A Fire in Their Hearts*, summarizes the reasons for that continuing adherence:

> The children of immigrants were attracted to socialist ideologies for several reasons. First, many American-born Jews, especially in the major cities, grew up in neighborhoods where socialist politics, ideas, organizations, and cultural activities fostered a general left-wing atmosphere. Second, many second-generation Jews themselves faced antisemitism as much as, if not more than, their parents did. Although more Americanized than immigrants, many second-generation Jews nonetheless still stood on the margins of American society.
>
> After all, antisemitism in the United States grew to new heights between World War I and World War II, the period in which many children of immigrants came of age. They encountered discrimination in housing, the job mar-

ket, and education precisely because they tried to make their way into the mainstream. Anti-Jewish quotas in universities, enacted extensively in the 1920s and 1930s, were a classic example. Third, the Great Depression, combined with antisemitism, limited the prospects of American-born Jews, causing much insecurity and downward mobility that made leftist solutions seem attractive. Fourth, many Jews looked to the USSR as a bulwark against Nazism and the best hope for solving the problems of capitalism and antisemitism. The USSR further appeared to be a defender of Jewish interests because of its staunch support for Israel in 1947–1948. The reality would later be a source of bitter disappointment for thousands of Soviet sympathizers. Fifth, no right-wing alternatives existed because the right wing during the Depression was generally xenophobic and antisemitic. By contrast, left-wing movements generally did not discriminate against Jews. Although leftists sometimes failed to appreciate the seriousness of antisemitism and objected to anything they perceived as Jewish nationalism, they put forward an attractive vision of a just society freed from bigotry and poverty. In short, second-generation, American-born Jews had plenty of reasons to be attracted to the left in one form or another: socialist, communist, anarchist, socialist Zionist, and so on.

Not all that many Americans sympathized with Jews or immigrants or the left. The opponents of Jewish immigration spoke in loud voices as they attempted to halt the entry into America of so many people who were foreign in so many senses of the word.

Broadway at the Bowling Green.

New arrivals on Lower Broadway. *Source: Courtesy of Brown Brothers.*

NINE

THE OPPONENTS
OF JEWISH IMMIGRATION

⚬⚬⚬

OR THE Jewish immigrants fleeing poverty and pogroms, America was a wonderful haven. The immigrants learned quickly that they could succeed and move out of the Lower East Side, that an education and hard work paid off in the Golden Land. And if German Jews had mixed feelings about the tidal wave of Eastern European Jews, the influx troubled some other Americans whose ancestors had come from Europe even more. These nativists were determined to stop what they considered the "grave dangers" of mass immigration.

THE EMERGENCE OF AMERICAN ANTI-SEMITISM

The rapid increase in immigration toward the end of the nineteenth century led to a strong reaction among some American Protestants—not just because of the sheer number of immigrants but even more because of the ethnic, religious, or national origins of those immigrants, so different from their own. The nativists favored the rights and interests of the people already living in the United States and wanted to maintain what they regarded as the nation's character by excluding such "aliens" as Irish, Chinese, Italians, and Jews.

"The Modern Moses," by Frederick Burr Opper and Joseph Keppler, 1881. *Source: Courtesy of Picture History.*

Thus the opposition wasn't to immigration itself, so it is inaccurate to label the nativists as anti-immigration. Opponents of immigration had a wide variety of motives. One came from the specific fact that a large number of the immigrants were Jewish.

The term *anti-Semitism* eventually came to be used to describe hatred of the Jews or the desire to exclude or physically harm the Jewish people. It was coined in 1879 by a German hater of Jews named Wilhelm Marr, who argued that Jews made up a race "inferior to the Aryans," the purported highest form of humanity. Most nativists subscribed to the division of humans into races and the subsequent ranking of races in terms of supposed quality. (Of course, it was the northern Europeans themselves, the self-proclaimed "Aryans," who were determining the ranking.) Soon European literature about race began to reach America.

American nativists, looking at the droves of immigrants arriving in the 1880s and 1890s, saw a flood of uneducated, poverty-stricken, religiously and linguistically different invaders who would destroy traditional American culture and never be able to assimilate. The nativists saw only trouble in allowing that sort of immigration.

The nativists channeled their concerns into political expression through the Populist Party. Other groups such as the American Protective Association, which mainly

TURNING BIAS INTO LAW

The ongoing battle between the nativists and Americans who favored immigrant rights was fought most consequentially within the political system. The most sweeping proposals, such as Lodge's, were ultimately defeated. Here are some of the most important acts that did end up becoming law:

- **1882**: Additions were made to the list of "excluded classes." Specifically cited were lunatics, idiots, and "any person unable to take care of himself or herself without becoming a public charge." (Obviously, this last phrase was vague enough to engender many disputes.) The same act forced ship owners to pay the costs for returning undesirable aliens back to Europe. This in turn led to the owners' setting up far stricter physical requirements at the various points of embarkation.

- **1891**: Still more "excluded classes" were added, including polygamists, paupers, and anyone having "a loathsome or dangerous contagious disease" and anyone whose steamship ticket had been paid for by someone else—a common practice among Jews.

- **1891**: Another act made the federal government rather than the states responsible for inspecting immigrants. The act also prohibited companies from advertising to promote immigration. Finally, the act strengthened the notion of returning "public charges" to Europe. This provision quickly made the rounds of the new immigrants who feared that their poverty would have dire implications. Ironically, the very vagueness and potential harshness of the act's provision forced Jews on the Lower East Side to work together for the common good to prevent such potential deportations.

- **1903**: An act blocked anarchists and "all persons who are of a low moral tendency or of unsavory reputation."

THROUGH A BIGOT'S EYES

A Protestant minister named A. E. Patton visited Ellis Island in 1912 and recorded his observations:

> For a real American to visit Ellis Island, and there look upon the Jewish hordes, ignorant of all true patriotism, filthy, vermin-infested, stealthy and furtive in manner, too lazy to enter into real labor, too cowardly to face frontier life, too lazy to work as every American farmer has to work, too filthy to adopt ideals of cleanliness from the start, too bigoted to surrender any racial traditions or to absorb any true Americanism, for a real American to see those items of a filthy, greedy, never patriotic stream flowing in to pollute all that has made America good as she is—is to awaken in his thoughtful mind desires to check and lessen this source of pollution.

opposed Catholic immigration, and the Immigration Restriction League joined forces to seek legislation limiting immigration, such as the effort by Henry Cabot Lodge to make entry dependent on passing a literacy test. Even after President Cleveland's veto of the bill, however, immigration restriction efforts did not cease. Presidents Taft (1913) and Wilson (1915) also vetoed bills prescribing literacy tests. But the nativists did have some successes.

Anti-Jewish sentiment that helped propel such legislation combined with the ever-increasing racial literature that was slowly infiltrating American life. In 1908, the so-called science of eugenics—a social philosophy whose advocates believed that hereditary traits in humans should be improved through the active intervention by society—was popularized in America by Alfred P. Schultz's book *Race or Mongrel?* The prominent magazine *Scientific American* urged Jews to adapt themselves quickly to America; the alternative was to face "a quiet but sure extermination" like that of the "native Indian."

ANTI-SEMITISM IN ACTION

The Jewish immigrants on the Lower East Side were profoundly affected by other famous anti-Semitic episodes—in the United States and beyond. Two most infamous cases of anti-Semitism were the Dreyfus Affair in France and the Leo Frank case in the American South.

THE DREYFUS AFFAIR (1894)

French intelligence officers accidentally obtained a secret military document that had been sent by an unidentified French officer to an officer of the German embassy in Paris. Suspicion immediately fell on Captain Alfred Dreyfus—because he was Jewish and because, it was claimed, his handwriting was similar to that on the document. Dreyfus was accused of treason and court-martialed. Found guilty, Dreyfus was sentenced to life imprisonment.

Two weeks after the conviction, Dreyfus was taken to a parade ground and dishonored by having his captain's insignia torn off.

Dreyfus was pardoned in September 1899, but the pardon seemed to include the suggestion that he was guilty. It took until 1906 to establish Dreyfus's complete innocence. He was readmitted to the army and fought for France in World War I.

THE LYNCHING OF LEO FRANK (1915)

Leo Frank had been accused of murdering a thirteen-year-old girl who worked in the Atlanta, Georgia, pencil factory he owned. The *New York Herald Tribune* said: "Mobs choked the area around the courthouse. Men with rifles stood at the open windows, some aimed at the jury, some aimed at the judge. These men repeated the chant: 'Hang the Jew. Hang the Jew.' . . ."

Frank was convicted, but Georgia's governor, noting how weak the case against Frank was, commuted the death sentence to life imprisonment. Two months later, a mob grabbed Frank from his prison farm and lynched him.

Anti-Semitism also emerged in the literary world. Sympathy for Jews had been the hallmark of American literature in the nineteenth century. Henry Wadsworth Longfellow, Walt Whitman, William Cullen Bryant, James Greenleaf Whittier, William Dean Howells, and Mark Twain had all expressed pro-Jewish sentiments.

However, after the surge in immigration and the emergence of nativist and racist ideologies, many writers began to allow their antipathy toward Jews to seep into their writing. Henry Adams, Henry James, and Edith Wharton expressed such sentiments. Their example would be emulated by a later generation of writers, including T. S. Eliot, Ezra Pound, Thomas Wolfe, and e. e. cummings.

COMMISSIONER BINGHAM

In 1908, Julia Richman, the Jewish-born district superintendent of schools in New York, approached Theodore Bingham, New York City's police commissioner. She wanted him to enforce regulations more strictly because, as she correctly asserted, many pushcart vendors did not have a license. The situation had come about because although the city required that all peddlers pay to get such a license, there were only four thousand licenses available. That meant that about ten thousand Jewish pushcart operators were acting illegally.

Most of those peddlers paid the police the standard $5 bribe and kept operating or used their voting power to get help from Tammany Hall. Other peddlers were arrested, either for selling their goods illegally on Sunday or for not having a license and not knowing what to do about it. Indeed, the "great Jewish crime wave" that some anti-immigrant advocates cited consisted for the most part of such peddler violations.

Commissioner Bingham, a general who had attended West Point and was retired from the army, was polite but reluctant. "You don't want to be too hard on the poor devils."

But Richman fired right back, "I say, if the poor devils cannot make a living without violating our laws, the immigration department should send them back to the country from which they came."

When her words became known, calls arose for her to resign. The furor was eclipsed later that year, however, when New York's Jews became even more incensed at Commissioner Bingham.

In September, Bingham published an article in the *North American Review* titled "Foreign Criminals in New York." In his most incendiary passage, he wrote, "It is not astonishing that with a million Hebrews, mostly Russian, in the city (one quarter of the population) perhaps half of the criminals should be of that race when we consider that ignorance of the language, more particularly among men not physically fit for hard labor, is conducive to crime. . . . They are burglars, firebugs, pickpockets and highway robbers—when they have the courage; but though all crime is their province, pocket-picking is the one to which they take most naturally."

Lower East Side residents were quickly reminded that a year earlier, Commissioner Bingham had observed that the police department's rogue's gallery included two thousand pictures of criminals and that twelve hundred were Jews.

Refutations of the charges came from various sources. One letter writer in the *Jewish Daily Forward*, signing himself only as "Gonif (Thief) from the Tombs," noted that as a professional thief for a decade himself, he was in an enviable position to know that the commissioner was incorrect. This correspondent blamed the charge on the fact that Jewish criminals were arrested more often because they refused to shoot a policeman trying to arrest them. The other reason, the thief noted, was that Jews were good prisoners and so left early, enabling them to return to their criminal ways sooner than their Gentile counterparts.

Eventually, the actual crime statistics revealed a picture far different from the one the commissioner had originally painted. In 1907, there were 2,848 felony convictions in New York County. Exactly 460 of those felons were Jewish; they thus constituted 16.4 percent of the convictions rather than the 50 percent the commissioner had originally claimed. Of every 10,000 criminals, 6.1 percent were Jewish; they were thus dramatically *underrepresented* in the criminal class. Finally, 88 percent of Jews who had been convicted of a felony were charged with crimes against property rather than against people. That is, the reality contradicted the perception and made the commissioner's charge inflammatory.

German Jews, who lived uptown, were concerned about overreacting to the incident. The downtown Jews wanted Bingham's badge, but eventually a compromise was reached: Bingham would retract the charges, and calls for his removal from office would cease.

In the retraction, Bingham claimed that "the figures used in the article were not compiled by myself, but were furnished me by others, and were unfortunately assumed to be correct. It now appears, however, that these figures were unreliable.

Hence it becomes my duty frankly to say so and repudiate them. . . . I withdraw the statements challenged frankly and without reserve."

EFFECTS OF THE ANTI-IMMIGRATION EFFORTS

The Bingham affair had some immediate effects. The first was that Jews realized that they lacked both organization and power. They needed to accelerate efforts at self-help communal organizations and to unite.

Perhaps even more significant, the episode and the ensuing fights among the wealthier German Jews and the poor Eastern European immigrants forced all members of the Jewish community to look at themselves and not turn away from unpleasant realities. Suddenly the Jewish community was aroused to rid itself of criminals.

The combined efforts of the anti-immigration forces had their most profound effect on immigrants and on American Jews in the decades following the First World War, when efforts to curb immigration were renewed. In a way that no one could foresee, it turned out that a race was occurring between increasing the number of European Jews who sought to immigrate to America and those who stayed behind to face first the unspeakable horror of the Holocaust and then the brutal regime of Stalin. The pro-immigration forces would fight long and hard, but they would eventually lose this battle too early.

And there were increasing signs in American life of hostility toward Jews. In 1920, Henry Ford, the founder of the Ford Motor Company and an enormously influential citizen politically, began publishing anti-Semitic articles in his newspaper, the *Dearborn Independent*. The newspaper's circulation was, at its height, half a million readers, though the effect—because of word of mouth, reporting on the articles, and the fact that it was Ford who was behind the effort—was much larger. Indeed, when Henry Ford's son Edsel commissioned a poll in 1940 to gauge the effect of the elder Ford's efforts, one stunning finding was that 78 percent of American males associated Ford with anti-Semitism.

In seven years, Ford ran more than one hundred articles, charging, for example, that German Jews had ordered their Eastern European coreligionists to emigrate to the United States. Most infamously, Ford's paper included the *Protocols of the Elders of Zion*, a notorious Russian forgery that claimed a Jewish effort at world domination.

Only after Jews began a boycott of Ford automobiles and instituted legal action did Ford apologize.

Ever at the mercy of Ford, the Ku Klux Klan, and other anti-Semitic people and organizations, American Jews found themselves increasingly isolated. When the Nazis rose to power in Germany in the early 1930s, Americans by and large wanted to remain isolated and didn't want to allow even endangered immigrants to enter the country. Their views contributed to the disaster that befell Europe's Jews.

American Jews on the Lower East Side, especially in the wake of the Bingham case, sought to help each other.

Sheet music for "A Brivele der Kale." *Source: Courtesy the Archives of the YIVO Institute for Jewish Research, New York.*

TEN

A HELPING HAND

⟫⟫×⟫⟨

THE GERMAN Jews who lived uptown, far from the immigrant world of the Lower East Side downtown, had mixed feelings toward the new immigrants. On the one hand, the German Jews were sympathetic toward other Jews, especially because of the terrible economic conditions and persecutions that had driven them to America. On the other hand, the German Jews were concerned about how the hordes of poverty-stricken workers who turned out to be attracted to socialist and other radical ideas would be seen by ordinary Americans who, by and large, had accepted German Jews. There had been incidents of discrimination, but the German Jews had by the beginning of the twentieth century successfully adapted to America. They were therefore deeply concerned about their own status. As the famed American leader Rabbi Kaufmann Kohler put it in 1889, "Will the Russian or Romanian Jew, now an object of pity owing to his defective education, his lack of culture, his pauperism, his utter helplessness, drag American Judaism down from the honorable position it has attained?"

Another famous religious leader, Rabbi Stephen Wise, drew the distinction between uptown Jews and downtown Jews in this way: "We are Israelites; they are Jews." The downtown Jews, somewhat less polite than Rabbi Wise, retorted by saying, "We are Jews; they are *goyim*."

The Jews who lived uptown were not in the working class. They were bankers and store owners. They were Reform. Downtown Jews associated Judaism only with Orthodoxy. Even the irreligious among them felt it was an Orthodox synagogue they refused to attend. The uptown Jews opposed unionism. For downtown Jews, unions were the pathway to justice and a decent life for their families.

However tentative the German Jews felt, it soon became obvious to them that whatever they said and whatever distinctions they made, the public would connect them to the Eastern European Jews whether either group wanted the connection or not. At any rate, the horrors of the pogroms genuinely affected them. So the German Jews, in their own self-interest and acting on the religious injunction of *tzedaka*—providing aid—began to develop organizations that would help the newcomers.

ORGANIZATIONS

Not all of the German Jewish efforts were truly humanitarian. Workers from the Hebrew Emigrant Aid Society were unduly mean to the very people they sought to help in their shelter on Ward's Island. Nor were the uptown Jews above efforts to force immigrants to drop their Jewish ways. The Clara de Hirsch Home for Girls refused to serve kosher food until 1913. Originally, no doctors at Mount Sinai Hospital spoke Yiddish.

But there is no disputing that German Jews did also try to help. They established the United Hebrew Charities, which provided basic help, such as food, housing, aid in searching for a job, and medical assistance. The National Council of Jewish Women, founded in 1893, focused on the much needed effort to protect immigrant women from abuses.

And the Jewish immigrants on the Lower East Side didn't just rely on help from uptown. They developed various organizations and societies to help themselves.

There were many organizations that, with varying degrees of effectiveness and in widely varying ways, aided the immigrants.

AMERICAN JEWISH COMMITTEE

Seeking to protect Jewish rights but to do so in an orderly manner, the uptown Jews established the American Jewish Committee (AJC) in 1906, with sixty original members. The AJC served to represent the interests of Jews against all kinds of discrimination by contacting America's national leaders directly. The AJC was very effective in its efforts to defeat literacy requirements and to have immigration authorities recognize both Hebrew and the less accepted but more commonly spoken Yiddish as legitimate languages. The AJC remains one of the principal organizations of American Jewish life.

INDUSTRIAL REMOVAL OFFICE

Operating from 1900 until 1917, the Industrial Removal Office attempted to encourage Lower East Side Jewish immigrants to relocate to other American cities. The effort was not extraordinarily successful, but eventually, about seventy-five thousand did move to such cities as Los Angeles and Saint Louis.

Jacob Schiff, a wealthy banker and leader of the uptown Jews, developed another plan to disperse the immigrants. In 1907, Schiff discussed some possibilities with Israel Zangwill, the British writer and territorialist who favored a Jewish homeland—not necessarily in the Land of Israel, but wherever Jews could find a haven. (Zangwill would become even more famous a year later with the opening of his play *The Melting Pot,* which seemed to advocate assimilation.) Zangwill reacted with an idea of his own: Schiff should use his wealth to purchase land in the southwestern United States for use as a Jewish homeland. The philanthropist declined, but he and Zangwill did work out an alternative: sending Jewish immigrants to Galveston, Texas. This became known as the Galveston Plan.

There was in fact already an active Jewish community in Galveston, headed by Rabbi Henry Cohen. Cohen would become known for saving a wrongly imprisoned man named Sidney Porter. Convinced of the man's innocence, Cohen took the case directly to the governor. When the grateful Porter was released, he came to Cohen and said, "I can't pay you for your help now, but I'm a writer, and I'll do what I can to help your people." Porter took the pen name O. Henry, and among his enormously popular stories was one about a rabbi who saved an innocent man from jail.

Even with Rabbi Cohen's help, though, the Galveston Plan had only limited success. A total of about ten thousand Jewish immigrants were sent to Galveston and settled there and in other parts of the Southwest.

Most Jews on the Lower East Side did not really want to leave the neighborhood; despite the oppressive conditions, it featured a familiar language, family and friends, and religious and cultural support. Of course, it is also likely that having uprooted themselves not so long ago, the new immigrants were in no hurry to make another life-altering change of residence. Furthermore, some other Jewish communities (and many Gentile communities) were not particularly eager to welcome Jews from New York City. These Jews and Gentiles had to be particularly careful about how they phrased their opposition. Southern Jews, who had inhabited the region since before the founding of the nation, frequently made the argument that the Jews from the North were conditioned to the cold and would have a terrible time trying to adapt to the warm southern climate.

HEBREW FREE LOAN SOCIETY

In 1892, eleven immigrants gathered in the Wilner Synagogue to consider how to help others. They pooled their money: $95. They then offered to loan money—at no interest—to Jews in need. Thus the Hebrew Free Loan Society was born. In the first year, the society loaned $1,205. The uptown Jews were impressed by this effort, and soon Jacob Schiff began sending substantial donations.

HEBREW ORPHAN ASYLUM

The Hebrew Orphan Asylum, though not located on the Lower East Side (it was at Amsterdam Avenue and 138th Street), nevertheless served many East Side children starting in 1880. Not everyone who went there was without parents, although many children were. Despair, disease, desertion, and dangerous work conditions combined to rob many children of their parents. Other parents simply didn't have money to support children and so turned the children over to the asylum. Perhaps the most famous alumnus of the Hebrew Orphan Asylum was the columnist and humorist Art Buchwald, who lived there for a month and a half when he was six years old. Even after he was placed with foster parents, however, Buchwald used to return to the asylum at various times to get clothes and have his teeth fixed.

HENRY STREET SETTLEMENT

If the Lower East Side produced its share of criminals and political rebels, it also produced honest, hardworking manufacturers, workers who quietly and heroically went about raising and supporting their families, and a few distinct individuals who had a profoundly positive effect on the Jewish community.

Lillian Wald was one of those people. Born in Cincinnati to a successful German Jewish family, she might well have lived a life of private luxury far from the din of the Lower East Side. Instead, at age twenty-two, Wald moved to New York,

Visiting nurses often went from tenement to tenement across the rooftops instead of descending to the street. *Source: Courtesy of the Visiting Nurse Service of New York.*

trained at the New York Hospital School of Nursing, and began work at the New York Juvenile Asylum, where she was horrified at the treatment of the children.

Wald began teaching nursing to Jewish immigrant women at the Louis Technical School on Henry Street. Then came an event that changed her life. A little girl approached her one day and asked that Ward accompany her to a tenement to visit someone who was ill. Wald went with the girl to a typically miserable two-room tenement that housed the seven members of the family and a variety of boarders. As she later noted, it took her half an hour to discover that helping the sick should be her life's work. She decided to move to the Lower East Side and help the tormented Jews who suffered there.

In 1893, Wald joined with Mary Brewster to establish the Visiting Nurse Service. Wald began providing any kind of nursing service that was needed. If a family could afford to pay, she charged a small fee. If the family had no money, the service was free.

FROM LILLIAN WALD'S CASE NOTES

Visit and care of typhoid patient, 182 Ludlow Street. Visit to 7 Hester Street where in rooms of Nathan S., found two children with measles. After much argument succeeded in bathing these two patients and the sick baby. The first time in their experience. They insisted no water and soap could be applied to anyone with measles before seven days. Brought clean dresses to the older children.

Annie P., 44 Allen Street, front tenement, second floor. Husband Louis P. came here three years ago and one year ago sent for wife and three children. From that time unfortunately, his trade, that of shoemaker, became less remunerative. She helped by washing and like labor, but two months ago he deserted her, though she stoutly maintains that he returned to Odessa to get his old work back. The youngest, Meyer P., age 5 years, fell from the table and injured his hip. He lay for 7 months in the Orthopedic Hospital, 42nd Street; he was discharged as incurable and supplied with a brace. . . . The mother is absolutely tied by her pregnant condition; the cripple is in pain and cries to be carried. They had no rooms of their own but paid $3 a month to Hannah A., a decent tailoress, who allowed the family to sleep on her floor. The $3 cannot be forthcoming now for the woman's accouchement is in three weeks. The children were unusually attractive, and later investigation showed that they all told the exact truth. Monday I filed application with Montefiore Home for Meyer's admission. The New York Hospital promised to look after the child until place was secured—if not too long. Tuesday I went to Hebrew Sheltering Guardian Society . . . and obtained promise of place for the two well children by Thursday. Necessary to procure committal first. . . . Obtained Judge Ryan's signature Thursday morning. Thursday afternoon, we washed and dressed the two children, and I left them in the afternoon at the Asylum, leaving my address. . . . They have absolutely no one in America but their mother. . . . I will take the mother to the Nursery and Child's Hospital where she will be cared for during confinement.

>⊶⊷<

During the summer of 1895, Wald moved to a redbrick row house at 265 Henry Street. It was a gift from Jacob Schiff, the banker and philanthropist, and began what was first known as the Nurses Settlement. The Settlement movement, part of a broader reform movement to aid the poor, got its name from the fact that those who aided the poor didn't just visit but "settled" among the people who needed their help. In 1902, the Settlement added buildings at 299, 301, and 303 Henry Street, which included a gymnasium.

The organization's name soon changed. A boy named Ernie Bronsky, who was on the Settlement's soccer team, complained to Wald that boys were mocking him and others from the "Noices" Settlement. The organization was promptly renamed the Henry Street Settlement.

Wald's Settlement House branched out beyond providing home nursing care. When Wald decided that neighborhood residents needed wholesome activities to help them recover and thrive, she opened one of the city's first playgrounds. By 1916, the Settlement was a mainstay of the community, and its hundred or so nurses were visiting more than two hundred thousand people a year.

Wald patiently struggled alongside the immigrants. If a drain needed unclogging, she taught the tenement dweller how to clear it. If medicines needed to be taken, Wald's quiet reassurance helped immigrants swallow the foul-tasting stuff. If cleanliness was a problem—how to get rid of the garbage, how to keep rats out, how to get rid of lice and bedbugs—Wald was there to help. She was calm and had a knack for getting agitated immigrants to relax. She held their hand, and she lived among them, so they trusted her. She had adopted a neighborhood that repulsed most others with its filth and its lack of culture.

Lillian Wald simply wanted to do good. She frequently explained her work by asking a simple question: "Have you ever seen a hungry child cry?"

HEBREW IMMIGRANT AID SOCIETY (HIAS)

In addition to its incredible work at Ellis Island, HIAS ran an employment bureau—open every night except Friday because of the Sabbath. The HIAS staff would get newspapers late at night and overnight would scour the ads trying to match new immigrants with available jobs.

In 1908, HIAS began publishing a journal that was sent abroad to give potential immigrants information about what the process involved and what such travelers might face at Ellis Island. HIAS was so helpful that at one point, the Russian government made an offer of 6,000 rubles annually to help the organization resettle Russian Jews in America. Fearing that the society might be compelled to provide information about those immigrants who had fled Russia illegally and that the American Jewish public would be shocked if HIAS accepted help from the hated tsarist government, the organization refused the money, saying it wanted to remain independent of any governmental help.

HIAS also eventually entered the political arena, working to defeat legislation that harmed the immigrants, such as bills that required literacy tests.

JEWISH COMMUNITY CENTERS
(YMHA AND YWHA)

The first Young Men's Hebrew Association was established in Baltimore in 1854. By 1874, Jews in New York had established a center at 112 West Twenty-First Street, but just four years later, the center moved away from downtown up to 110 West Forty-Second Street. Realizing that there was a need for a downtown center, a branch was established in 1882. That branch later evolved into the Educational Alliance. In general, the YMHAs wanted immigrant Jews to learn American ways.

THE KEHILLAH

In the wake of the Commissioner Bingham incident, the Jewish community realized that it needed a clear voice to defend the community from any future attacks and to uproot crime in Jewish neighborhoods both to protect Jewish victims and to forestall further embarrassing claims by high officials.

In 1909, Rabbi Judah Magnes founded the Kehillah (the Hebrew word for "community") to represent more than two hundred organizations, from both uptown and downtown.

Magnes, an associate rabbi of the uptown Reform movement's Temple Emanu-El, was a natural bridge builder. Over the course of his extraordinary life, Magnes was a constant boundary crosser. He was born in Oakland, California, but came east. Ordained in the Reform tradition, he later became a Conservative rabbi. He was an ardent Zionist and an advocate of peace between Arabs and Jews. He was the first president of Hebrew University in Jerusalem.

Despite Magnes's youth (he was thirty-one), attractive appearance, genuine concern, and proven abilities, he still represented the German Jews in the eyes of the others, and the downtown Jews worried about being led by a member of a group they didn't trust, a group that disdained Yiddish and its culture and saw assimilation as the principal goal of its efforts.

The Kehillah set up a Welfare Committee, which, in conjunction with local police, sought to remove crime from the Jewish areas. In a then famous case, the Kehillah was vital in breaking up the Yiddish Blackhand Association, an extortion ring that specialized in poisoning the horses of business owners who refused to pay protection money. The Kehillah, working through Abe Shoenfeld, its principal investigator, aided police in shutting down over one hundred houses of prostitution.

One of its controversial activities was to publish Hebrew textbooks through its Bureau of Jewish Education. Some uptown Jews were disheartened at such an effort because learning Hebrew, they believed, would put a brake on the assimilation of the immigrants into American life.

The Kehillah injected itself into the commercial, religious, and legal life of the Jewish community as well. For example, it helped settle a strike in the fur trade.

The decline of the Kehillah came because the uptown Jews withdrew their support of the effort. The pacifist Magnes had opposed entry into World War I, a position many of the downtown socialists also advocated. That opposition infuriated the more nationalistic uptowners.

LANDSMANSHAFTEN

The need for help was often exacerbated by the sometimes contradictory intense longing for the familiarity of the shtetl the immigrants had left behind. They had no nostalgia for the hardships or the Gentile peasant neighbors or the poverty or the strict rules, but they did miss the close-knit Jewish community. They missed their homes, however flimsy; their streets, however muddy; their synagogues, however tattered; and their longtime friends and neighbors.

Soon these new Americans began to form associations known as *landsman-shaften*, self-help societies organized according to the various hometowns they had fled (*landsman* is the Yiddish word for a person from the same place of origin; the plural is *landslayt*). Thus they managed to re-create the communal support of the shtetl in a Golden Land that was often too demanding on the individual. The notion of such associations was deeply embedded in Jewish history. When exiles from Judea were sent to Babylon in the sixth century B.C.E., they organized according to the town from which they had come in the Land of Israel.

LANDSMANSHAFT FUNDRAISING

Mollie Hyman, who worked in the garment industry, recalled her experience about how the associations raised money:

> Every landsmanshaft, if they wanted to raise a little money for the destitute member or the organization, they would buy tickets in blocks and sell them to the members. We'd go to all the operas and concerts. You never had enough money to get a seat. You go standing for a quarter or fifty cents. You had to come early because they let in only so many standees. You'd end up spending two hours standing on the line to get in. Then you wait an hour until the show starts. Still, you wanted to go there.
>
> You had all those Jewish shows on Second Avenue, the Thalia on the bowery, the Jacob Adler, and there were a few more smaller theaters. These theaters uplifted the quality of life in the neighborhood.

The landsmanshaften provided help for the immigrants who might otherwise not be able to afford a burial or a doctor or be able to survive between jobs. They provided strike insurance and disability payments. They reserved burial plots. Starting with Beth Israel in 1889, the associations started their own hospitals. They opened homes for the aged and for orphans. The landsmanshaften raised funds in various ways, including mounting benefit shows at theaters. According to one reasonable estimate, there were some three thousand landsmanshaften with a total membership of about four hundred thousand people—a quarter of the Jewish population of the Lower East Side. Since the associations were mostly male— many were exclusively male—the proportion of Jewish males who joined was staggering.

Membership in such an association, therefore, must have been of paramount emotional importance to the immigrant men. Trapped in tiny apartments, guilty about being unable to support their families, struggling with endless hours of difficult

HOW LANDSMANSHAFTEN CAME TO BE

In 1938, the Yiddish Writers Group, part of the Federal Writers Project, conducted a survey to determine why the landsmanshaften had originally been formed. Here are some of the responses they got:

> The men here felt miserable, they had left wives or brides back home, so they used to get together in the house of a married landsman to drink tea or play cards.

> A landsman was about to be deported because he was sick, so the landslayt realized the importance of having their own organization for self-help.

> A landsman died in the factory. People think he is a Greek and bury him in Potter's Field. Landslayt hear about it, his body is dug up, and the decision taken to start our own organization with a cemetery.

━━✕━━

labor, confused about the changing roles of their wives and the strange American ways of their children, the immigrant men found in the associations their own declaration of survival and of independence from the harsh world in which they lived.

The men would gather together to play pinochle, argue—always with gusto—about politics, and deal with the problems of their families, the Jewish community, the wider world, or one of their own officials who absconded with the association's treasury.

Perhaps most important, the landsmanshaften were halfway houses between the Old World and the New. The associations were crucial in letting immigrant men, at least in part, determine the depth and pace of their adaptation to American life. The associations were safe havens in which to test out what was palatable and what was not.

At their start, landsmanshaften formed not just as associations but also as congregations so that people from the same town could pray together, chanting familiar tunes in familiar accents, and also have a chance to talk about news from the Old World and perhaps share a memory or two. Fairly quickly, by the turn of the twentieth century, though, the associations stopped organizing religious events and instead focused on the more worldly aspects of gatherings of friends and charitable support.

It soon became apparent that if a few men could gain more power and provide help by joining together to form an association, a few of these associations joining together would have still greater power. Federations of associations from various regions in Eastern Europe soon sprang up.

The landsmanshaften were great rules keepers. Each had its own constitution, filled with the sorts of precise requirements that defined the culture and morality as the association saw it. The Pukhoveritser constitution admonished its members to dress appropriately at a funeral, not to arrive late, and not to smoke. The First Kalisher Benevolent Association insisted that if one of its members married, a committee would accompany the new wife to a doctor for certification of her health; without such a certification, the constitution duly noted, the member would have to remain single or would not be qualified to obtain the usual death benefit for his wife. Some of the constitutions delicately denied health benefits to members with an "immoral disease."

Beyond companionship, it was the benefits that most of the members needed. The landsmanshaften depended on the "assessment system." That is, when money was needed because of, for example, a death, all the other members of the society would pay a tax. Originally, the system worked well, but as the average age of members increased and more and more death benefits were required, the resulting taxes on the surviving members became more and more burdensome. Eventually, a number of societies faced bankruptcy. This trend was accelerated when younger members looked at the large number of older members, projected what the following few years would mean in terms of taxes, and left to form a new organization with men of their own age. They often found a way to incorporate the word *young* into the name of the new association.

HELP FROM OUTSIDERS

The incredible sights and sounds of the Lower East Side often intrigued Gentile observers. Social workers, educational reformers (like John Dewey, who formed a close friendship with the writer Anzia Yezierska), government officials—all were curious about the Jewish immigrants. Their sympathy and support helped the Jewish immigrants feel more like Americans and helped Gentile Americans be more hospitable toward the newcomers.

Reporters and writers had the most immediate effect because their words were widely read. For example, Lincoln Steffens, the most renowned reporter of this era, was intrigued by a neighborhood close to Nassau Street, known as Newspaper Row because several of New York City's major dailies were published there. Steffens started his inquiries by looking up the author of the novel *Yekl: A Tale of the Ghetto*. For his part, Abraham Cahan, a great Yiddish journalist himself, must have been overwhelmed by Steffens's interest in him as a guide and the Lower East Side as a fascinating reportorial beat. Steffens enlisted Cahan to write for the *New York Evening Post* and later for the *Commercial Advertiser*. Cahan's columns provide fascinating glimpses into Jewish immigrant life. The training Cahan got on these papers enhanced his skills immeasurably and gave him access to a journalistic world he had only dreamed about.

Steffens was also kind to other journalists who sought to explore the seemingly foreign world of the Lower East Side. As he later wrote, "At the time, I was almost a Jew. I had become as infatuated with the Ghetto as eastern boys were with the wilds of the west, and nailed a mezuzah to my office door."

Hutchins Hapgood, one of the men Steffens helped, was the author of *The Spirit of the Ghetto*. Published in 1902, the book was filled with sympathetic portraits. Previous efforts by writers to describe "Jewtown," as the Lower East Side was sometimes mockingly nicknamed, were done almost at arm's length, as though an unpalatable or dangerous specimen was being held up for examination because it was so different. The immigrants, before Hapgood, were portrayed in books as incapable of ever becoming "real" Americans and impossible to civilize.

Hapgood had Steffens as his editor and Cahan as his colleague. Cahan guided the curious Hapgood around the neighborhood. When Hapgood was ready to publish his book, he sought out an artist to provide accompanying illustrations. Again he turned to Cahan, and the guide provided a suggestion: a young man named Jacob Epstein, who would go on to become a world-famous sculptor and eventually be knighted by the king of England. Epstein, who had been born on the Lower East Side, found himself driven by its energy. Indeed, after his parents moved away to a better area of the city, Epstein moved back for artistic inspiration.

Although these writers were sympathetic, not all journalists felt exactly the same. Hapgood found the Jews on the Lower East Side genuinely fascinating, but he had still another colleague, Jacob Riis, also working with Steffens, who saw instead a Jewish ghetto filled with unpleasant people.

Riis was not anti-Jewish. Nor was he, like the nativists, attempting to defend a supposedly pure American culture from the foreignness of such people as the Jews. Indeed, Riis himself had been born in Denmark, so such a stance against immigrants would have been untenable. Instead, as a writer and a photographer, Riis both chronicled and railed against an American political system that would permit the conditions, especially the poverty, that he saw on the Lower East Side.

He was part of the tradition of muckrakers, journalists who sought to improve intolerable conditions by describing them and making people aware of them. In his book *How the Other Half Lives*, Riis offered blistering attacks on the conditions he found.

But however reform-minded Riis was and however much his photographs and reporting may have provoked sympathy for the Jews, he was not warmhearted about the people whose plight he described. As he wrote in 1890, "Hardly less aggressive than the Italian, the Russian and Polish Jew, having overrun the district between Rivington and Division Streets, east of the Bowery, to the point of suffocation, is filling the tenements of the Old Seventh Ward to the river front, and disputing with the Italian every foot of available space in the back alleys of Mulberry Street. The two races, differing hopelessly in much, have this in common: they carry their slums with them wherever they go, if allowed to do it."

Still, whatever his personal feelings, the work that Riis produced provided stunning evidence of the difficult conditions under which the Jews were forced to live and in that way came to the aid of the Jewish residents of the area.

Help came from a variety of sources. For some Jewish immigrants, the greatest help of all came from the solace of religion.

READING FROM THE SCROLL.

Orthodox Jews at worship in a *shul. Source: Courtesy of the Eldridge Street Project.*

ELEVEN

RELIGION AND ITS REBELS

><><

O RTHODOX JUDAISM had a hard time making the trip across the Atlantic. Most of the devoutly Orthodox wouldn't even contemplate going to a wild land like America, preferring even the poverty and periodic persecutions in a world they understood to what they saw as certain to be a world that was corrupting and unreligious.

RELIGIOUS CHALLENGES

The young people who made the journey tended to be the most fiercely independent, the least learned, and the most indifferent or hostile to tradition. This demographic reality was compounded by the fact that the working classes who came to America became radicalized there by the socialist intellectuals among them, the conditions under which they lived and labored, and the predominantly German socialists who had preceded them. Finally, the realities of American life made it difficult to maintain a strictly traditional way of life. It was difficult to find a job that didn't require work on the Sabbath. The lures of America, which undermined the moral strictures of Judaism, were immensely attractive. There was intense pressure from family and friends to adjust to the New World, to discard clothes and rituals, prayer shawls and religious law. The very Constitution of the United States made a

ONE FAMILY'S RELIGION

Jacob Javits, the extraordinary senator from New York who served from 1957 until 1980, was born on the Lower East Side in 1904. In his autobiography, he recalled how religion affected his family:

> My mother welcomed and appreciated the Sabbath and the Holy Days as a respite from her daily grind. They provided a chance to spend a few extra hours with her family. To my father, however, religion meant much more. The rituals of Orthodox Judaism were the core of his life; despite all of his life's vicissitudes, he never forgot his rabbinical training and never lost his passionate faith in the law of the Torah. Upon arising in the morning, he strapped to his forehead and to his left arm the little leather-bound *tefillin*, phylacteries, containing prayers and passages from the Torah. Then, with these symbols of the Hebrew faith near his mind and his heart, he would pray. Except on the Sabbath and on Jewish holidays—which required of him longer, more intricate rituals and prayers—my father prayed with his phylacteries every morning of his life.

formal separation between religion and state. Democracy meant that power, at least in theory, was supposed to flow from the bottom up, not from the top down, as it had in the authoritarian countries from which the Jews had fled. This American antiauthoritarianism worked against Orthodoxy and central Orthodox virtues, values, beliefs, rituals, leaders, and dreams.

The numbers revealed the challenges Orthodox Judaism faced. In 1916, there were three million Jews in the United States. Only 12 percent of them belonged to a synagogue. Only 25 percent of elementary school–aged children received any religious training. Of those old enough to attend high school, a staggeringly low 1 percent went for religious training.

Of course, these figures belie the complexity of the immigrants themselves. Many, though young, had been brought up keeping the Sabbath and keeping kosher. It was a natural part of their lives. They measured time with a Jewish mind and on a Jewish calendar. When, for example, on December 17, 1903, the Wright brothers made four flights in their new flying machine, the Jews remembered the date as the third day of Hanukkah.

Older immigrants felt even deeper attachments to the tradition. And some of the immigrants were fervently Orthodox, though it should be said that some people who called themselves Orthodox worked on the Sabbath or attended a performance of the Yiddish theater on the day of rest. And even in the yeshivas (the Jewish schools), students rebelled when they weren't allowed to study English, science, or literature.

KOSHER FOOD

Many Jews, even if they weren't Orthodox, continued to keep kosher out of habit and tradition, although their children were much less willing to do so. In 1897, the manager of a slaughterhouse on the Lower East Side reported that he kept between fifteen hundred and eighteen hundred head of cattle reserved, though only about 70 percent of those were considered usable. The slaughterhouse kept a refrigerated area where there was a supply of chuck. Chuck was the forequarter of the steer and the only part that was used for kosher meat. The fifth rib of the steer was used as the dividing line between the front and middle of the steer. Jews were not supposed to eat cuts from the hindquarters—the filets, porterhouse steaks, and tenderloins prized by many Gentile consumers.

The frozen compartment where the meat was stored was kept at 36 degrees Fahrenheit. The top halves of the animals hung on hooks with their necks facing downward. Each hanging beef has its own tags and labels indicating it had passed a government inspection and that it was kosher.

The killing of the animals took place by separating the windpipe by pressing it with a knife. The goal was for the ritual slaughterer, the *shochet*, not to shake his hand so as to cause the animal unnecessary suffering. The knife he used had to be sharp and smooth, without any indentations.

The process was kept far from eyes of the consumers of the beef, who saw it prepared to look appetizing. The kosher meat dealers liked to emphasize that kosher meat was healthier for consumers and that the sacrificed animal had suffered far less at the hands of a kosher slaughterer than a nonkosher one.

THE PLIGHT OF RABBIS

Rabbis in America not only had lost their traditional authority but also in many cases their means of earning a living. Many rabbis had to struggle with different jobs. They resented having to teach young boys whose minds were on baseball. Finding someone a husband or wife may have been a mitzvah, but it was also a source of constant complaining by the various families. Rabbis became specialists in peddling or writing letters.

To the young boys who studied Hebrew, the rebbe who taught them—a real rabbi or a tutor who came to their apartment—was frequently seen as a quaint, unpleasant presence. In his memoir *The Time That Was Then*, Harry Roskolenko offered a vivid picture of such teachers:

> The Rebbe was usually an old man who wheezed, coughed, sneezed in your face, and smoked broken cigarettes. He looked all dead except around his sparkling eyes. His hair was a mass of wool, when he was not all bald. His hat, which was black, made him appear even more pious. . . . He moved about in a long, untidy black coat, often of satin and lined. . . . It was a coat which the Rebbe filled up with Yiddish newspapers, torn letters from relatives in Russia, tattered books that he pulled out—to show his scholarship. The pockets—and it was a coat consisting more of pockets than coat—were his repositories for the day, for the week, for the year, for all of his peripatetic ways as a talker about God.

RELIGIOUS CONFLICT

The Orthodox among the Jewish immigrants were quick to note the laxity with which many of their coreligionists observed the *mitzvot*, the commandments. Friction was increasing among those who sought to maintain Orthodoxy; the uptown mostly Reform Jews; the anarchists who held Yom Kippur dances; the socialists who saw in religion generally a false belief system that served to blind workers from the true conditions of society; the indifferent who just wanted to have fun, make money, or get on with life; the Zionists; the emerging Conservative movement; and the various other strains of religious or irreligious belief in the community.

The Orthodox were the most shocked at the behavior of the young and of other Jews. They were profoundly concerned about the future and still-forming identity of these new American Jews. This concern sometimes took the form of confrontation.

A FRUSTRATED RABBI

The *New York Commercial Advertiser* noted the letter-writing work of a frustrated rabbi in its July 23, 1898, edition:

A bonnetless young woman with a letter in her hand was gazing about her, as if in search of something, as she leisurely proceeded on her way along Ludlow Street. . . .

"Do you know a letter writer around here?"

"My rabbi writes letters cheap and good. He lives around the corner. Shall I show you where it is?". . .

[She went to] a basement window with a little signboard which read: Hebrew taught. Letters written in Yiddish, English, German, Russian, and Hebrew. The rabbi was found at the head of a class of dirty boys lazily singing over huge open books. "Louder or I'll break every bone in . . ." The threat was suddenly broken off by the appearance of the newcomers. The boys cast furtive glances at the strangers. "Where do you keep your eyes, Gentile boys that you are? Look at your Bible or I'll make you look the Angel of Death in the face."

The chapter finished, the rabbi reached out his hand for the woman's letter. "Have you anything particular to write, young woman?"

"Tell my sister that I am sending her ten American dollars, and that I hope to the uppermost that her husband will get well. Tell her also that mother sends her love. Tell her also that God has given me a crown for a husband and that he kisses my footprints and that he sends the money gladly, and . . . and . . . and . . . Don't you know of anything else to write, rabbi?"

"You have got enough. You don't want me to be writing a whole year for five cents, do you?"

For example, on the evening of September 25, 1898, right after Yom Kippur had ended, hundreds of religious Jews rioted at Canal and Division Streets. They had gathered around a restaurant at 141 Division Street. The owners had put an ad in the *Jewish Daily Forward* informing the public that the restaurant would be open on Yom Kippur. This was unusual, since restaurants traditionally kept closed on a holy day that required fasting out of courtesy to the community and their customers. The restaurant was crowded during Yom Kippur itself, and all seemed calm.

In the evening, the religiously fervent began to gather in protest. As three diners emerged from the restaurant, the crowd attacked them and began to beat the men. The three escaped by jumping on a horsecar.

A policeman named Baker was the only law enforcement officer on the scene; realizing he needed support, he called for backup. The acting captain ordered his men not to club the protesters but to use enough force to push them back to Rutgers Street. It took the police half a dozen surges into the crowd to move them.

The police waited as frightened patrons of the restaurant emerged. As each left, six police officers would lift the man and throw him into passing horsecars, startling the passengers already aboard.

Protests like that suggest that the Orthodox were deeply influenced by the emerging labor movement. One other clear case of this influence can be seen in the kosher meat boycott of 1902. In mid-May of that year, the cost of kosher meat jumped 50 percent—from 12 to 18 cents a pound. The kosher butchers protested for a week by not selling the meat they got from wholesalers, but the price did not drop. Soon Jewish women organized and refused to buy any kosher beef.

Fanny Levy, wife of a cloak worker, and Sarah Edelson, a restaurant owner, led the organizational efforts, literally going from one tenement to the next to get support. The strike reached a climax on May 15 when a reported twenty thousand women charged into kosher butcher shops, grabbed the meat, took it into the streets, poured gasoline on it, and set the meat on fire. The strikers used sticks to take meat from women who had made purchases. Seventy Jewish women were arrested. The boycott spread, so that by June 9, the price finally dropped, to 14 cents a pound. That ended the boycott.

The Orthodox on the Lower East Side had much to be concerned about besides kosher meat. The deepening desire of immigrant Jews to become part of American life led a few to marry Gentile partners. There were Christmas exercises in the public schools. Reform Judaism in particular was providing an alternative for those who wished to leave Orthodoxy without leaving the religion entirely. And Christian missionaries were making frequent and determined forays into the Lower East Side in search of new adherents.

SHULS

The immigrants may not have come from the most religious among those living in Eastern Europe, but they were often homesick for their parents, their wives, their friends, or even the visual memory of their hometown. In America, the need for connecting to their past was met, in part, by the landsmanshaften. But it was also met by going to synagogue, or *shul*.

The Jews on the Lower East Side organized into shuls by their town of origin. Since there were so many towns, there were, correspondingly, an enormous number of shuls. Some were in storefronts or tenement flats or meeting halls. Most of the new shuls were in small rooms, *shtieblach*, which might once have been a living room, an attic, or a basement. The Jews didn't traditionally have lavish religious observances. A bar mitzvah might cost $8 for a bottle of whiskey, some cakes, a dollar or two to rent the synagogue, and—if a rabbi officiated—a dollar for him.

There were also holiday customs. It was common in preparing for Passoverf, for example, for people to go to Streit's Matzos. Streit's had begun life in a small shop at 65 Pitt Street. The owners' specialty was making matzoh by hand. The store moved to Rivington Street in 1925 and eventually expanded to include 148–154 Rivington. There were long lines waiting to buy the 5-pound boxes. After getting the matzoh, the journey continued to Schapiro's to purchase some wine from the large casks. Schapiro's had begun in 1899 as a small restaurant on Attorney Street. In 1908, Sam Schapiro concluded that so many people asked for the kosher wine he produced, he abandoned the restaurant and moved to 126 Rivington Street to open a winery. People sampled from different kinds of wine before they bought, and as one immigrant recalled, "By the time you bought the wine, you were dead drunk." One favorite across the years was the Extra Heavy Concord wine, which became famous because of the motto attached to it: "Wine so thick, you can almost cut it with a knife."

The variety of shuls was confusing to the immigrants because they had characteristically come from a shtetl where there was only one shul, and that shul had one rabbi. It is therefore not surprising that in an attempt to impose some order on the religious chaos, an effort was mounted in the late 1880s to name a "chief rabbi." The designated leader, Jacob Joseph from Vilna, was not able to get the various congregations to agree on their religious activities. Indeed, in the Old Country, a rabbi who came to a town stayed there for life. On the Lower East Side, it was more typical to give a rabbi a contract for a year so that the congregants—especially the *balbatim*, the influential congregants—could determine whether he should be retained.

Synagogues did prove popular. In 1880, there were 270 in New York City. There were 1,000 in 1916. There were also religious schools (*talmudai torah*)—335 in 1905—and many Bible and Hebrew classes in a single room. Religious seminaries also began.

While prayers were the center of religious activity in shul, the Jews also came to shul to hear the cantors. Famous cantors came for the High Holy Days, and some cantors drew applause from the congregants after their performance. Rabbis were often jealous of the intense attachment the congregants felt toward the cantors; in some shuls, rabbis posted men at the exits to prevent people from leaving after the cantor had finished and before the rabbi had begun. Many people simply didn't understand the Hebrew the rabbi spoke and the cantor sang, but that didn't prevent them from enjoying the beauty of the cantor's voice. As English-speaking rabbis emerged who reduced the amount of Hebrew in the service, the role of the cantor in those shuls simultaneously was reduced.

Many of the cantors became famous. Josef "Yossele" Rosenblatt arrived in New York in 1912 and sang at Congregation Ohab Zadek for $2,400 a year, an enormous salary at the time. Rosenblatt also sang in concert halls and composed music. However, Rosenblatt was torn because he was Orthodox. Unlike performers who compromised their religious beliefs or didn't even think about them, Rosenblatt faced many difficult choices. In vaudeville, he would not perform with women. He refused to have an organ accompany his act. But Yossele Rosenblatt did make one significant contribution to American culture: he provided the voice in *The Jazz Singer,* the first significant motion picture with sound.

There were many famous shuls, and not all of them were built for Jews from Eastern Europe. For example, Congregation Kehila Keosha Janina was built in 1927 by Romaniote Jews from Janina, Greece. It still operates at 280 Broome Street.

Congregation Shearith Israel, the Spanish and Portuguese Synagogue, was founded in 1654, the oldest Jewish congregation in North America and the only Jewish congregation in New York from its founding until 1825. Its first synagogue was on the Lower East Side (the synagogue now is on Central Park West at Seventieth Street). The congregation also had the oldest surviving Jewish cemetery, at 55 Saint James Place, which was in use from 1682 to 1828.

ANSHE CHESED (PEOPLE OF KINDNESS) AND ANSHE SLONIM (PEOPLE OF SLONIM)

What was once Anshe Chesed, located at 172 Norfolk Street, is the oldest surviving building in New York that was originally designed as a synagogue. It was the first shul built on the Lower East Side. When it was built in 1850, it was the largest synagogue in the country.

The congregation of Anshe Chesed moved uptown and was replaced by Anshe Slonim. Anshe Slonim ceased functioning as a synagogue in 1974. The Angel Orensanz Foundation for the Arts, which was established in 1992, currently occupies the site.

BETH HAMEDRASH HAGADOL (GREAT HOUSE OF STUDY)

This congregation at 60 Norfolk Street began life as a Baptist church, but Hungarian Jews purchased it in 1885. This oldest Orthodox shul of Russian immigrants was a center of Orthodox life; indeed, it was Beth Hamedrash Hagadol that first brought Rabbi Jacob Joseph from Vilna in an attempt to create the position of chief rabbi for the Lower East Side. The poor rabbi, a Talmudic scholar not ready for the raucous factionalism of New York City Jewish life, was a disappointment as a chief rabbi but a great success with his congregation. He died in 1902.

Rabbi Jacob Joseph's funeral was an important event on the Lower East Side for several reasons. First of all, the sheer size of the funeral was newsworthy. Estimates of up to one hundred thousand people participated in the procession. The rabbi's casket was taken from one synagogue to another.

The second reason for the funeral's fame was a confrontation it ignited. As the procession passed the R. H. Hoe printing plant on Grand Street, the predominantly Irish workers in the plant began to yell at and otherwise harass the members of the procession. Police officers supposed to protect the crowd encouraged the workers. This struggle was widely seen as a symbolic battle between the Irish and Jewish immigrants over the question of exactly whose Lower East Side it was.

BIALYSTOKER SYNAGOGUE

In 1878, a group of men from Bialystok, Poland, met as a congregation in a loft on the first floor of 100 Hester Street. They eventually purchased a house at 82 Orchard Street and transformed it into a synagogue.

A second group of people from Bialystok organized into another congregation on Grand Street. The two groups would eventually merge. Because of a 1905 pogrom in Bialystok, the number of immigrants from there grew. In 1905, the congregation took over the Willett Street Methodist Episcopal Church. (Willett Street would eventually be renamed Bialystoker Place.) The synagogue is remarkable for its three-story ark, which came from Italy. The sanctuary's ceiling is decorated with paintings of zodiac symbols that correspond to Jewish months. There is also a provocative historical possibility concerning a door in the synagogue. The door is concealed in a corner of the women's gallery. When the door is open, it leads to a wooden ladder that stretches up to the attic. This hidden area might be interpreted to mean that the congregation was a stop on the Underground Railroad where slaves headed for Canada stayed overnight on their journey.

CONGREGATION B'NAI ISRAEL KALWARIE

This synagogue, at 15 Pike Street, was originally above stores. The synagogue grew from congregants who had left another synagogue and then joined with people who had come from the village of Kalwarie. Known most familiarly as the Pike Street Synagogue, the congregation was large and popular. Eddie Cantor attended Hebrew school there and celebrated his bar mitzvah there in 1905.

The synagogue was also famous for a religious dispute. In 1911, the well-known Reform Rabbi Stephen S. Wise gave a speech at Clinton Hall, at 151 Clinton Street. The speech was notable for several reasons. First, it was in English. More important, while Wise hoped to inform his somewhat skeptical audience about what he saw as the virtues of the Reform movement, he also wanted to get support. And so at this Friday evening lecture (which was therefore taking place on the Sabbath), he sought to raise money by passing a basket to gather funds. Carrying and handling money on the Sabbath was strictly forbidden by Orthodox standards. Angered, a group of people in the audience stormed out.

Determined to provide an alternative to Rabbi Wise, those angered by the lecture and the money raising called on Rabbi Judah Magnes to speak on behalf of

Orthodoxy. His speeches were to take place at the Pike Street Synagogue. Most particularly, those opposed to Rabbi Wise sought to locate within Orthodoxy a way to lead traditional Jewish religious lives but to do so in a specifically American way. They wanted to speak English. They wanted to be able to speak—or even dance— with women. This search ultimately led to the formation of the Young Israel movement.

Rabbi Magnes's lecture at the Pike Street Synagogue was meant as a founding act of that organization. So resonant was the message that Rabbi Magnes was preparing to offer that on the night of his lecture, thousands of people who wanted to hear the rabbi speak pushed and shoved each other so forcefully as they tried to get into the synagogue that police were called to control them. Young Israel quickly grew and began its efforts by inaugurating a series of Friday evening lectures in English about various subjects of Jewish interest.

The synagogue closed in 1994.

ELDRIDGE STREET SYNAGOGUE

The Eldridge Street Synagogue, at 12–16 Eldridge Street, was a statement as well as a shul. In the Old Country, a shul was a modest—sometimes very modest— building, but in America, with its material wealth, German Jews had already constructed lavish synagogues. The Eastern European Jews who built the Eldridge Street Synagogue in 1886–1887 for congregants of K'hal Adath Jeshurun who came from Russia, Romania, and Poland didn't want just a shul; they wanted to stake their claim to American life. Deliberately meant to show that the "downtown" Jews could be prosperous and to separate their synagogue from the standard vision of a Lower East Side shul as a tiny place in a storefront, the congregants at Eldridge Street commissioned the Herter brothers, Protestant architects from Germany, to built a masterpiece.

The congregants got their wish. The synagogue was the first truly magnificent synagogue built on the Lower East Side. It had 70-foot ceilings. There was a velvet-lined ark (made in Italy from solid walnut inlaid with mosaic) that could hold twenty-four Torah scrolls, a trompe l'oeil mural that worked very well as an illusion, stained-glass windows, skylights, and an incredible exterior.

The Eldridge Street Project has restored the Eldridge Street Synagogue, and its majesty remains impressive.

Sheet music for "Sholom Aleichem." *Source: Courtesy the Archives of the YIVO Institute for Jewish Research, New York.*

FIRST ROUMANIAN-AMERICAN CONGREGATION (SHAARI SHOMOYIN)

In 1860, a group of Romanian immigrants formed a congregation at 70 Hester Street. In 1902, the Congregation moved into a redbrick building at 89–93 Rivington Street. The synagogue had an unusual past; it had passed back and forth between Christian and Jewish congregations. At one point it was a missionary church whose members sought to effect the conversion of Jewish immigrants to Christianity. Given the huge number of new Jews, their desperate circumstances, and their willingness to cross physical boundaries—and so, the missionaries thought, their possible willingness to cross spiritual boundaries as well—a large number of Christian missionaries were active on the Lower East Side. They were singularly unsuccessful, however, and so, in the case of the owners of this building, eventually the effort was abandoned.

The First Roumanian-American Congregation became famous as "the Cantor's Carnegie Hall." Many of the famous cantors in their day sang here. Moshe Koussevitzky, famous for hitting high notes in an extraordinary fashion; Yossele Rosenblatt; and later, Moishe Oysher and Jacob Pincus—who would go on to achieve fame as the opera star Jan Peerce. Great cantors were drawn by the synagogue's magnificent acoustics.

Soon many Jews who were not Romanians joined what was the largest synagogue on the Lower East Side (it could seat seventeen hundred). The entertainers Eddie Cantor and Red Buttons were in the congregation's choir. George Burns was a member. The synagogue was torn down on March 3, 2006.

Synagogues nourished the spiritual hunger of the new American residents. But sometimes the immigrants on the Lower East Side just needed to escape their tenements, their jobs, their bosses, and even their families. They sought, individually or with friends, some refuge from the harshness of their everyday lives.

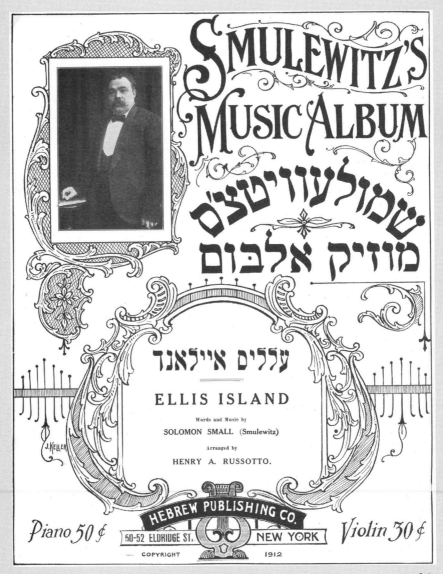

Sheet music for "Ellis Island" by Solomon Small (Smulewitz). *Source: Courtesy of the Lower East Side Tenement Museum.*

TWELVE

REFUGE ON THE LOWER EAST SIDE

>✠✕✠<

T HE JEWISH immigrants on the Lower East Side prized their rare moments of free time. They were hungry for relief, for companionship, for friends, for relaxation, for a refuge away from their drudgery.

They found such refuge wherever they could congregate. Some people went to barbershops to sit around and play cards. Others headed to pool halls to smoke and hear the latest jokes. Others liked to gamble. Stuss was one popular game. It was a type of faro. No elaborate gambling palace was required for those who wished to bet. A simple table was needed in what were known as stuss houses. Pictures of the thirteen cards that made up a suit were painted on the table. Players put their money on one of the pictures. The dealer would then turn over a card from the deck. If players bet on the first card that was turned, they lost; players who bet on the second card won.

There were also popular saloons, including the bar on Essex Street run by "Silver Dollar" Smith. Charles Smith (born either Charles Solomon or Solomon Finkelstein) had been a Republican assemblyman who switched sides in reaction to Republican attempts to curb immigration. Smith gave campaign speeches by inviting the crowds back to his bar for a drink. The bar, directly across from the Essex Market Courthouse, had a unique interior. A thousand silver dollars were embedded in the floor. There were five hundred on a chandelier. Additional silver dollars formed a star and crescent behind the bar counter.

Women took refuge on their stoops, chatting with neighbors and keeping their eyes on their children.

Younger immigrants especially loved the movies. Two favorite houses were the Gem on East Houston and the Odeon on Norfolk Street. Two young people could get in for a nickel. This fact resulted in many fights because one would have to pay 3 cents and the other 2 cents. Candy cost a penny, so the decision really mattered. On Clinton Street, a firehouse was turned into a silent movie theater.

Because many of the immigrants couldn't read the movie subtitles, a man and woman wielding microphones would sometimes read for the audience. Harry Golden called this an experimentation with "talking pictures." On summer mornings, the movies opened at 8:30, and two hundred children would jam in. Anxious ushers trying to deal with the crowds would go down the aisles and force children to sit two in each seat. This resulted in clever children who had 3 cents selecting an especially skinny partner with 2 cents. In the wintry cold weather, when theaters didn't have so many customers, the theater owners reluctantly lowered the price so that two children could get in for 4 cents.

When children entered the theater, the usher gave them a "late check," a card with the theater's name emblazoned on it with the dreaded words "Late Check." At the end of the show, the ushers collected the cards, trying to prevent customers from seeing a movie more than once. Of course, after their card was collected, children were free to sit through the entire next show until the cards were collected again. Vendors called candy butchers roamed the aisles offering peanuts, oranges, and Cracker-Jacks. Popcorn was not yet a movie house staple. The movies themselves in this era before Charlie Chaplin or Mary Pickford or Fatty Arbuckle were mostly westerns with the cavalry riding in to rescue a besieged fort.

Adults liked the movies as well, but they sometimes had more serious matters on their minds, and sometimes they sought human company rather than a film. The Lower East Side offered a wide range of refuges.

ADULT LEARNING

Jewish immigrants concluded early on that if they couldn't master English and American life, their children had to. But many adults as well wanted to get a better job or be able to enter the wider world beyond the confines of what was called the Jewish ghetto, or "Jewtown."

In addition to their practical ambitions, the Jews on the Lower East Side also had a subtler reason for wanting to learn and to argue, to hear disputes from all sides and to absorb knowledge about even arcane subjects. They had fled a regime that suffocated the freedom of expression, that saw modernity and thought as challenges to the regime. For the Jews, stifled for so long so efficiently, the chance to read and hear what they wanted, to be able to express their ideas freely and even be praised for it, was remarkably heady.

For various reasons, then, the vast majority of immigrants wanted to participate more fully in American life. To do so, they had to learn English. Some of the immigrants attempted to teach themselves the new language just by practicing with the people they encountered. Others turned to the dictionaries of Alexander Harkavy. Harkavy, who had been the first person HIAS sent to Ellis Island, provided Yiddish-to-English and English-to-Yiddish translations in his dictionaries. He also composed *Englisher Lerer,* a Yiddish language textbook for those studying English. More than a hundred thousand copies were sold.

Harkavy lived at 130 Madison Street, among the people he taught. He had arrived from Russia in 1882 at the age of eighteen. His goal was for the new immigrants to study English, and he determined to help them. He began by teaching English in private lessons in the evening for 30 or 40 cents an hour. It was while teaching them that he realized that a dictionary was vital and took on the task of creating one.

But not all immigrants were so ambitious. They needed some kind of formal education, but they couldn't pay for it. New York City aided their efforts by providing free evening schools. The classes were run three or four times weekly in public schools. The best and funniest fictional rendition of how such classes were fondly remembered by some can be found in Leo Rosten's book *The Education of Hyman Kaplan,* an extraordinary collection of fifteen tales published by the then twenty-four-year-old author in 1937 under the pseudonym Leonard Q. Ross. Of course, the evening schools faced daunting challenges. There were people from widely varied backgrounds speaking different languages. Much of the material taught in language classes was really designed for children, a fact that some of the adult students resented. But without question, enormous numbers of adults availed themselves of the opportunity to get a free education.

In 1889, the *New York World* suggested that the Board of Education establish a similarly free series of lectures. By 1897, one hundred thousand people thronged to the thousand free lectures available in the city. The enthusiastic Jewish audiences journeyed to the YMHA, the Metropolitan Museum of Art, a neighborhood school, or the Educational Alliance for lectures that supplemented the ones available in synagogues.

Jewish audiences loved the lectures. They might hear Emma Goldman speaking about anarchism or Abraham Cahan on socialism or Felix Adler on Ethical Culture, his secular alternative to Judaism. They could go to talks on Darwin, rallies at the Workmen's Circle, or any of the vast number of talks offered. They could also go to the Educational Alliance.

EDUCATIONAL ALLIANCE

The Educational Alliance, at 197 East Broadway, was a hybrid institution, the principal goal of which was to transform the greenhorn immigrants into English-speaking, economically independent Americans—that is, to help them become absorbed into American life.

German-Jewish philanthropists founded the Alliance in 1889. As always, the German Jews had conflicting motivations. They wanted to help poor Jews, and in some way, they wanted to help themselves by not having the Eastern European Jews make Americans look with suspicion on all Jews in the United States, including the well-assimilated German Jews.

Regardless of their mixed intentions, the institutions they founded were remarkable. They provided enormous amounts of funds and gave of their time as well.

The Downtown Hebrew Institute, as the Alliance was first named, was meant to aid and educate the community. It provided a school and a library and served as a branch of the YMHA. The institute was restructured in 1893 and took the name Educational Alliance.

The Alliance became especially effective when David Blaustein was appointed superintendent in 1898. Blaustein, as an immigrant himself, understood the emotions of the people who came to the Alliance. He had graduated from Harvard and served for a short while as a rabbi. He was thus the archetype of a successful American Jew—steeped in tradition and triumphant in navigating America's waters. Blaustein lightened the heavy hand the Alliance had used to make immigrants into Americans. He listened carefully to what the attendees had to say. He was a brilliant, tireless organizer.

Classes at what was nicknamed the "Palace of Immigrants" were held from nine in the morning until ten at night. Its library collection was eventually transferred across the street to the Seward Park branch of the library. There were concerts and theatrical presentations. Immigrants learned etiquette and Jewish culture. They celebrated American holidays and sang patriotic songs, activities that not all the immigrants always appreciated. The immigrants got copies of the Declaration of Independence—in Yiddish. During a single week in the years 1900–1910, up to thirty-seven thousand people attended one of the three branches of the Alliance.

Mark Twain and Sholem Aleichem were among those who read from their writing there. Arthur Murray learned to dance there. David Sarnoff learned English there. Eddie Cantor made his first stage appearance at the Educational Alliance. Other graduates included Supreme Court justice Felix Frankfurter, the philosopher Morris Raphael Cohen, George and Ira Gershwin, and later, Zero Mostel.

The Alliance became particularly famed for its art school. Lessons cost 3 cents. Artists who either taught or learned there include Jo Davidson, Sir Jacob Epstein, Chaim Gross, Louise Nevelson, Mark Rothko, Ben Shahn, Raphael Moses, and Isaac Soyer.

Teachers often went far beyond their normal duties. One teacher named Sam Franko, who taught the young George Gershwin, would frequently take the thirty-five members of his class, ranging in age from ten to fifteen, to a restaurant and let them choose what they wanted to eat.

Morris Raphael Cohen recalled in particular his teacher Thomas Davidson, who was Presbyterian. Davidson organized the Breadwinners' Circle to provide an education to men who worked. He also supported a summer camp where students studied classical literature.

Over time, the Alliance modified its originally intense zeal to change the immigrants into the German-Jewish version of a good American. The internal institutional struggles about whether to emphasize Yiddish and Hebrew culture or American were never truly resolved. Orthodox Jews on the Lower East Side didn't like what they considered impious changes in the prayer service. The socialists thought the Alliance was dealing with individual problems when it should have raised its eyes and dealt with the social conditions that caused those problems. Some of those who went there resented what they saw as the blunt assimilationist tactics. As the journalist Eugene Lyons recalled, with some anger, "We were 'Americanized' about as gently as horses are broken in."

But the Alliance was much more commonly beloved by those who attended its programs, and it was truly eclectic in offering those programs. It would try whatever people wanted, and in that way, it was a unique, indispensable institution.

BATHHOUSES

It is unsurprising that one form of escape for Jews who lived in squalor, worked in filth, and wandered through crowded streets would be a place where they could get clean. Many blocks on the Lower East Side were without any bathtubs. In 1897, for example, only 8 percent of homes had any form of a bath. Of course, bathing before the Sabbath was an age-old Jewish tradition.

Therefore, the *shvitz*—from the German *Schwitzbad,* a sweat bath—was a popular hangout. A typical shvitz started with hot coals. Cold water was poured on the coals. This created some steam, and according to those who went regularly, the steam created a sense of calmness. Men who gathered for a shvitz might play cards, eat some food, or swap gossip, stories, and jokes. Some men underwent what then qualified as a massage. Workers held birch leaves tied together and hit the customer. Less hardy customers could go from the steam to a cold shower. By 1897, there were about sixty Jewish bathhouses.

Some of these were floating bathhouses on the East and Hudson Rivers just off Lower Manhattan. They operated from the 1870s to the 1910s. There were also public bathhouses, the first of which was the People's Bath, which opened in 1891.

Traditional women, of course, went to the mikvah, the Jewish ritual bath.

CAFÉS

German immigrants originally used the cafés on Second Avenue to promote their political socialism. Eventually, the new Jewish immigrants populated the area, and so the avenue got nicknamed "Knish Alley." The Jews were not frequent customers at saloons. They drank liquor, but at home, in private. Tea was their public drink, so they needed places to go that were alternatives to saloons.

They also needed a place to argue. The cafés became the intellectual centers of life on the Lower East Side. They were a place to test out an argument, tell a joke, or play a game. The Russian Jews especially were avid chess enthusiasts.

The proprietors of cafés were constantly walking among the tables and talking to the patrons, being the perfect host and providing up-to-date information on an enormous number of subjects.

Harry Roskolenko, in his memoir *The Time That Was Then*, recalled the culture of cafés:

> A café, to my father, was a place where they served tea and talk, mixing unequal doses of philosophy, indignant politics, diatribes against some union leader, reverence for some rabbi, endless anger about sweatshop conditions—and whatever else was in the newspapers that evening. . . . The cafés were often stinking saloons, smelly damp cellars that made the beer . . . and the schnapps taste sour. There were barrels containing wine—and men sat on them as if they had sprouted up, glass in hand, with an open mouth. . . . There were young children bringing home a pint of beer [in a bucket], trying not to spill too much—or have it taken away from them by an overly drunk drunk out of money. . . . It was easy to be both mirthful and miserable within a minute in response to the sights inside or outside. . . .
>
> There were also cafés for domino players who drank nothing alcoholic and seldom talked. . . .
>
> Cafés and saloons opened early and closed late. Many sold food—bean soup, borsht, cold fish, Russian dishes, Jewish dishes. . . . Tea came out of samovars in classical Russian style. The sugar was in an open bowl—huge lumps, unbroken. . . . Granulated sugar was impossible, unthinkable, with Jewish drinkers of tea. The lemon, too, was sucked when it was not put into the glass.

CAFÉ ROYAL

The Café Royal opened in 1911 at Second Avenue and Twelfth Street and was a major gathering place for actors and writers. Many Jewish intellectuals as well went there for *a glezele tey* (a glass of tea) and a piece of pastry. But Gentiles were also attracted to the café and found it a perfect place to debate the political and artistic issues of the day. At various times, Theodore Dreiser, Charlie Chaplin, and Leon Trotsky came for the atmosphere.

SACH'S CAFÉ SOCIETY

The customers of Sach's Café had fond memories of its hospitality for radical intellectuals. It was there in 1889 that Emma Goldman, having escaped from a failed married, met Alexander "Sasha" Berkman, the love of her life. As one customer of Sach's wrote:

There the "cream" of the *radikalen* gathered nightly, and over Mrs. Sach's fine coffee and famous cheesecake discussed the problems and philosophies of the day. . . . There was no gesticulation or noisy argument. These were mannerly . . . intellectuals, exiles and martyrs of world revolution, graduates of many famous universities.

At one table would be Comrade Solataroff, well-known lecturer and exponent of world revolution. Beside him Comrade Kats, editor of . . . the Yiddish anarchist weekly. . . . At Comrade Yanofsky's table sat the "Poet of Revolt," Edelstadt, the "Yiddisher Francois Villon," reciting his latest epic to a fascinated audience. There was "Granpa" Netter, a bearded patriarch, a great Talmudist, who in his old age repudiated Orthodoxy and joined the Comrades. With him was his daughter Chaverte . . . , young and good-looking and devoted to the holy cause. At other tables were slummers, members of the English-language press looking for local color, and occasionally members of the Bomb Squad, in very evident disguise.

~✕~

Crowds also came for Herman, the busboy. Herman Tantzer was famous for his many skills—as a keeper of secrets, as a dispenser of funds (for actors, never ever writers), as a promoter (for an appropriate fee, he would page a customer who sought to impress a guest), and as an all-around attraction. Oscar Szatmarie, the headwaiter at the Café Royal, had "won" Herman and the entire café in a Hungarian card game of klabiash.

SEGAL'S CAFÉ

Segal's at 76 Second Avenue was not the usual café; it was a gathering place for criminals. The café was owned by Louis "Little" Segal and Aaron "Big Aleck" Horlig, who also ran a house of prostitution. Dopey Benny Fein, a notorious enforcer, went there. Gamblers, pickpockets, prostitutes, pimps, and other assorted miscreants all came to Segal's to relax, play cards, and one might presume, swap crime tips and gossip.

ZUM ESSEX

Zum Essex was prized for its food, carefully prepared by Sigmund Manilescu, the cook who owned the place. This basement hangout served lavish five-course meals. Customers could have all the pumpernickel bread they could eat. The cost of such a meal was just 12 cents. Regular customers would come in any time they wished and be served a free glass of seltzer. Friday nights were a specialty because the Sabbath meal included gefilte fish and Manilescu's homemade horseradish. Thirsty customers could buy one of the variously colored bottles, each one of which contained a different flavor of soda water—seltzer and syrup. The drink cost a penny, though the restaurant offered a bigger glass and more syrup for 2 cents.

CANDY STORES

The candy store, nicknamed a "Cheap Charlie," with its egg creams, Hooton's Bars, and Mell-O-Rolls that delighted children and some people who weren't children anymore, was a principal gathering place. The store patrons formed their own sorts of associations and used the stores as their clubhouses. Men would come to the candy store and stay for hours catching up on the lives of those around them, relaxing, steeling themselves for a return to the dull routines of life.

Without question, Auster's at Third Street and Avenue D was the candy store most prized for egg creams. In the summer, owners made 52 quarts of egg creams a day—enough to fill the five thousand orders a day being sold in the summer. They always sold their egg creams in glasses. Cups were never used because the owners didn't think the taste in them was as good.

As at some other candy stores, patrons of Auster's not only could get the famous drink but also could gamble at the numbers business in the establishment, and bookmakers congregated there. The bookmakers were constantly trying to outwit the police. The nearest station was only three blocks away, and the place was famous, so the "bulls" were in Auster's a lot, sometimes walking a bunch of gamblers back to the station. Some of the bookmakers used to write the numbers on the marble wall in the hallway. They kept their hands on the wall, and if a cop arrived, the bookmakers just rubbed the numbers off with their fingers. Of course, the police soon figured out the trick; at one point, they simply removed the entire marble slate from the wall.

There were quite a few of these candy stores, these social centers—in 1900, it was estimated that there were fifty of them in the Tenth Ward. They were all remarkably similar in appearance.

A counter ran along the length of the store. On it, customers could find inexpensive candies and some cigars. Cigarettes and cigars were also on the shelving behind the counter. On the wall, perhaps some pictures that accompanied packs of cigarettes. A soda fountain was the center of the place. Some stores attempted to be fancier and set off a room that was designated as an "ice-cream parlor," the "elegance" of which was marked off by a table or two and a few chairs. If it lacked charm, the parlor was still a perfect place for a meeting.

Young boys of fifteen or sixteen, anxious to enter show business as comedians, would jam the parlor with a dozen boys and try out their material. The would-be stars knew they would never face a tougher audience.

The owner provided a lot of advice—sometimes wanted, sometimes less so—to the customers, especially the young boys who came in after school and perhaps asked advice concerning problems they were having with a parent, teacher, boarder, or sibling.

LIBRARIES

Libraries were extraordinarily popular among Lower East Side residents. There was a branch at Chatham Square, and children raced there after school and took out, on average, a thousand books a day. As one reporter noted, "The Jewish child has more than an eagerness for mental food; it is an intellectual mania. He wants to learn everything in the library and everything the librarians know. He is interested not only in knowledge that will be of practical benefits, but in knowledge for its own sake."

The children, almost all of whom were Jewish, would form a line that snaked down the two flights of stairs in the library and overflowed out into the street. The library needed to keep a complete shelf just of Bibles because they were so popular. The young patrons also enjoyed children's versions of the Bible stories. The two best candidates for the single most popular book was *The Story of the Chosen People* and *Uncle Tom's Cabin*. Readers also liked *The Wandering Jew* and *The Merchant of Venice*.

There was only one table, at the rear of the ground floor; nowhere else could the young, avid readers just sit.

There were some mild incidents involving the children's fiercely Jewish attachments in a world they understood as being deeply divided between Jews and Christians. At one point, the library put out books that contained great works of art. The librarians noted that the explicitly Christian symbols in those books were returned with the symbols cut out or defaced.

The young patrons adored the librarians. It was common for a child to write a letter to them with passages like "I send you so many kisses as there are stars in the sky," give them a present, or run an errand for them. The children thought of them as teachers.

The librarians were absorbed by the quaint ways that English came out of the young readers. They might say, "He's come to be joined into the library," or "He's a murder" to describe an unpleasant person, or "I have a mad on her" to indicate an argument. Librarians were also astonished by some of the excuses they heard for books returned with some damage. Until the emergence of the Jewish immigrants, those librarians had never encountered an excuse like "The baby dropped it in the herring," which was the favorite excuse when the cover was dirty.

The Seward Park Branch, at 192 East Broadway, was one of what were known as the Carnegie libraries. There were sixty-seven in all, gifts from Andrew Carnegie, who in 1901 donated $5.2 million to build them.

The site was a familiar one to Jewish library patrons. In 1886, some German Jews had created the Aguilar Free Library Society (named for Grace Aguilar, a Sephardic Jewish writer). The society operated four libraries in New York, all of them free. In 1890, the society purchased the land and built the small library there. The newer building was constructed in 1909.

The library attracted many famous visitors. Leon Trotsky, who lived in New York in 1917, used to come to the Seward Branch to read.

BRIDGES AND PARKS

The Brooklyn Bridge was the first of three bridges that eventually connected Manhattan and Brooklyn. It opened in 1883. The Williamsburg Bridge opened in 1903, and the Manhattan Bridge on the last day of 1909. Although all three bridges were scenic, walking across the Brooklyn Bridge was the most satisfying. In terms of affecting the Lower East Side Jewish immigrants, though, the Williamsburg Bridge, at the eastern end of Delancey Street, was the most crucial. People could envision crossing the East River into Brooklyn after the Williamsburg was built. A trolley ride across the bridge, introduced in 1905, cost 3 cents, and new housing in Brooklyn and a pedestrian bridge that allowed Sabbath observers to cross over from Brooklyn back to the Lower East Side for synagogue services made escape from the Lower East Side possible, and so the exodus from the Lower East Side slowly began. The journey east was taken by so many Jews that one newspaper nicknamed the Williamsburg Bridge "Jews' Highway."

Prior to 1897, Tompkins Square Park was the only park located south of Fourteenth Street on the East Side. It was, however, more of just an open space than a genuine park.

JACKSON PARK

Jackson Park was meant for families, and indeed, it was always crowded. It didn't have all the amenities of other parks. There were many benches on the asphalt, which was uninterrupted by trees or grass. There was also a stone pavilion that would house small brass bands. Visitors, in the park to escape from the stifling heat, could stop to buy a glass of milk for a penny. Men walked around in their undershirts. Couples sat on benches. Bums stopped anyone, bothering them for money. Children without shoes scooted around playing their own games. Jackson Park was extraordinarily popular for those on the East Side unable to afford more costly recreation.

SEWARD PARK

Lillian Wald, in her irrepressible efforts to improve the lives of people living on the Lower East Side, realized that children needed a safe, pleasant alternative to the overflowing streets to use as a playground. Therefore, in 1898, she helped found the Outdoor Recreation League. The league sought to provide for public parks and playgrounds. Among its efforts, it raised funds to improve Seward Park, which eventually became the first municipal playground in the city. In its first four years, the league was responsible for opening nine parks and playgrounds.

Seward Park—named after William Henry Seward, who as secretary of state purchased Alaska and who was a supporter of immigrants—came to be built after a series of tenements were condemned in 1897. The tenements were torn down, and the park, stretching from East Broadway to Hester Street between Essex and Jefferson Streets, was built. It was, however, not a true park. There was a fence and little else. It was the Outdoor Recreation League that set about to transform its landscape. It raised the funds for plants, trees, benches, and walking paths.

It was not until 1903 that New York City took control of the administration of the park. The city installed a running track, bathhouses, and much else.

RESTAURANTS

Restaurants represented a place outside the crowded tenement flat to gather, a chance to talk with family in an atmosphere less emotionally charged than a home, a place to meet friends, an escape from having to cook, and an opportunity to sample new and tasty foods. In short, restaurants were irresistible.

GARDEN CAFETERIA

This famed gathering place opened at 165 East Broadway in 1911. In true cafeteria style, customers received a ticket when they entered. The person serving them punched the cost of the food or drink on the ticket, and the customer would give the ticket to the cashier when leaving.

The Garden Cafeteria was the home of a thousand arguments an hour. Anarchists and socialists solved the world's problems by yelling at each other over a glass of burning tea. The food was dairy, and so the blintzes and matzoh ball soup provided pleasant interruptions to the arguments. The cafeteria became even more famous later when Isaac Bashevis Singer was a frequent customer and wrote a short story set there.

KATZ'S DELICATESSEN

The delicatessen has achieved mythic status in American culinary life. Its delicacies are, like bagels and bialys, intimately associated with Jews. However, had such meat distributors as the German Jewish Isaac Gellis not moved to the Lower East Side, and had Eastern European foods prevailed, Jews would not be so fully associated with delicatessens.

One of the most famous delis in New York, Katz's, at 205 East Houston Street, was originally established by the Kostagin brothers in 1888—making it the oldest delicatessen in New York City—and it officially became Katz's in 1912. The place was especially popular with actors from the Yiddish theater, perhaps because of its large, perfectly carved sandwiches and hanging salamis.

Later in its life, Katz's became world famous for sending salamis to men in the armed forces of the United States. Its appropriate slogan was "Send a salami to your boy in the Army." Later still, the deli became the setting for a famous scene in the film *When Harry Met Sally*.

MOSKOWITZ AND LUPOWITZ

Founded in 1909 by two Romanians who decorated the restaurant walls with murals of their homeland's country landscapes, Moskowitz and Lupowitz was a fancy place for the Lower East Side. Located at Second Avenue and Second Street (and proud of it—the menus were adorned with "2 + 2" across the top), the restaurant featured waiters in black tie. Perhaps because of its opulent aspirations and appearance, the restaurant was especially popular with people, often entertainers, from uptown.

RATNER'S

If Katz's Delicatessen was a haven for meat dishes, Ratner's was the haven for dairy foods. It was especially popular for brunch; typically, twelve hundred people were served there on a Sunday morning. The crowds were so large that people had to stand in line behind velvet ropes. With the much-prized hot onion rolls and black bread filling baskets that accompanied every meal, customers happily ordered kreplach, potato pancakes, blintzes, or other items on the menu.

Ratner's also became famous for its waiters. They were an assertive bunch declaring the food the customers really wanted, regardless of whatever it was that they might have ordered. The waiters hovered over the table. They developed an endearing rudeness. Though some customers found the act annoying, most just saw the waiters as characters.

Originally opened on Pitt Street in 1905, the restaurant moved to 138 Delancey Street in 1915. Two brothers-in-law, Morris Ratner and Jacob Harmatz, founded the establishment and determined whose name it would bear by tossing a coin. Ratner's was a hangout for the gangsters Meyer Lansky and Bugsy Siegel, who spent much time in the backroom. Al Jolson and Groucho Marx were among the restaurant's more famous customers.

Ratner's closed in 2002 but opened for one final time to celebrate the restaurant's one-hundredth anniversary.

YONAH SCHIMMEL'S KNISH BAKERY

Yonah Schimmel, a rabbi who had emigrated from Bulgaria, couldn't make enough money from his religious profession, so he decided to open a bakery at 137 East Houston Street in 1910. The bakery may be small, but its worldwide reputation as the mecca of knishdom belies its physical size.

VAUDEVILLE

When Jewish entertainers first entered the American consciousness, they did it through vaudeville. That is no surprise, since vaudeville was so popular among immigrant audiences, Jews among them.

Vaudeville became nationally popular just as the Jews were immigrating into the country. Prior to vaudeville, the minstrel show had been America's most popular entertainment, but by the turn of the twentieth century, the vaudeville show had become dominant. Because entertainers in general were considered unsavory by most people in the country, there were opportunities for Jews in this new arena that others didn't want. Jews became stage managers, booking agents, and owners of vaudeville theaters as well.

Immigrant audiences loved vaudeville in the era before movies and radio rendered it superfluous. Vaudeville was a perfect escape, filled as it was with entertainment and wonder. Vaudeville moved quickly. Each performer was on stage for seventeen to twenty minutes. There were lots of sights and sounds. In that way, vaudeville mimicked the rhythms of urban life and made Lower East Side audiences in particular very comfortable because they recognized the emotional environment in which they were entertained. Although ethnic humor was later deemed denigrating, immigrant audiences grew up with it and, for better or worse, enjoyed the stereotyping of groups. "Hebrew" masks were sold, for example, so audience members could perform the Jewish dialect humor at home.

In a typical Jewish ethnic vaudeville act, the "straight man" (a creation of Jewish comedy teams) would come out and sing. Then some shots would be heard offstage. Suddenly the Jewish comic—inevitably clad in an ill-fitting suit, adorned by a long beard, and wearing a hat that went over his ears—came running on stage:

STRAIGHT MAN: Mr. Cohen, what are you running for?
COHEN: I'm trying to keep two fellows from fighting.
STRAIGHT MAN: Who are the fellows?
COHEN: An Irishman and me.

There were several prominent Jewish comedians in early vaudeville. The most famous were Joseph Weber and Lew Fields. Weber, the child of immigrants from Poland, was rescued one day from a menacing gang of boys by a youngster named Lew Schanfeld, whose father ran a sweatshop.

The two boys began performing together at the age of ten. They went to beer dives and dime museums, taking material where they could find it, sizing up audience tastes. They developed comic "Dutch" (the term used for Germans) characters—a con man and his dupe—and gave them all of the ethnic stereotypes then admired. Their "Dutch" characters had unmistakably Yiddish accents. The two had pointed goatees, thick accents, derby hats, and mismatched ill-fitting clothes. In 1887, they uttered the exchange that led to vaudeville's most famous line. Weber said to Fields, "Who is that lady I saw you with last night?" Fields responded, "She ain't no lady. She's my wife." Their specialty was physical humor, then called knockabout, and wordplay like this:

WEBER: You got a good job?
FIELDS: Pretty good.
WEBER: What are you doing?
FIELDS: I'm dyeing.
WEBER: You look good.

Sheet music for "The Jewish King Lear." *Source: Courtesy the Archives of the YIVO Institute for Jewish Research, New York.*

The wordplay was fun for the immigrant audiences because they had to struggle so much with language. The incessant violence had a subtler attraction. The knock-about humor, to be sure, was a release of anger at bosses, spouses, annoying neighbors, and others. But it also provided audience members an emotional outlet for

Sheet music for "Long Live the Land of the Free." *Source: Courtesy the Archives of the YIVO Institute for Jewish Research, New York.*

their anxieties. The immigrants had a great need, a hunger to succeed. After all, their entire identity was at stake. They had abandoned their homes, in many cases their families, and in some cases the rituals and beliefs of their religious heritage. They had gambled all in the belief that the Promised Land would provide them with a good life. Failure was acceptable in the Old World but not the New. This anxiety about success was released as audiences enjoyed the slapstick physical violence on the vaudeville stage. It was only as the children of immigrants grew up and became embarrassed by the ethnic stereotypes and knockabout humor that it ended in the 1920s.

Vaudeville also allowed immigrant audiences a crucial psychological way to escape. That escape came, of course, from the entertainment; but more crucially, in the rough, ethnic humor of vaudeville and its naughtier cousin, burlesque, audiences could laugh at themselves and their community's foibles and at the urban culture in which they were trying to survive.

Vaudeville shows varied, but a typical short one had five acts; the longer, two-hour shows had as many as eight or nine acts. Vaudeville shows opened with a "dumb act," one in which no language was used. The act might be acrobats or a trick dog or cyclists. Because vaudeville was aimed at everyone, the "dumb acts" were particularly good for those whose English wasn't yet advanced. More practically, the silent acts opened the show because in that way, latecomers into the theater wouldn't disrupt any dialogue on stage. The second act would be a musical number or bit of comedy performed in front of the curtain to allow the setting up of scenery. The headliner, the principal star, finished the first half of the show. The last act was very loud, deliberately aimed at letting the audience hear over the sounds of anyone leaving.

Shows were produced from early in the morning until late into the evening.

There were other escapes, other refuges as well. Some of those escapes—the Yiddish theater, newspapers, and literature—deserve their own story.

The legendary Jacob Adler as Shylock in *The Merchant of Venice. Source: Photo by Marianne Barcellona, courtesy of Time Life Pictures/Getty Images.*

THIRTEEN

YIDDISH THEATER

⤜⤛

T HE RELIGIOUS community had its synagogues. The radicals had their rallies
and their cafés. There were associations and all sorts of places to seek out
friends. But as a community meeting place on the Lower East Side, no other
location could match the Yiddish theater.

Audiences wailed during the sad scenes of the deeply emotional plays they
loved, grew nostalgic as the inevitably warmhearted portraits of Yiddishe mamas
unfolded on the stage, marveled at the props (called "handoffs" by the actors), wondered if they could find an English translation of that great Yiddish play *King Lear,*
and worshiped the acting gods and goddesses whose glossy pictures were displayed
on the playboards outside the theaters. The *patrioten,* rabid fans who followed individual performers, gathered together to applaud whatever the object of their adora-
tion might do. The plays were operatic renditions of classic biblical tales, comedies
about the tribulations of immigrant life, and tear-inducing melodramas about parents and children in the Old World and the New.

The early Yiddish theaters themselves were not the golden palaces of Broadway. Plays were often presented in auditoriums, and the raucous nature of East Side
life was reflected in the theatrical experience, which included noisy peddlers and
audience members unwrapping their snacks and drinks—typically apples, candy,
peanuts, and soda—with great urgency so that they didn't let the stage performance
interfere with their desire to eat. They enjoyed talking to each other. Crying babies

were not hushed. There were constant calls of "Sha!" or "Shut up!" from other patrons trying to hear the performance. But whatever struggles they might have had in hearing a performance, audiences wanted it to go on forever.

The shows characteristically lasted a long while and often would not end until midnight. Audiences might interrupt the performance, wanting a beloved song to be sung again. The playwright associated with one acting troupe would often disparage a rival troupe in clever wordplay. Audiences especially liked poetic couplets that did this. Villains would be booed. Handsome actors would be met with a wave of sighs. Actors were both distant and close. They were separate from ordinary folk but part of them. An actor might, for example, invite the entire audience to his upcoming wedding or plaintively reveal the deteriorating status of his marriage.

To the Yiddish-speaking immigrants, untutored in the ways of theatrical etiquette, unaware of the opulence of Broadway or even some vaudeville theaters, the experience of attending a play was deeply emotionally satisfying. Their lives were dreary. The days were long and scarred by a constant struggle to survive. The theater provided a great escape. It was the immigrant dream factory. The audience could cry and laugh at the same time. There, in the dark, they could look on stage and see brave Jewish heroes. They could, by projection, be the actors or the heroes themselves. They could return to the ancient days of glory with the biblical sages and kings, fighters and prophets or the simple family life in a shtetl. For a while, they could be leading not their own lives but the lives of the great. And those lives were delivered in an extraordinary brew of songs, dance, music, melodrama, and humor. But their theatrical ignorance could also lead them astray. At least one reporter noted that after a Shakespearean play that the audience particularly enjoyed, calls rang out for "Author! Author!"

THE DEVELOPMENT OF YIDDISH THEATER

Beloved as it was, Yiddish theater was a relatively new phenomenon in Jewish life. The Enlightenment was slow to come to Eastern Europe, where music was the only real entertainment, and religious authorities were anxious to keep out what they saw as the undermining effects of modernity. But as Jews moved into cities and yearned for secular studies and a release from Orthodox strictures, they wanted entertainment that reflected those attitudes.

Always religiously mindful not to use imagery that might represent God, Jewish communities' embrace of music meant that as their tentative experimentation with plays began, it started with minstrels. The *Broder Zinger,* from Brody, began this tradition and traveled across Eastern Europe. As troupes of minstrels increased, inevitably some of the singers began to talk to their audiences, to wear costumes and makeup, to use props, and to seek a dramatic structure to their presentations.

In 1876, Abraham Goldfaden, a Russian poet whose words had frequently been set to music, was in Jassy, Romania, at the Green Tree, a wine cellar. The owners offered him money for a public performance of some of his songs after one of his songs, written by Israel Grodner, one of the Broder singers, became particularly popular.

Goldfaden expanded the idea, adding a dramatic structure to the songs. Much of the dialogue was improvised, but the general idea of the scene was explained to the performers. Yiddish theatrical history was made on October 5 and 9, 1876, when this "musical" was performed. Its success led Goldfaden to take his troupe touring in Eastern Europe.

He began writing plays, including in 1877 the successful *Shmendrik,* a comedy whose title character's name was the Yiddish word for a nice but naïve person. In the 1880s, Goldfaden sought to expand his repertoire beyond satirical humor. In 1883, the Russian government forbade the performance of Yiddish plays, and so the various troupes scattered, including to such places as New York. Goldfaden went to New York but was overwhelmed by the enormous number of new troupes, went back to Europe, and then returned to New York in 1903, where his plays were mocked as simplistic and without literary merit. Only a subsidy provided by Yiddish actors enabled him to survive. His final play was *Ben Ami,* written after the death of Theodor Herzl, the founder of modern political Zionism. The play was an attempt to adapt George Eliot's novel *Daniel Deronda,* which supported Jewish nationalism. It finally made its debut in New York on December 25, 1907. Goldfaden attended then and for the following four evenings. On the fifth evening, he fell ill and died. Seventy-five thousand people attended the funeral of "the Jewish Shakespeare," the father of the Yiddish theater, a man unknown in the Gentile world and revered in the Jew-ish one.

Yiddish theater had begun in New York on August 12, 1882, on East Fourth Street with a production of Goldfaden's play *The Sorceress.* Joseph Lateiner was responsible, with his partner, Sophia Karp, for the Grand Theater, the first building

BEHIND THE SCENES
OF THE EARLY YIDDISH THEATER

Life for Yiddish actors in Eastern Europe was very difficult. The actor David Kessler provided a vivid account of the acting life there in his unpublished memoir, as translated in Irving Howe and Kenneth Libo's book *How We Lived:*

> Our theater always was some rented loft that was standing vacant at the time. Our stage consisted of some boards which we had banged together, with a sheet of some sort serving as our curtain. Without any food, we used to drag ourselves around, performing, encouraging one another, arguing, quarreling, and complaining. The poverty of our troupe was so acute that we simply did not have any clothes we could use in public. Costumes and theatrical clothes were out of the question. I had only one costume. Occasionally we would run across some good-hearted enthusiast of the Yiddish theater, who would give us some sort of support. For instance, a certain wealthy tie manufacturer took us into his home, supplied us with all the necessities, and even lent us a few hundred rubles. In another place we all barged in on an uncle of mine. But if there was no such opportunity, then we would go hungry.

in New York specifically constructed to house a Yiddish theater. By 1900, there were three Yiddish theaters on the Bowery with eighty actors performing the works of a dozen playwrights. Two of the most popular were Moshe Hurwitz (Morris Horowitz) and Lateiner. These playwrights were, to put it delicately, not universally admired. One critic said Hurwitz's efforts were "full of historical plunder." Hutchins Hapgood, the sympathetic Gentile observer of Lower East Side life, noted that Lateiner wrote one hundred plays, "no one of which has form or ideas." The

The Grand Theater. *Source: Courtesy of Brown Brothers.*

writer Ronald Sanders later suggested that these playwrights "together brought Yiddish theater to a new low." One writer noted that Lateiner's technique was "to take a foreign play, squeeze every drop of juice out of it, change the Gentile names to Jewish ones, slap on manly beards and *peyes* [sidelocks] and let them parade across the stage as Jews."

The inferior melodramas they produced may partially be excused by the fact that they had to write quickly, for two reasons. First, frequently a play only had three or four performances. Plays that ran for more than a dozen times were rare. And second, playwrights only got between $25 and $85 for the theatrical rights to their work, so to make a living, they had to turn out plays very quickly. The required speed adversely affected the quality of these early efforts.

Yiddish theater survived because its audience was enthralled by the very existence of performances on stage and by the great actors.

YIDDISH ACTORS

Boris Thomashefsky was a master of the melodrama. Although youthful and overweight, with a head topped by curly black hair, the young women of the ghetto thought him extraordinarily attractive. Thomashefsky, who liked to refer to himself as "America's Darling," reciprocated the admiration. He was famed far and wide for his unflinching attempts to seduce any young woman he encountered.

Thomashefsky had immigrated to New York at age twelve in 1881. He began singing in the Henry Street Synagogue and worked in a sweatshop making cigarettes. Other workers began singing songs they recalled from the Yiddish theater in Europe. Immediately, the young singer decided that such theater should be brought here.

One of those coworkers had brothers associated with the theater in the Old Country. The brothers wished to come to America. So the precociously charismatic Thomashefsky convinced a tavern owner to pay for the steamship tickets. When the brothers, along with four other actors, arrived in New York, the tavern owner rented a hall and put on Goldfaden's operetta *Koldunya*.

But the play had its problems. Many uptown Jews did not want the coarse sounds of Yiddish put in the service of theater. The female lead of the play was even bribed to claim she had a sore throat and could not perform. This potential disaster did not stop Thomashefsky. With the help of his father, he simply put on a dress, padding, and a wig and performed her role. The audience gave him a standing ovation.

Boris Thomashefsky was thirteen.

He soon founded a touring troupe and became beloved throughout the Yiddish theatrical world. One theatrical person recalled a Thomashefsky performance:

He had a vibrating, crackling voice, somewhere between baritone and tenor. . . .
No matter if the scene was laid in the hot sandy desert or the Halls of the Inquisition, Thomashefsky always managed to get in a song about Mama. . . .

In the early days he often appeared on horseback, naked to the waist, with his legs in golden tights. . . . The theatre was drafty and Thomashefsky suffered from continual colds.

Michael Tilson Thomas, the acclaimed conductor and composer, and currently the music director of the San Francisco Symphony, is Boris Thomashefsky's grandson.

Jacob P. Adler, founder of a renowned acting family (Celia, Stella, and Luther Adler were his children), was Thomashefsky's principal rival for the affections of the Yiddish audience. Adler had been part of Goldfaden's traveling troupe.

Adler was in many ways a more serious actor, certainly more accomplished. His voice was thin, and he didn't have a good ear for music. His personality and this defect were crucial for the development of Yiddish theater, however, because the combination made him seek to turn away from the musical operetta and the melodrama. He eventually became most famous for his portrayal of Shylock in *The Merchant of Venice*.

Like Thomashefsky, Adler enjoyed the company of adoring women. Two of his wives had left their husbands to marry him, but that sacrifice failed to keep him faithful to either one.

David Kessler also began as part of Goldfaden's troupe. He was known for his rough-and-tumble roles and for his method of insulting actors who did not perform the way he wanted them to act. He would, along with Adler, play a crucial role in transforming the nature of Yiddish theater.

Men were not the only beloved Yiddish performers. Jacob Adler's third wife, Sarah, and Boris Thomashefsky's wife, Bessie, were very popular. Among the early women performers, though, Bertha Kalisch was the most accomplished. She had arrived in the United States in 1896, age twenty-four, with years of theatrical experience under her belt.

By 1903, she was ready to shock the Yiddish theater. She performed in the title role in the Yiddish version of *Hamlet*. She was not the first Jewish woman to appear in the role; Sarah Bernhardt had done so the year before in London. But Yiddish audiences were not British ones. They were unfamiliar with theatrical history. Kalisch's experiment paid off. Critics and audiences loved it.

Because the stars ruled the Yiddish theater, the other actors in the company were frequently paid very low wages. Seeking redress, some formed the Hebrew

David Kessler. *Source: Courtesy of the Museum of the City of New York, Theatre Collection.*

Bertha Kalisch in *The Lights from St. Agnes. Source: Courtesy of the Museum of the City of New York, Theatre Collection.*

Actors Union, the first actors' union in the United States, in 1899. Actors were not allowed to join the union automatically. There was a rule, for example, that actors had to perform first beyond New York City. Still, by 1925, there were about three hundred members of the union.

THE YIDDISH THEATER GETS REAL

Jacob Adler's performance as Shylock proved that Yiddish actors could perform serious works and be well received by the audience. He began to look for serious plays, the very sort of plays that some members of the Yiddish intelligentsia had

A placard announcing the performance of the famous Boris Thomashefsky in the title role in *Hamlet*, 1901. *Source: The Dorot Jewish Division, New York Public Library, Astor, Lenox, and Tilden Foundations.*

been calling for to take the place of the light operettas they didn't much like. Those plays, which they derided as *shund,* or trash, were characterized by ridiculous coincidences and stock situations—the favorite one of which was a pregnant daughter. These intellectuals sought to find a playwright who would be their Jewish version of Ibsen, Strindberg, or Shaw.

Adler's search and the quest by Yiddish intellectuals would be ended when Adler found Jacob Gordin.

Gordin was in his late thirties when he came to America and soon became a journalist. Although he had never even seen a Yiddish production and didn't know much about the theater, he knew he wanted to try to write a play. A comic in Adler's acting troupe read one of Gordin's Russian-language pieces and mentioned it to Adler. The great actor and his comic met Gordin in a café. Adler told him that the plays available for Yiddish actors were not serious enough. They didn't deal with real life; what was needed was dramatic works with real artistic sensibilities.

For his part, Gordin was pleasantly surprised upon meeting the actor:

I was curious to meet a Yiddish actor. . . . I thought that as soon as I told him I wanted to write a play, he would start emoting: wipe his nose on his sleeve, jump on a chair, and recite one of the popular tunes of the day. . . . Imagine my surprise on meeting gentlemen with silk hats and handkerchiefs who talked intelligently. In their eyes I even detected a spark of talent. But if Yiddish actors are like other actors, why shouldn't Yiddish theatre be like all other theatres? At my first visit to the Yiddish theatre [which had taken place previously], everything I saw was far removed from Jewish life: vulgar, false, immoral.

The man who would be a new force in Yiddish theater was ready to get to work. Adler agreed to have Gordin write a play. In 1891, Gordin finished his play *Siberia*, and it was produced on stage in November of that year. The story, meant to be a heart tugger but grounded in real life, was about a young Jew sentenced to Siberia who escapes, takes another name, and acquires wealth, only to be turned in to the police by a business competitor.

There were some songs and dances, but on opening night, the audience did not appreciate this story set in the present day, not the glorious, infamous, or beloved past, and filled with realistic rather than fabulous images. According to a later playwright, Adler was so disturbed at the audience that just before the third act, he went out on stage to berate the crowd: "I am ashamed of you because you do not appreciate this masterpiece. . . . If you understood how great this play is, you wouldn't laugh." Adler began crying. The audience, seeing the great Adler in tears, burst into applause.

Gordin became a major Yiddish playwright. He wrote almost sixty plays. He was widely admired, but not by all. Most famously, Gordin entered into a dispute with Abraham Cahan, who would eventually become the powerhouse editor of the

Jewish Daily Forward. At the time of the dispute, which started in 1895, Cahan was a journalist and socialist activist in the labor movement.

The feud began with Gordin's play *The Russian Jew in America.* In the play, Gordin mercilessly attacked corrupt American life as represented by a variety of unsavory characters. Huzdak, a Jewish labor leader, was one of the characters. Huzdak was always willing to sacrifice any principles for material gains for the union.

"What do I need brains for when I've got a Constitution?" was a refrain he uttered throughout the play.

When Cahan attended the performance, he was outraged that a labor leader would be presented in such a way. As Huzdak uttered his famous phrase for the first time, Cahan screamed out in Russian that such a claim was a lie.

The feud continued in 1902 when Cahan told an actor backstage that Gordin's dialogue was not realistic; that was a true insult for the founder of Yiddish realism.

Gordin, who was by now famous for appearing onstage between the acts of his plays to denounce his critics, could take it no more. Cahan was subjected to such a public attack. Cahan vowed he would never again see a Gordin play.

The fierceness of the public disputes, an extension of the Lower East Side's passion for political and cultural arguments, provided the sort of gossip that audiences loved. They could take sides, watch a good fight, and enjoy themselves at a new level when they went to a performance.

Following Gordin, Leon Kobrin, the man who told the tale of Adler's weepy support of Gordin, was the other great realist of the era. He brought realistic plays close to the immigrant home in such efforts as *The East Side Ghetto; Minna, or the Ruined Family from Downtown;* and *Sonia from East Broadway.*

THEATERS

There were four principal Yiddish theaters in the Bowery area at the turn of the twentieth century. They had come a long way from the beginnings of Yiddish theater in small halls or auditoriums and now collectively provided eleven hundred performances a year for two million customers.

The theaters were the Thalia, with its three thousand seats and its reputation for high quality and more literary plays; the Grand, with Jacob Adler as the manager; the Windsor, which opened in 1893 and had thirty-five hundred seats, making it the largest of the Yiddish theaters; and the People's, which Thomashefsky leased. The People's, arguably, had the longest-running plays. *Dos Pintele Yid* ("The Jewish Spark") was performed in 1907 and lasted throughout the season. Tens of thousands of immigrants saw the play.

These theaters survived by attracting audiences for specific reasons. Theater parties were popular, but hosting them meant that theaters had to offer a lot of different plays. They solved the problem by developing a repertoire and the company learned all the plays at the same time so that in any given week, various plays from that repertoire would be performed.

It was particularly difficult to attract audiences on the first four nights of the week. Theaters developed the idea of benefits. One of the hundreds of Jewish organizations or associations would get all the tickets for a performance at a discount of sometimes up to 75 percent off the regular price. The organization would then charge its members full price. The theater filled what would be an otherwise near-empty performance, and the organization raised funds.

The benefit audiences were particularly attracted to lighter fare. The actors didn't always appreciate the benefit performances. Any Yiddish production had its share of audience chatter and movement, but at a benefit audience, members were often friends. Theater managers went crazy trying to get them to be quiet so that the show could go on. The actors had to react by improvising unimportant lines and not allowing the principal actor to appear until there was some semblance of quiet.

The weekends were reserved for the successful current play, and the full price of anywhere between a quarter and a dollar was charged. In 1902, the average worker earned $10 a week, so attending the theater several times a week was an enormous economic sacrifice, one that Lower East Siders were glad to make because the theater contributed so much to making the rest of their lives bearable.

THE POSTIMMIGRANT GENERATION

The Yiddish theater in New York thrived during the First World War. More money was spent, and responding to the times, the theaters presented lavish spectacles instead of realistic plays. This prosperity in turn led to a full-scale relocation of the theatrical district from the Bowery to Second Avenue between Houston and Fourteenth Streets. The movement to Second Avenue had actually started much earlier; the first Yiddish theater there, the Second Avenue Theater, had already opened in 1911, and the National Theater, a $1 million structure specifically constructed for Thomashefsky had been built in 1912. Additional theaters were built on Second Avenue through the mid-1920s.

But the end of the First World War in 1918 marks turning point in the history of the Yiddish theater in America. The resurgence of popularity in the 1920s and early 1930s, that Golden Age of Second Avenue, was a watershed in the history of the theater itself but not truly part of immigrant history. For by then, the immigrants had mostly moved out of the Lower East Side. They had achieved some economic security and developed a very different aesthetic sensibility, considerably more refined than the original immigrant sensibility. The immigrants' children had gone to college and knew much more about the American cultural world than their parents. And the world had itself changed radically because of the war. Russia had had its revolution, antiradical feelings had burst forth in postwar America, and much else was very different from the days before the war.

There were just under twenty Yiddish theaters in New York in 1918, including in Brooklyn. Younger actors emerged, people like Jacob Ben Ami, Maurice Schwartz, and Paul Muni (Muni Weisenfreund), who were more focused than their predecessors on acting skills and serious dramatic performances. There were also stars like Joseph Buloff and Molly Picon and Menashe Skulnik who survived into the late 1930s.

Molly Picon was "the sweetheart of Second Avenue." Her comic songs and dances and the assertive, winning characters she played were especially beloved in New York by the second generation of Jews. Picon had grown up in Philadelphia and first appeared on stage at age six. She determined to be a vaudeville star. In 1919, at age twenty-one, she was in Boston without work and in need of some cab fare to get home. Picon wandered into a Yiddish theater and met Jacob Kalich, the manager. They soon fell in love and married. Kalich took Picon to Europe so that her Yiddish could improve. By 1923, she was back in the United States enjoying enormous success.

These were great years for the Yiddish theater, but they reflected the last bright flickering lights of a time when Yiddish had dominated American Jewish life. The stars slowly went out. Joseph Gordin had died in 1909, Adler in 1926. Thomashefsky lived until 1939 but he was just past seventy when he died, hardly able to perform at the level that he had as a young man.

The popular Molly Picon in an appearance at the
Second Avenue Theater. *Source: Photograph by
Rappoport Studios. Courtesy of the Museum of the City
of New York, Theatre Collection.*

Within a generation or two, American Jews had by and large lost their ability to
speak Yiddish. By the late 1930s, only seven thousand people a year were attending
a Yiddish theatrical performance anywhere in the United States. English had
become the language of American Jews. The Holocaust would destroy the heart
of the Yiddish-speaking world, so that there weren't to be any new immigrants or
audiences. Yiddish theater would never fully die, but the immigrant generation
would have been shocked at how rapidly it declined.

Its tradition lives today in the Folksbiene Yiddish Theatre. The Folksbiene
("the People's Stage") was a theater company that began in 1915 operating under

the aegis of the Workmen's Circle. It sought to present plays that were socially conscious. Today, it is the last surviving Yiddish theatrical company.

The dominance of Yiddish in the immigrant generation was not reflected only in the theater but also in the wide range of Yiddish-language newspapers available for the immigrants, who yearned for news, laughter, advice, and escape.

A newsboy selling the *Forward. Source: Courtesy of Brown Brothers.*

FOURTEEN

YIDDISH JOURNALISM

꘎꘎꘎

L IKE THE Yiddish theater and the landsmanshaften, the Yiddish press was as much
a part of the daily lives of the Lower East Side Jewish immigrants as their
loving, noisy, large, annoying family and their accursed work. Used to
strong family bonds from Eastern Europe, the Jewish immigrants sought ways to
mimic it in their strange new land.

All the Yiddish culture they embraced was meant to reflect Yiddishkeit, Jewishness—a particular culture united by language, an emotional attachment to the Jewish people not exclusively through religion but as part of a group that had pursued a
particular way of life.

Yiddish had its struggles. The early Jewish socialists didn't like it because it
focused on the particularity of a people rather than on the universality of the class
struggle. Zionists didn't like it because it was the language of exile.

But its very particularity and its exilic origins gave Yiddish its power. It was a
language of marginality. Its writers couldn't overly adapt European modernism
without diluting Yiddish and the folk culture it represented—that is, without
destroying the Jews' very identity. Of course, that fact worked in the opposite way
as well. By being unable to adapt modern cultural influences, the Yiddish intellectuals were in danger of remaining frozen in time. Yiddishkeit was the symbol of having one foot in the Jewish world and the other foot in the modern world. As a
language, it was the perfect symbol for being Jewish.

It was common for Jewish families to read several Yiddish dailies, to argue with their friends over a paper's contents or its unspeakable lack of good taste or its deplorable critical judgments.

One hundred different Jewish newspapers were produced between 1885 and 1900. The Yiddish papers were filled with ideas, but they also made a sport of mocking each other. If one Yiddish paper praised a play, that was enough for its rivals to pan it. The political and religious disputes were fierce.

People generally bought their newspapers from newsboys who would gather outside a synagogue or a workplace or wherever large crowds would pass when the boys left school and on Sunday mornings. The newsboys developed a keen sense of marketing. They were not above yelling "Extra!" when the news was quite ordinary. Since so many of the Jews on the Lower East Side hated Russia, the boys would look for any story that might put Russia in a negative light and scream about that story.

Not everyone who bought a Yiddish paper did so exclusively for its news or literary value. Because there were no paper bags yet available, peddlers on the Lower East Side would wrap their herring or their vegetables in a page of one of the Yiddish newspapers.

Of all the Yiddish newspapers, one stands out: the *Jewish Daily Forward*.

THE *JEWISH DAILY FORWARD*

For dedicated socialists and ordinary workers and their families who wished to understand and adapt to their new homeland, there was no substitute for the largest and most influential of the Yiddish newspapers, the *Jewish Daily Forward*. It was their Bible, the mirror that was held up to their lives and then reflected in plain Yiddish for all the world to see. In a society without television or the Internet, the *Forward* became the principal connection between the masses of Jews and the confusing outside world of America.

The *Forward* began in 1897 when a group of socialists split from the Socialist Labor Party and became determined to start a paper to reflect what they considered their practical yet noble social concerns. They met in Valhalla Hall and gave their money, pocket watches, jewelry, and whatever else of value they had to make their journalistic dreams come true. The *Forvets*, the *Jewish Daily Forward*, was born. Its first issue, priced at 1 cent, was published on April 22 of that year.

The great Abraham ("Abe") Cahan, founding editor of the *Jewish Daily Forward. Source: Courtesy of* Forward.

ABE CAHAN

Abraham Cahan, the founding editor, was a professional journalist as much as a professional socialist. With a shock of curly hair atop his head, his bushy moustache, and round glasses shielding determined eyes, he wanted a paper that reported the news. He didn't want a party organ, one that filtered the Lower East Side's reality through a socialist lens or reprinted tracts or reported the minutes of some endless debate. That integrity led to many arguments, and he ultimately quit the paper. But as it turned out, the paper needed him, and he had the vision to see what the *Forvets* might become. He rejoined the paper in 1902.

He immediately made changes based on his experience writing for English-language papers during his four-year absence. Suddenly there were large headlines. This was, after all, the era of William Randolph Hearst's sensationalistic newspapers.

Hearst ran for mayor of New York City and, in 1906, governor of the state. In both elections, he carried the Jews on the Lower East Side. Hearst actively sought their vote; his own papers included Yiddish sections. He made sure to tell the immigrant Jews that he shared their hostility toward Tammany Hall, and of course that he hated the tsar in Russia. So carried away was Hearst with winning the vote that he actually started a Yiddish newspaper—as sensationalistic as his English-language papers—but it lasted only a few weeks.

Cahan also followed the lead of the sensationalist papers in capturing a realistic Yiddish in the paper, the Yiddish that was spoken on the streets, not in literary salons—a dialect his critics called "Potato Yiddish," the language of peasants. When Cahan was uncertain about the prose he was about to publish, he was famous for trying it out on the elevator operator. If the operator understood it, Cahan reasoned, so would ordinary readers. Cahan was a tough, demanding boss.

Cahan had keen literary instincts, but he believed that his literary insights were so valuable that they shouldn't be ignored. He gave space to many writers who would become famous, including, starting in the mid-1930s, a new immigrant named Isaac Bashevis Singer, who would go on to win the Nobel Prize for literature. Singer was not impressed by Cahan's critical eye and later characterized the editor as "dictatorial."

Cahan had escaped from Vilna when he was twenty-two, already a determined revolutionary. After studying a grammar book to learn English, his facility with the language was so amazing that he taught English in a public school for a dozen years. Soon his zeal and writing skills led to his copublishing a socialist newspaper, and that led to his efforts to found the *Forward*.

Cahan would gain his greatest national fame with the publication of *The Rise of David Levinsky*—a novel he wrote in English—in 1917. Born in 1860—the same year as Theodor Herzl—Cahan lived until 1951 and so witnessed the ongoing assimilation of the children and grandchildren of his readers and the extraordinary decline of Yiddish.

Abe Cahan's sympathy for his ordinary readers was crucial to the *Forward*'s success. It certainly had a political tinge; no one ever doubted that its ideology was socialistic. He railed against the tenements as tinderboxes and complained about landlords and sweatshops. He helped unions in every way. When it eventually started a radio station, the paper selected WEVD as the station's call letters, in honor of Eugene V. Debs, who had been imprisoned on a charge of contempt of court in a labor dispute (the famous Pullman Strike in Chicago) and later for speaking out against America's participation in World War I. Debs eventually ran five times for president on the Socialist Party ticket.

LEARNING TO LIVE IN AMERICA

But the *Forward,* unlike other strict socialist publications, didn't mock religion. It understood the deepest yearnings of its readers. It saw itself as being not above the lives of its readers but on their level. Cahan tried to explain baseball and employed a diagram of the Polo Grounds, home of the New York Giants. He tried to explain thermometers and hats. He offered advice on how to can peaches. He emphasized the value of citizenship and gave guidance on how to become citizens and participate more fully in American life.

He wrote about Jewish subjects and tried to help his readers understand the mores of the New World. For example, it was difficult for the immigrants to accept the use of a handkerchief and even more difficult to grasp the very notion of good manners. In the crowded streets, people frequently bumped into each other, and that inevitably led to much anger and raised voices, sometimes accompanied by curses of one sort or another.

Cahan tried to teach his readers how to say, "Excuse me," and to answer, "I'm sorry," as an appropriate response to such an apology. The immigrants, for their part, were dumbfounded that a simple expression of a few words should serve to rid them of the anger. And Cahan tried to give them culture. He personally translated *Madame Bovary* into Yiddish so that the plumbers and factory workers who read his paper could enjoy Flaubert's masterpiece.

The *Forward* also served a crucial psychological role for the workers who read it. Their dire lives were marked by struggle and frequently by self-doubt and concerns that their families and neighbors saw them as failures. The *Forward* gave them pride in themselves. They were, in its pages, struggling as a community. Theirs was not a lonely crowd.

Cahan could, in his dramatic, direct way, give voice to his readers' deepest passions. The day after the Triangle Fire, for example, the *Forward* ran the headline "Our Daughters in Ashes." Such a horrific image, so intimately tied to the Jewish emphasis on family, helped Jewish readers get their unbounded sorrow out in the open and eventually under control.

And Cahan kept track of trends in the community. In 1903, he noted the existence of a brand-new Yiddish word, *oysesn,* "outside eating," conveying the meaning

Home of the *Jewish Daily Forward. Source: Courtesy of Brown Brothers.*

that the family ate not in its own home or that of a relative or friend but outside the home, in a real restaurant. No one ever did that in Russia, and Cahan was amazed at how quickly Lower East Siders adapted to this novel experience.

Cahan was also quick to note the attractions of escaping from the city to the relatively open land in upstate New York; the *Forward* ran its first ad for a Catskills resort in 1902. There were then three such resorts catering to Jews seeking some respite from the crowds and the noise and the grime. It would still take several decades for the major resorts to be built, but the immigrant Jews were learning, slowly, how to incorporate the idea of vacation into their lives.

The *Forward*'s home, starting in 1908, was an imposing building at 175 East Broadway. The structure was ten stories high, with a clock above the paper's name. Above the entrance to the building were engravings of four socialist leaders, including Karl Marx. It eventually had the largest Yiddish neon sign ever. The building, beyond the newspaper, was a center for Yiddish culture and socialist thought. Leon Trotsky debated there. The *Folksbiene* theater group performed there for almost twenty years. Without it, the Socialist Party and various Jewish unions would have had a much tougher time organizing.

When Cahan had returned to edit the paper in 1902, it had six thousand subscribers; by the 1920s, it had a quarter of a million.

THE BINTEL BRIEF

The *Forward* had many popular writers. B. Kovner was one of the favorites. (The author's real name was Jacob Adler, and since the actor with that name had already made it famous, Cahan bestowed a pen name on Adler, B. Kovner, "someone from Kovno," a city in Lithuania.) Kovner wrote a beloved humor column. He created several characters, the best known of which were Yente Telebende, a woman who could wield words as weapons, and Moyshe Kapoyer ("Moses Upside Down"), a man who marched to the beat of his own Yiddish drummer, a bit of an eccentric.

Without question, the most popular of all the paper's features was the letters column in which readers emptied their hearts onto paper and sought solace and advice.

Cahan had always liked having new sections. One day, an assistant came to him with a bunch of letters that didn't fit into any of the existing sections. Cahan decided to start a new section—titled *A Bintel Brief* ("a bunch or bundle of letters"). So eager were some people to write to the Bintel Brief and to see their words in print that they would hire someone else to write the letter for them. But however those letters were written, they filled the paper's office. Sometimes the editors had to correct some spelling or condense the expansive story of a wounded soul, but most ran unretouched.

The column began—with three letters and an introduction—on January 20, 1906, with Abe Cahan himself writing the responses for a while. Cahan used the column to help his perplexed readers make their way through the maze of American life. With his deep compassion for the masses of immigrants, he fully understood why they needed a forum to express their most private feelings and ask for guidance.

As he wrote in his memoirs, "People often need the opportunity to be able to pour out their heavy-laden hearts. Among our immigrant masses this need was very marked. Hundreds of thousands of people, torn from their homes and their dear ones, were lonely souls who thirsted for expression, who wanted to hear an opinion, who wanted advice in solving their weighty problems. The 'Bintel Brief' created just this opportunity for them."

The Bintel Brief did more than give advice and serve as a forum for self-expression. It provided literal help. Mothers found their children; one mother who had been separated from her infant child was reunited twenty years later by the Bintel Brief. It was a public forum for expressing outrage. One writer in 1906 protested against his boss for deducting 2 cents from wages owed a thirteen-year-old boy. The boy had come to work ten minutes late and only earned $2.50 a week.

The letters in the Bintel Brief were capsule biographies of all the types of people on the Lower East Side. Readers of the letters got caught up in a world of degrading poverty, aching hunger, guilt because no job could be found, young women driven by circumstances into a life of prostitution, horrifying illness, anguish at family members incapable of understanding each other, longing for a dead relative, anger at a husband who deserted, and all the other minute joys and heartaches that cumulatively stitched together an immigrant's life.

Even the simplest of family disputes could find its way to the Bintel Brief: "Is it a sin to use face powder? Shouldn't a girl look beautiful? My father does not want me to use face powder."

Because the *Forward* was a socialist paper, it got many letters from people on the left with problems, such as, "I am a Socialist and my boss is a fine man. I know he's a Capitalist but I like him. Am I doing something wrong?"

Here is a letter and a response from 1906:

Dear Editor,

I am a Russian revolutionist and a freethinker. Here in America I became acquainted with a girl who is also a freethinker. We decided to marry, but the problem is that she has Orthodox parents, and for their sake we must have a religious ceremony. If we refuse the ceremony we will be cut off from them forever. Her parents also want me to go to the synagogue with them before the wedding, and I don't know what to do. Therefore I ask you to advise me how to act.

Respectfully,

J.B.

The advice is that there are times when it pays to give in to old parents and not grieve them. It depends on the circumstances. When one can get along with kindness it is better not to break off relations with the parents.

And Cahan and his editors weren't afraid of bluntness, especially when it came to Old World superstitions:

> Dear Editor:
>
> I am a young man of twenty-five, and I recently met a fine girl. She has a flaw, however—a dimple in her chin. It is said that people who have this lose their first husband or wife. I love her very much. But I'm afraid to marry her lest I die because of the dimple.
>
> *The tragedy is not that the girl has a dimple in her chin but that some people have a screw loose in their heads.*

The *Jewish Daily Forward* had its critics. Orthodox readers were unhappy with what they saw as its sparseness of coverage of religious issues. Communists and anarchists didn't like its politics or what some saw as its watered-down socialism. In some way, the most fundamental of criticisms against Cahan was that he had made the *Forward* into an agent of assimilation. But he was simply responding to his readers. They voted with their subscriptions. His readers wanted to become Americans; he didn't impose that view on them.

OTHER YIDDISH NEWSPAPERS

As noted earlier, there were a large number of other Yiddish newspapers besides the *Jewish Daily Forward*, including the *Arbeiter Tseitung*, the newspaper of the Socialist Labor Party, and *Der Groisser Kundess* ("The Big Stick"), a humorous weekly. And there were additional papers aimed at Sephardic and German Jews.

DER TAG

Begun as a Zionist paper and one politically supporting the Democrats, *Der Tag* ("The Day") developed into a journal that was more literary and scholarly. It even had an English section to make language instruction easier for its readers. Sarah Bronstein Smith was many readers' favorite columnist. She wrote of domestic problems in emotionally moving melodramatic Yiddish.

DI YIDISHE TSAYTUNG

On March 1, 1870, the *Tsaytung* ("The Jewish Newspaper") published the first edition of the first Yiddish newspaper in America. The paper was, to put it mildly, not well received by the English-language Jewish press published uptown. The *Jewish Times* expressed a widely held opinion that the paper was "a weekly publication written in Jewish and German-Polish jargon, and its contents are as laughable as its language. It provides reading material entirely suited to the recently imported Russian Jews, and is a shining example of Middle Ages superstition and naiveté." Despite its content, much of which was adapted from European publications and politically loyal to Tammany Hall, the *Tsaytung*'s publisher knew before anyone else that such a paper would be needed. Due to its elevated price—6 cents—it lasted only seven years.

FREIE ARBEITER SHTIMME

David Edelstadt, an anarchist poet, founded the *Freie Arbeiter Shtimme* ("Free Worker's Voice") in 1890. Edelstadt was deliberately provocative, especially enjoying a frontal assault on Orthodox customs. He died young, at twenty-six in 1892, and his successor softened the ideological approach and opened the paper's pages to more literary works.

FREIHEIT

The *Freiheit* ("Freedom") was created by the American Communist Party in 1922, after the initial wave of immigrants and so not a genuine part of the Lower East Side story. It had the distinction of being the first communist newspaper in America. Moissye Olgin, the paper's first editor, was known for his acidic prose and his delight in attacking critics. He also had a sensitive literary eye. Many writers new to the country found they could experiment with prose more readily in the *Freiheit* than Abe Cahan would allow in the *Forward*. The paper was well received for a few years until it became clear that the editors had the same ideological positions as the Communist Party in Russia did, even when those positions were clearly at odds with the best interests of the Jewish people.

MORGEN ZHURNAL

The *Jewish Morning Journal* was the first Yiddish daily morning newspaper. It began on July 2, 1901. The *Journal* politically supported the Republican Party, was pro-Zionist, and was deliberately aimed at what it saw as a high class of Orthodox readers. Its Orthodoxy was hardly strict; the paper proudly supported efforts to help the immigrants adapt quickly to American life and in practice was far more secular than its announced ideology would indicate.

YIDDISHER TAGEBLATT

The *Yiddisher Tageblatt* ("Jewish Daily News"), founded in 1885, was the first Yiddish daily newspaper aimed at an Orthodox readership. The paper was historically important because its success proved that there was a readership for Yiddish papers of its kind. The immigrants, after all, had no tradition of reading newspapers; amazingly, at the time of the *Tageblatt*'s birth, there was not a single Yiddish newspaper in all of Europe. The paper was not only explicitly religious but also antisocialist. It later merged with the *Morning Journal*.

In 1917, around the height of the cumulative readership of the Yiddish press, the four most popular papers and their circulation were as follows:

Jewish Daily Forward, 148,560

Jewish Morning Journal, 87,322

Der Tag, 65,369

Jewish Daily News, 55,000

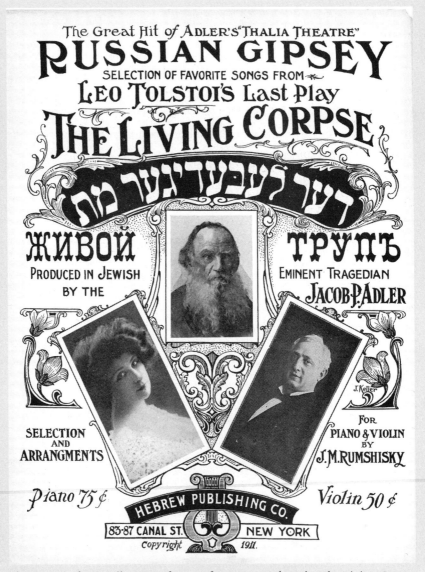

Sheet music for a collection of songs from Leo Tolstoy's *The Living Corpse*.
Source: Courtesy the Archives of the YIVO Institute for Jewish Research, New York.

FIFTEEN

YIDDISH LITERATURE

>><

YIDDISH LITERATURE had flowered in Eastern Europe in the late nineteenth and early twentieth centuries. Its unofficial origins went back to the Middle Ages, when Jewish minstrels sang romances they had translated from non-Jewish sources. Originally, Jewish literary minds focused on biblical and religious themes.

But by the nineteenth century, Eastern European Jews were being exposed to new intellectual and physical worlds. The Haskalah (Enlightenment) sought to make Jews familiar with the great Western culture they had mostly sealed themselves off from. While Jewish Enlightenment figures didn't much care for Yiddish, they wrote in it because they wanted people to understand what they had to say. The Hasidic movement had emphasized the Yiddish language and Jewish culture. Furthermore, the increasing pogroms and other attacks on Jews made it necessary for Jews to fight back in the only way they could. Deprived of weapons and political or economic power, they focused on pride in their own culture as a source of solidarity and emotional self-protection.

The new era produced three extraordinary prose masters whose fiction spoke directly to the Jewish people. Shalom Jacob Abramowitz took the pen name Mendele Mokher Sefarim (the name means "Mendel, the wandering bookseller"). Mendele was the first to use Yiddish for his passionate fiction; his literary world was marked by the close attachment he had to the people he wrote about but also his

Sholem Aleichem. *Source: Pictorial Parade/Hulton Archive/Getty Images.*

belief that they were being held back by religious customs and that the lives they led were hemmed in by those ancient traditions.

Sholem Aleichem was the most beloved of all the Yiddish writers. His humor, wisdom, warmth, sadness, and sharp eye combined to create characters completely recognizable to his audience. That the characters were also universal was proved a century later when the musical *Fiddler on the Roof* recounted the story of some of those characters.

I. L. Peretz was less interested in folk customs than the other writers and more inspired by the Russian prose masters. Like Dostoyevsky, Peretz focused on the psychological aspects of his characters.

Only Sholem Aleichem made it to the United States, and then only at the end of his life for a relatively brief time.

In the United States, there was at first not much cultural sophistication among the writers of Jewish literature. No prose writer was even able to approximate the extraordinary skills of the Jewish masters in Eastern Europe. The particular circumstances of the early immigrant experience contributed to this. Writers produced fiery political tracts and romances called *shundromanen* ("trash novels") that aimed at providing cheap emotional thrills for the masses.

But if Yiddish prose was stilted in the New World, a new Yiddish literature nevertheless did arise. Poetry, without much of a Jewish tradition in Eastern Europe, blossomed. It was poetry at odds with the passive Jewish voices in Eastern European literary circles.

POETS

Poetry, in which the pent-up feelings of the oppressed Jews could be given shape and life by language, and in which the highly personal, highly idiosyncratic demons could be set loose or the angels embraced, was popular on the Lower East Side. Poetry could be read quickly, and its compressed emotion perfectly suited the needs of its readers. The immigrants sought from their poetry what every reader sought from literature. They wanted to understand themselves and their lives more clearly. They wanted models of behavior. They wanted emotional rehearsals for dealing with problems that they would one day face or were facing then. They wanted guidelines about how to stop being a foreigner and become an American.

And they sought this poetry beyond the page. There was a tall man who roamed Hester Street offering to quote poems from Edgar Allan Poe for a dime; Shakespeare cost a quarter.

There were various schools of poetry in the Lower East Side's literary world. The first of these was known as the "sweatshop poets." The sweatshop poets, writing most productively in the final decade of the nineteenth century and the first decade of the twentieth, focused on the oppressive nature of their working lives and their desperate need to struggle against their condition. They wanted to foment some sort of revolution that would free the Jewish workers from the sweatshop system. This group of poets, all working in the same emotional and physical area, forged the first Yiddish poetry movement ever. And not only did they write about the sweatshop system, but most of them also worked in the sweatshops themselves.

Four major poets came out of the "sweatshop school": Joseph Bovshover, David Edelstadt, Morris Rosenfeld, and Morris Winchevsky. Edelstadt—the editor of the anarchist paper *Freie Arbeiter Shtimme*—died of tuberculosis, known on the East Side as "the sweatshop disease." Winchevsky was the only one of these poets who did not work in a sweatshop; he was a journalist who believed his poetry could make workers see not only why they had to work under such horrible conditions but also the radical solution to their problems.

Rosenfeld, the "Dante of the Sweatshops," was the most accomplished and most famous of these poets. His poem "I Am a Millionaire of Tears" was widely quoted. He was interested less in overthrowing capitalism and more in explaining the painful realities of sweatshop life to readers who didn't fully understand it. He finally left the sweatshops when in 1898 Leo Wiener, a language professor at Harvard, published an English translation of Rosenfeld's poetry under the title *Songs of the Ghetto*. Rosenfeld escaped the sweatshops by opening a candy store. He soon became a journalist, but he was unhappy with the low wages he got from the *Jewish Daily Forward*. He died penniless.

In his poem "In the Shop," Rosenfeld provided a vivid description:

> The sweatshop at midday—I will draw you a picture:
> A battlefield bloody; the conflict at rest,
> Around and about me the corpses are lying;
> The blood cries aloud from the earth's gory breast
> A moment . . . and hark! The loud signal is sounded,
> And dead rise again and renewed is the fight. . . .
> They struggle, these corpses; for strangers, for strangers!
> They struggle, they fall, and they sink into night.

In 1907, a younger group of poets issued a journal named *Di Yugnt* ("Youth"), and so they acquired the name *Di Yunge* ("the young ones"). They did not want their poetry to be constricted by political needs and sought inspiration instead from the larger world, especially its more beautiful aspects. They thought the sweatshop poets focused too much on the needs of an entire people and not enough on the needs of the individual. *Di Yunge* focused on aesthetics and the value of art, much as the Romantic poets had done a century earlier in England. The principal poets in this group were Mani Leib, H. Leivick, and Moshe Leib Halpern. There were, in addition to poets, some prose writers in *Di Yunge*. The most prominent of those were David Ignatoff and Isaac Raboy.

Mani Leib Brahinsky (Mani Leib's real name), one of the movement's founders, was a shoemaker and leatherworker. As he described his moment of self-discovery in his poem "I Am," Mani Leib realized that he was not a shoemaker who wrote poems but a poet who was a shoemaker.

Leivick was born Leivick Halper, but he changed his name because people confused him with Moshe Leib Halpern. Leivick was an ascetic. He believed that only by his personal experience with pain could he fully identify with his people and that the suffering provided him with a sort of redemption. He had escaped from a prison term in Siberia before arriving in New York. After leaving the sweatshops, he became a paperhanger. He became known for poems about the Jewish longing for the Messiah.

M. L. Halpern didn't like being considered part of any group. He wrote of his inability, though, to separate himself from a God he didn't believe in, the Jewish people he didn't feel part of, and himself, whom he struggled to understand.

By 1919, as the first generation of Lower East Side immigrants were moving out and as immigration was about to stop, another school of poetry emerged, the *Inzikhistn*, the "introspective" poets. The arc from the social (the sweatshop poets) to the personal (the young poets) reached its peak with the *Inzikhistn*, who believed that the constructs of meaning came only from within themselves, not the outer world. The "real" world mattered to them only insofar as it was reflected within them.

The *Inzikhistn* were poetic experimenters. They wrote in free verse. They didn't like the symbols, the lyrical excesses, or the emotional moods created by *Di Yunge*. The major poets in this movement were Jacob Glatstein, Aron Glantz-Leyeles, and N. B. Minkov.

NOVELISTS AND PROSE WRITERS

Yiddish fiction in America lagged behind poetry and developed as an art form only after the First World War, that is, after the era of the initial immigration. Sholem Asch, I. J. Singer, and Joseph Opatashu, among others, not only produced their work later but also seemed uneasy dealing with New World subjects. (The major exception to this generalization is I. J. Singer's novel *The Brothers Ashkenazi.*) Thus Yiddish fiction in America did not have the literary merit of Yiddish poetry.

It did have controversy, though, that took place many years after the immigrant experience. Sholem Asch was the most popular of the Yiddish novelists between the world wars. Artists, almost by nature, cross boundaries. Yiddish writers and their avid readers sometimes crossed ideological, political, and religious ones. Some were radicals or atheists. But whatever they felt—including disdain—toward Orthodox practices and the idea of a supernatural deity, they didn't flirt with Christianity. Asch seemed to do so. He wrote three novels with Christian content, the first of which, *The Nazarene,* was published—in English—in 1939. Abe Cahan was so incensed that a gifted writer whose work had been published in the *Forward* would publish such a work that he refused to have any further contact with Asch and, of course, adamantly refused to serialize the novel.

Asch, though intimately familiar with the Bible, including the Christian New Testament, vociferously argued against the charges, claiming that he simply wanted to show just how Jewish a life the early Christians led. More precisely, he was attempting to show that the religions were the same and so should be united. This was, of course, religious heresy. But the Yiddish literary world also interpreted his stance as abandoning the Jewish people culturally and never forgave him. In 1955, Asch moved to Israel. His son, Moe Asch, was the founder of the legendary Folkways Records, a company that recorded and preserved music from all the various American cultures and the archives and recordings of which are now the basis of the Smithsonian collection of American folk music.

Abe Cahan was the most successful immigrant Jewish writer in English. While between his jobs at the *Jewish Daily Forward,* Cahan went to work at an English-language newspaper, under the American novelist William Dean Howells. The American was an exponent of literary realism; he wanted to portray the gritty truth of American life for his readers. Howells became fascinated by Jewish immigrant life and asked Cahan to serve as his guide as he wandered through the crowded, boisterous streets of the Lower East Side. He told Cahan that the Yiddish world there needed someone to write about it.

Cahan, ever ambitious, determined to try his hand at such an effort. The result was his novella *Yekl: A Tale of the New York Ghetto,* published in 1896. Cahan told of a greenhorn anxious to rid himself of the old customs, including his old-fashioned, religious wife. The novella became the basis of Joan Micklin Silver's extraordinary

1975 film *Hester Street*. The ambivalence of the novella's hero toward the New World and the loss of much of what was valuable as it is sacrificed for material goods became Cahan's favorite themes.

In 1898, Cahan published *The Imported Bridegroom and Other Stories of the New York Ghetto*. The most famous of the volume's five stories is "A Ghetto Wedding," about Goldy and Nathan, both of whom work in sweatshops. Cahan drew a vivid picture of an Orthodox wedding and the redemptive power of love in a very tough world.

The best of Cahan's prose works, and the most famous, was his 1917 masterpiece *The Rise of David Levinsky*, a powerful tale of a poor young man who becomes a successful manufacturer in the garment industry. Despite his accumulation of enormous wealth, Levinsky finds himself dissatisfied, bereft of spiritual moorings, and unsure how the early part of his life even connected to the present. For someone whose journalism had helped so many immigrants become Americans, the dark uncertainty of the novel was a grim reminder of how difficult the immigrants found American life even when they seemed to surmount its initial difficulties.

As noted earlier, *The Melting Pot* was the most controversial play presented during the immigrant era. Produced in 1908, it was written by Israel Zangwill, a British Jew who had already made a name for himself as a chronicler of life in London's Jewish section. The play was dedicated to President Theodore Roosevelt, who thoroughly enjoyed it; so did Jane Addams. It makes a passionate plea for Jewish assimilation and argues that as all the various immigrant groups are tossed into the large pot that is America, the particularities of the various groups would disappear as they became Americans. David, the play's Jewish hero, is a violinist in love with Vera, a Gentile.

David concludes that in the new country, "Germans and Frenchmen, Irishmen and Englishmen, Jews and Russians—into the Crucible with you all! God is making the American." It was ahead of its time in arguing that in America, romantic love was more important than tradition.

However dubious the play's literary merits might have been, it is indisputable that Zangwill precisely dramatized the central question of immigrant life: should the new Jewish immigrants transplant their traditions from the Old World and continue them in the New? Should the immigrants surrender their Jewishness as easily as they shed their old clothes and adopt a thoroughly American identity? Or, as most wanted, should they try to find some way to be American without losing their Jewish identity and be Jewish without losing their American identity? These were issues that framed the thinking of American Jewish life then and have continued to do so ever since.

Novelists writing in English about the Lower East Side would flourish in the 1920s. But the vital and extraordinary flowering of American Yiddish culture—in the theater, press, and literature—turned out to be a shooting star in Jewish life. As Jews began to prosper, as they yearned to escape the sweatshops and the tenements, as their children, nimble in English and confident in outlook, began to succeed in American life, the world of the Lower East Side began to crumble. This happened at the same time as the opponents of further immigration triumphed. So the old immigrants were leaving, and there were few new ones to take their place.

Eddie Cantor. *Source: Courtesy of the Brian Gari Archives.*

SIXTEEN

THE END OF AN ERA

><><

THE COMPACT world of the Lower East Side lasted only a generation. The immigrants themselves wanted to escape the tenements and the sweatshops, and many did. Their children, less aware of the difficulties of their parents' lives, simply moved for the adventure of it or to go to college or to take jobs. Of course, some Jewish immigrants continued to live in the neighborhood, struggling financially, especially after the immigration restrictions of the 1920s.

Soon there were large numbers of Jews living in the brownstones along Prospect Park in Brooklyn, or as African Americans moved into Harlem, the Jews headed north into the Bronx or Queens or the Upper West Side on Central Park West or West End Avenue or maybe even to a residence on the exclusive Riverside Drive. All this was a precursor to their own children's migrations to New Jersey or Long Island—or Beverly Hills or Palm Beach.

The children of the immigrants also changed their names. They were hungry for all that was American, even if what they understood as truly American was filtered through an advertisement or a publicity agent. The children of the immigrants in that sense were great mimics; they learned to imitate what they thought of as really American. Of course, not all had such abilities or wanted them, but many in the second generation were determined to leave the past behind them and be reborn as fully American.

FAMOUS CHANGED NAMES

Many American Jews who later became famous changed their names either upon entering the country or sometime later. Here are the original names and professional names of some prominent American Jews, most of whom were not immigrants themselves.

Original Name	Occupation	Professional Name
Hyman Arluck	songwriter	Harold Arlen
Israel Baline	songwriter	Irving Berlin
Rosine Bernard	actress	Sarah Bernhardt
Nathan Birnbaum	comedian	George Burns
Fania Borach	entertainer	Fanny Brice
Ellen Naomi Cohen	singer	"Mama" Cass Elliott
Howard Cohen	sports announcer	Howard Cosell
Issur Danielovich Demsky	actor	Kirk Douglas
Albert Einstein	actor, director	Albert Brooks
Sophie Feldman	comedian	Totie Fields
Bernice Frankel	actress	Bea Arthur
Jacob Gershowitz	composer	George Gershwin
Edward Israel Iskowitz	performer	Eddie Cantor
Sonia Kalish	vaudeville performer	Sophie Tucker
Allen Stewart Konigsberg	comedian, director	Woody Allen
Benjamin Kubelsky	comedian	Jack Benny
Archibald Leach	actor	Cary Grant
Joseph Levitch	comedian, director	Jerry Lewis
Joan Molinsky	comedian	Joan Rivers
Bernard Schwartz	actor	Tony Curtis
Jerome Silberman	actor	Gene Wilder
Muni Weisenfreund	actor	Paul Muni
Asa Yoelson	singer	Al Jolson

RISING IN THE NEW WORLD

The children of the immigrants looked for success in a variety of places. The Jewish gangsters didn't want their children to enter the family business, so professional Jewish criminals became much rarer. Higher education had long been a dream of Jewish parents. After all, learning, like religion, was portable. The anti-Semites couldn't take away what the mind had learned or what the heart believed. In America—was it possible?—Jews were allowed, even encouraged, to get a college education. Many entered professional lives. Other Jews left the sweatshops to become small business owners.

DAVID SARNOFF

Some of the Jews from the Lower East Side became enormously successful and transformed American life. David Sarnoff was one of those people.

David Sarnoff was ambitious from the start. Four days after his family landed in New York, the nine-year-old had a job selling newspapers. Quick-witted and having to help support his family, Sarnoff realized that he could be more mobile than the other boys if he had a cart. He built one himself and soon was selling three hundred copies of the *Tageblatt* each day. On the Sabbath—his day off from work—he picked up another $1.50 by singing in a synagogue choir.

He dreamed of buying his own newsstand but could not afford the astronomical $200 needed to make the purchase.

One day, as Sarnoff returned to his home on Monroe Street, he encountered a mysterious woman he didn't recognize near the tenement doorway. She asked about his father; Abe Sarnoff had been a painter who had gone without food so that he could save enough money to bring his family from the Old Country. He was ill and now couldn't work. She asked if what she had heard was true, that David, now thirteen, supported the entire family. When David answered, the woman gave him an envelope containing the $200 he needed for the newsstand.

The newsstand was a success, and Sarnoff got his younger brothers to help take care of it while he got an additional job at the Commercial Cable Company. He had actually wanted a job as a newspaper reporter and had decided to ask about a job at the *New York Herald*, but by mistake, he had walked into the building next door—the Cable Company. By sheer luck, young David Sarnoff found himself at the very bottom of the radio industry, an industry that he would one day help shape and cause to prosper.

David Sarnoff as a young newsboy in 1887.
Source: © Bettmann/CORBIS.

Sarnoff's principal job was delivering telegraph dispatches, and he realized that it would help him immensely if he could learn the Morse Code. In 1906, he asked his employer to let him have the Jewish holy days off; instead, they fired him.

Sarnoff went to work as an office boy for the Marconi Wireless Telegraph Company—a job that would change his life. Sarnoff rose steadily in the company. By 1912, his job entailed sitting in a small radio studio at Wanamaker's Department Store, which had installed it as a curiosity to attract customers. Sarnoff sent and received messages between New York and Wanamaker's other store in Philadelphia.

And then came April 14, 1912.

Suddenly, Sarnoff received a faint signal. He determined that it came from the S.S. *Olympic,* a ship in the North Atlantic. The message was that the famous new ship, *Titanic,* had hit an iceberg and was sinking. Sarnoff radioed other ships in the area. He called newspapers, telling them of the story so they could get extra editions on the streets. Wanamaker's kept the store open through the night. Crowds gathered, waiting to hear news. The police had to barricade Sarnoff from the anxious crowd. President Taft ordered all radio stations in the United States to shut off so there would be no signal interference for David Sarnoff.

At 2:20 A.M., Sarnoff received the fateful message: the *Titanic* had sunk.

Sarnoff stayed in the radio studio for seventy-two hours, copying down the names of the survivors. Soon another list started accumulating—the list of those who had perished.

David Sarnoff had become an international hero. He was twenty-one years old. The boy from the Lower East Side, who would go on to oversee the dominance of radio and the emergence of television in American life, had found his way out of immigrant life.

But there were some Lower East Siders who did not become pioneers in broadcasting or accountants, lawyers, teachers, doctors, professors, or business owners. They went in a different direction.

ATHLETES

Many of the children of immigrants became ardent sports fans. At one point, a writer for the *Der Tag* ruefully observed, "The grandfather studies the Torah, the father the business section, the son the sports page."

Some of the children became athletes themselves.

Benny Leonard was the most famous of the Jewish boxers. Born Benjamin Leiner in 1896, Benny was a lightweight who became a professional fighter at fifteen. "The Ghetto Wizard" went through some painful fights before acquiring the punching skills that later made him famous. He became the world lightweight champion in 1917 and held the title until 1925, when he retired unbeaten. He did return to the ring in 1931 because of the economic effects of the Great Depression. He won eighteen more fights, fought another opponent to a draw, and then finally lost. It was then that he quit boxing for good.

Other Jewish boxers included "Slapsie" Maxie Rosenbloom, Barney Ross, and Al Singer. There was also a boxer named Max Baer, who, despite the fact that he wore a Star of David on his trunks to attract fans, was not Jewish.

Baseball had a special attraction for Jewish boys. They loved to play it, and they loved to watch it. Knowing this, the teams, especially in New York, were searching for a great Jewish player. In 1923, the New York Giants thought they found him. Moe Solomon, "The Rabbi of Swat," was thought to be a rival for Babe Ruth (the "Sultan of Swat"), but sadly for all his fans, Solomon, though an excellent hitter, was terrible as a fielding first baseman and outfielder. He turned out not to be much of a rival for Ruth. In later years, when Hank Greenberg came along, those Jewish fans would have somebody to root for. In 1938, he almost broke Babe Ruth's record of 60 home runs; Greenberg hit 58. His legendary batting skills made him an icon in the Jewish community.

One of the most famous athletes was not a boxer or a baseball player. And he was as much an entertainer as an athlete. Zisha (Sigmund) Breitbart was a strongman.

Breitbart was popular in the mid-1920s in Yiddish vaudeville houses. "The Pride of the Yidn," widely considered the strongest man in the world, broke coins between his fingers, lifted weights with his teeth, tore chains just using his hands, and drove nails into a board using his fists. He would lie on his back and have an automobile—filled with ten passengers—placed on top of him. He would lift a baby elephant and then climb a ladder and perform other feats on the ladder while still holding the elephant.

He formulated the idea of training other Jews to enter an army with him to liberate the Land of Israel. He wanted to go to the ancient Jewish homeland to re-create Samson's great feats of strength.

Jewish mothers would warn their children who tried such feats, "Don't be a Breitbart."

The movie *Invincible* starring Tim Roth was based on Breitbart's life.

ENTERTAINERS

For those on the Lower East Side who didn't relish life in a factory or a store, who for one reason or another didn't like school or do well there, but who did have some talent, or perhaps just a little talent and a burning desire, there were other opportunities. The Lower East Side produced its share of great entertainers, people who had learned to sing or tell jokes on the stoops of the tenements and in the streets, young people who were characteristically poor, with weak or absent fathers, who didn't find much that was morally problematic about stealing, and who were very bright, although not in any way that their schoolteachers would have admired.

Vaudeville and the music business and the movies were open to them. More settled Americans looked down on entertainers in general as immoral. But the need for actors and performers was enormous.

The Jews were about to make their mark. Some of them had only a brief experience on the Lower East Side. Fanny Brice was born there but left at age four. Al Jolson was a member of the Eldridge Street Synagogue. Edward G. Robinson lived on Broome Street for a while and celebrated his bar mitzvah at the First Roumanian-American Congregation before heading off to City College.

But the area had a more lasting presence in the lives of some other immortal artists and entertainers.

IRVING BERLIN

Berlin never learned to read or write music. He played the piano in F-sharp, using just the black keys. He knew no other key. (To write in other keys, he had to employ a specially built piano.) Born in Russia and subject to excruciating poverty on the Lower East Side, Irving Berlin was an unlikely candidate to one day be a contender for the title of greatest American songwriter who ever lived.

Berlin began his musical life leading a singing beggar into the cafés. Blind Sol let Berlin sing with him once in a while, and the young boy found that he enjoyed the experience so much that he began singing in the cafés himself. He was soon hired to be a song plugger—someone who sang songs from a particular publisher so that customers would buy the sheet music.

In 1906, Berlin became a singing waiter at Pelham's Café, inventing risqué lyrics to parody current hits. Two singing waiters at another café had published a song aimed at Italians, and the song had been successful. Pelham's decided it had better get in the song business as well and had its piano player compose a similar song. Berlin's lyrics were used, and so his first song, "Marie from Sunny Italy," was published on May 8, 1907, three days before his nineteenth birthday.

He would go on to write such American standards as "Alexander's Ragtime Band," "Puttin' On the Ritz," "God Bless America," "There's No Business Like Show Business," "Always," "Let's Face the Music and Dance," and "White Christmas."

Irving Berlin in 1928. *Source: © Bettmann/CORBIS.*

GEORGE BURNS

George Burns was born at 95 Pitt Street on January 20, 1896. His birth certificate records the birth name as Naftaly Birnbaum, though he was Nathan or Nat to his friends. He and his eight brothers and sisters slept on a single mattress. Three more children would soon arrive, so the family moved to 259 Rivington Street. Young Nat's father Louis, or Lipa, tried different jobs, none too successfully. On August 22, 1903, Lipa was sitting by the window reading a prayer book when he slumped over and died. Nat, age seven, was devastated and determined that it was time to earn money for his family.

He might have entered a life of crime. That was common enough for boys his age and in his circumstances. Certainly, school was not an option for him. By age ten, despite an amazingly quick wit, he was struggling just to read and write. He had already lost a battle with arithmetic. It was torturous for his mind to unscramble letters or recognize words. He left school.

STEPPING INTO SHOW BUSINESS

George Burns had a partner in the dancing school he started at fourteen. Ed Renard also became a partner in an ill-fated attempt to enter show business. Renard recorded his memories:

> I had a dancing school with George Burns. We had mostly foreigners that wanted to learn how to dance; the girls would sit on one side of the hall and the boys on the other side. We used to go and give exhibitions for dancers for a cup. Burns would be the judge, so I won the cup. Then I would be the judge, so Burns won the cup.
>
> Then I had an act with Burns. . . . We went to Brooklyn for the matinee and the manager takes one look at us and closes us.

>◝×◝

But he knew what he loved. At seven, he had been part of the "Peewee Quartet," singing on street corners or wherever they could. He tried different jobs, including an attempt to start a life in show business as a dancer.

By fourteen, he had helped start a dancing school.

On September 5, 1917, Burns married Hannah Siegel at her family apartment at 247 Broome Street. Burns was twenty-one and listed himself as a "performer" on the marriage certificate. That marriage would not last long, however, and Burns, having tried to work in the garment industry and gotten fired for standing on a table and singing and dancing for his coworkers, kept trying show business. Siegel would go on to marry again but never achieved fame.

Burns's life would change in 1923 when he met Gracie Allen. After a long courtship, the two would eventually marry and make show business history. Burns and Allen would go on to conquer radio and television and become the most successful husband-and-wife comedy team in history. In 1926, Burns and Allen played

BURNS AND ALLEN ROUTINES

Burns and Allen developed some of the most beloved routines ever. When they first started to attract attention, they were using routines like this one:

GRACIE: All great singers have their trials. Look at Caruso. Thirty years on a desert island with all those cannibals.

GEORGE: You've got the wrong man.

GRACIE: No. You're the man for me.

GEORGE: But they say I'm through as a singer. I'm extinct.

GRACIE: You do not!

GEORGE: Gracie, let me ask you something. Did the nurse ever happen to drop you on your head when you were a baby?

GRACIE: Oh, no, we couldn't afford a nurse. My mother had to do it.

GEORGE: You had a smart mother.

GRACIE: Smartness runs in my family. When I went to school I was so smart my teacher was in my class for five years.

GEORGE: Gracie, what school did you go to?

GRACIE: I'm not allowed to tell.

GEORGE: Why not?

GRACIE: The school pays me $25 a month not to tell.

GEORGE: Gracie, this family of yours, do you all live together?

GRACIE: Oh, sure. My father, my brother, my uncle, my cousin, and my nephew all sleep in one bed, and . . .

GEORGE: In one bed? I'm surprised your grandfather doesn't sleep with them.

GRACIE: Oh, he did, but he died, so they made him get up.

Jack Benny. *Source: CORBIS © John Springer Collection.*

the Palace in New York, the top theater in vaudeville. Friends like Jack Benny and Archie Leach, who earned $5 a week walking stilts at Coney Island but who would soon change his name to Cary Grant, were in the audience.

EDDIE CANTOR

Eddie Cantor (born Israel Iskowitz in 1892) had a difficult time, even by the standards of the Lower East Side. His mother died of a lung disease a few months before the boy turned two. His father either died or disappeared before he was three, and so his grandmother, Esther Kantrowitz, had to raise him. Poor herself, she could afford only a basement apartment at 47 Henry Street. The apartment had three rooms. She sold candles and ran an agency for young women seeking employment as servants. He sometimes stole from pushcarts. There was some misunderstanding as he was being signed up for school, and the boy ended up with the last name of Cantor. He was not a great success at school, though more of one when he attended the Henry Street Settlement.

He began to juggle, tell funny stories, and sing in the streets. His first legitimate job was at a delicatessen that sold meat products from the famed Isaac Gellis factory. Cantor picked up the meat from the factory at 37 Essex Street and delivered it to the deli in a basket. He got paid two sandwiches.

Soon he began to win some local talent contests. He acquired the name "Eddie" because Ida, the young woman he began going out with seriously and would soon marry, wanted a boyfriend with that name.

He had various early jobs in entertainment, such as being both a performer and waiter at a saloon on Coney Island where an aspiring Italian kid named Jimmy Durante accompanied him on the piano.

On stage, Eddie was known as "the Apostle of Pep" because he always seemed to be in motion. His "banjo eyes" became his trademark. He remained close to his audience. His energy, his nonstop action, mimicked the energies of immigrant life, and his audiences loved him for caring about them. They loved his funny ad-libs.

Eddie Cantor became an extraordinarily successful star on stage, on radio, in the movies, and on television. His songs such as "If You Knew Susie" and "Making Whoopee" became wildly popular.

GEORGE GERSHWIN

George Gershwin's parents decided to purchase a piano so that his brother Ira could learn the instrument. It was 1910, when George was twelve, and the boys were fascinated as the piano movers maneuvered to raise the piano from the street through the apartment window on the second floor. But Ira didn't much like pianos, and he was shocked that George immediately sat down and played a popular tune. Somehow he had learned using a player piano at a friend's house.

By age fourteen, Gershwin had learned all he could from the local piano teachers when he met Charles Hambitzer, who taught Gershwin all the classical composers while Gershwin just wanted to play more modern music.

Gershwin achieved great fame in 1920 when Al Jolson recorded "Swanee." More than two million copies of the song were sold. He would go on to write such standards as "Fascinating Rhythm," "The Man I Love," "I Got Rhythm," "Embraceable You," "Someone to Watch over Me," "Summertime," and many others. He also wrote his classical work "Rhapsody in Blue," "An American in Paris," and the remarkable folk opera "Porgy and Bess." He died of a brain tumor at the age of thirty-eight.

George Gershwin around 1920. *Source© CORBIS.*

THE CLOSING OF THE GOLDEN DOOR

The heart of the Jewish Lower East Side story was gone by the time World War I was over.

The area had undergone enormous changes between 1880 and 1918. By the end of the Great War, the pushcarts were mostly gone; the Jewish peddlers had become store owners or factory workers. The streets were asphalt. Non-Jewish immigrants were coming in to take the place of the Jews who were leaving.

Beyond the changes in the neighborhood, national and international events effectively ended the immigrant era.

America had entered the war in 1917, and that impeded most immigration. When the war ended, the nativist and isolationist elements in America grew stronger, and restrictive laws abounded. The entire society seemed to want to cleanse itself, and foreigners were regarded with suspicion. Don't forget, this is the same era in which social engineering took the upper hand and Prohibition began. Although the Russian Revolution in 1917 was greeted with joy by the socialists on the Lower East Side, by the end of the war, such foreign ideologies as Marxism—whether communistic or anarchistic—were increasingly viewed as antithetical to American values. There was a "Red Scare" culminating in the Palmer Raids in 1919, led by A. Mitchell Palmer, the attorney general whose house had been bombed by an anarchist, in which radicals were rounded up and deported. Ironically, those deported were sent overseas through Ellis Island.

The Zionists on the Lower East Side welcomed the 1917 Balfour Declaration, giving British approval to the revival of a Jewish homeland in Palestine.

Dislike of foreigners and Jews had been building even before the war. In 1916, Woodrow Wilson had nominated Louis Brandeis to become the first Jewish justice on the Supreme Court. There was widespread opposition, led by the president of Harvard University. The war stirred up the fear of foreigners. The Ku Klux Klan was revived in Georgia in 1915. Henry Ford began publishing his anti-Semitic tirades. Racist literature began to appear all across America, with Madison Grant's 1916 best-selling book *The Passing of the Great Race* being one of the most influential. The author, an anthropologist at the American Museum of Natural History, railed against immigrants not of northern European heritage, whom he declared inferior to the British, Germans, and Scandinavians who formed the racial heritage of America.

Thus the entire United States was completely different from what it once had been, now inhospitable to new immigrants or children of immigrants who didn't want to become fully Americanized. Americans had become distrustful of urban values. The rapid growth of cities that accompanied the industrialization of America after the Civil War was a shock to rural, agrarian Americans who felt out of place in the new economy that was emerging. They experienced economic depressions and decreasing wages. They saw themselves in a battle to defend their vision of the "true America" against the invasion of alien hordes who had come here to steal jobs, become criminals, and live in dirt. And fear was widespread that the ethnic groups that formed the bulk of the immigrants would somehow dilute the "racial purity" of the native stock.

The nativist distrust of foreigners had a seemingly unlikely ally—labor unions. The unions wanted restrictions on immigration to keep out potential job competitors.

In 1917, Congress passed a bill—over Woodrow Wilson's veto—that defined three categories of foreigners who should not be allowed to immigrate. One of those categories was anyone over sixteen who could not read a language, a category that affected many Jews as well as Gentiles. Once the war ended and immigrants began again to enter America, there was renewed effort to stop the flow. In 1921, with Wilson gone from the White House and replaced by Warren G. Harding, Congress restricted the number of immigrants based on their national origins.

In 1924, the Johnson-Reed Act effectively stopped immigration. The act provided for a maximum of 150,000 immigrants a year and established a quota declaring how many immigrants from each nation would be allowed to enter. The quota was 2 percent of the number of immigrants from that nation already in the United States before 1890. Only six senators voted against the act.

The effect on Jewish immigration was, of course, enormous. In 1924, fifty thousand Jewish immigrants entered the country; the following year, only ten thousand did. The Johnson-Reed Act would govern immigration until 1965. Jews who sought to flee from the Holocaust would find few ships to sail by the Statue of Liberty, no annoying officials on Ellis Island, no Lower East Side to serve as a way station as they entered American life.

The Golden Door had slammed shut.

Home of the Lower East Side Tenement Museum. *Source: Courtesy of the Lower East Side Tenement Museum.*

SEVENTEEN

THE LEGACY
OF THE LOWER EAST SIDE

><><

B Y 1927, fewer than 15 percent of the Jews living in New York City were residents of the Lower East Side. The Jewish presence there began to be replaced by Jewish memory. New York's Jews—indeed, America's Jews—came to think of the area as a sacred place, a place of mythic collective origins for a lot of them, a place to visit, to reconnect to that past, and to be energized. The Lower East Side became a landmark.

Despite the incredible hardships endured by the immigrants there, the Lower East Side was a place where, perhaps for the only time in their American experience, large numbers of them formed a community. The Jews, in a sense, had their own country in America. Everyone spoke a Jewish language, married someone Jewish, ate Jewish food, and even if they mocked Judaism, they did so as Jews. It was a time of hope, of a belief in a better world for Jews and for all humanity. This lost world became enshrined for its memory, not the reality of existence there. For example, the Lower East Side was never exclusively Jewish. Indeed, during the immigrant generation, it wasn't even generally called the Lower East Side. That would come later as Jews reflected on its attraction.

For many Eastern European Jews, life on the Lower East Side became the first chapter in the narrative of their American Jewish experience. It was a starting point from which to try to make sense of whatever present the American Jews inhabited.

LOWER EAST SIDE MEMORIES: PERSONAL AND SCHOLARLY

Professor Hasia R. Diner has written several scholarly books about the Lower East Side. Here she considers why she writes about it.

Scholarship drew me to the Lower East Side. After all, so much of what we know about the great Jewish immigration to the United States played itself out on the jumble of New York streets below Houston and east of the Bowery. Labor activism, Yiddish journalism, religious fervor, political radicalism, the theater, and Jewish street life of shopping, playing, and just being there made this chunk of space America's most Jewish of places. Historians have rightly pointed out that this neighborhood served as the epicenter of the Jewish immigrant drama on this side of the Atlantic.

I must admit a personal side to my fascination. Having grown up in a distinctly different place—Milwaukee—where only the faintest echoes of this kind of pulsating Jewishness could be felt—made me imagine New York and the Lower East Side as places I had to visit and somehow become part of. From the first time that I ventured on to these streets whose names resonated in the literature—Essex, Hester, Rivington, Delancey—I felt, I am embarrassed to admit, the sense of being a time traveler. Intellectually, I knew that these streets differed profoundly from the streets of my imagination, but that did not stop me as I created a set of imaginary scenes in my head of an era that had come to an end decades before I was born. I also knew that the Lower East Side of my fantasy little resembled the Lower East Side of history.

What I have hoped to do as a historian is bring together the empirical with the imaginary, the scholarly with the romantic, and explore why I and so many other American Jews needed the Lower East Side.

They could go back and compare where they were to their beginnings at the tip of Manhattan. The journey of the immigrants, their stay on the Lower East Side, and their eventual acceptance into American life became the story arc of Jewish life in the United States. It was a story that needed to be retold in each generation.

During the 1960s and 1970s, for example, when ethnic attachments were deemed crucial in the construction of a personal identity, when the search for roots became a national pastime, the Lower East Side became a natural destination for searching Jews. It was the home address of American Jewish roots.

Jews do their remembering in a number of ways beyond actually visiting the Lower East Side. Scholars and researchers were fortunate in having records. The vanished world of Ashkenazic Eastern Europe Jewry and the Yiddish cultural traditions of the Lower East Side and the wider American Jewish community left behind an enormous number of books and documents. The YIVO Institute for Jewish Research was founded in 1925 in Vilna to gather crucial materials and provide a resource center to make those materials available.

After the emergence of Nazism and the seizure of YIVO's archives, a new headquarters opened in New York City in 1940. Much surviving material of the original archives was discovered in Frankfurt after the war and was then forwarded to New York.

YIVO's library has more than 360,000 volumes in twelve languages. There are 23 million manuscripts, documents, photographs, sound recordings, sheet music, film, and other artifacts in its archives.

Much additional information can be gleaned from the enormous number of memoirs about growing up on the Lower East Side, most written in Yiddish. In 1942, YIVO ran a contest for immigrant memoirs. Nine of the best entries are translated into English in *My Future Is in America: Autobiographies of Eastern European Jewish Immigrants* by Jocelyn Cohen and Daniel Soyer.

Readers interested in learning about the Lower East Side can study the photographs of Jacob Riis or Lewis Hine. They can even read a variety of novels and view films and television programs.

ENGLISH-LANGUAGE NOVELS

Life on the Lower East Side was filled with fabulous stories of poverty and triumph, family miseries and tensions, love and betrayal, the desire to maintain traditions and

MEMOIRS IN ENGLISH

Interesting memoirs have been written by a number of celebrities, including Eddie Cantor and George Burns. Here are eighteen of the best English-language autobiographies by less famous people who wrote about leaving the Old Country, the journey across the Atlantic, and Jewish immigrant life on the Lower East Side.

Emma Beckerman, *Not So Long Ago: A Recollection*

Louis Borgenicht, *The Happiest Man*

Samuel Chotzinoff, *A Lost Paradise*

Rose Cohen, *Out of the Shadow: A Russian Jewish Girlhood on the Lower East Side*

Philip Cowen, *Memories of an American Jew*

Gertrude Ford, *81 Sheriff Street*

Benjamin A. Gordon, *Between Two Worlds*

Morris Hillquit, *Loose Leaves from a Busy Life*

Bernard Horwich, *My First Eighty Years*

Israel Kasovich, *The Days of Our Lives*

Ephraim Lisitzky, *In the Grip of Cross Currents*

Carole Malkin, *The Journeys of David Toback: As Retold by His Granddaughter*

Marcus Ravage, *An American in the Making*

Harry Roskolenko, *The Time That Was Then*

Sophie Ruskay, *Horsecars and Cobblestones*

Bella Cohen Spewack, *Streets: A Memoir of the Lower East Side*

Benjamin Stolberg, *Tailor's Progress*

Gregory Weinstein, *The Ardent Eighties*

the yearning for the new and forbidden. Such a life was a natural source of material for Jewish novelists.

HAUNCH, PAUNCH, AND JOWL (1923)

Samuel Ornitz was born on Hester Street in 1890. He published *Haunch, Paunch, and Jowl* anonymously. It was serialized in the *Freiheit* and sold over one hundred thousand copies. The book is thematically similar to *The Rise of David Levinsky*. Meyer Hirsch, the protagonist who narrates the story, describes his journey from petty thief to crooked lawyer to judge. It is a tale of someone who seems connected to other Jews but uses them to get ahead. Like David Levinsky, he sacrificed his Jewishness for American success, and the sacrifice corrodes his life. Some rabbis denounced the book, but other Jewish readers praised its painfully accurate portrayal of the deceits needed to survive and the deals with life that many immigrant Jews had made.

Ornitz became a screenwriter; he was one of the Hollywood Ten during the McCarthy era and served a year in prison charged with contempt of court.

BREAD GIVERS (1925)

Anzia Yezierska was the poet of the immigrant heart. She and her family had arrived in the United States in 1901, when she was sixteen. After working as a servant, sewing buttons in a tailor's sweatshop, and toiling in a factory, she decided to become a writer. Her freethinking ideas put her at odds with her traditional father, and her writings are filled with emotionally charged prose about their impossible relationship. *Hungry Hearts,* her first collection of short stories, was published in 1920. It was an overpowering description of excruciating poverty.

One afternoon after the publication of the book, Yezierska was sipping tea in her rooming house on Hester Street. She was thinking that the landlady was not around because there was no money to pay the rent. Just then someone called out her name. She sensed that she would be evicted.

She went to the door, opened it, and saw a group of people surrounding a messenger from Western Union. Such a message almost inevitably meant someone had died. Yezierska took the envelope and opened it. The message read: TELEPHONE IMMEDIATELY FOR AN APPOINTMENT TO DISCUSS MOTION PICTURE RIGHTS FOR HUNGRY HEARTS.

The agent, R. L. Giffen, had sent it, and Yezierska couldn't believe what she was reading. The book had earned $200 in royalties, but that had been spent long ago.

But to call him, she needed a nickel for the phone. To get to his office, she needed a dime for the streetcar. Desperate, she decided to pawn her mother's shawl for the money. She got a quarter for the shawl and went to the agent's office. He told her that various Hollywood producers wanted her book. They had offered $5,000, but he was holding out for $10,000.

She was excited and asked if the agent could advance her a dollar. He smiled and gave her a $10 bill.

She walked across the street to Child's Restaurant, where she had often stood outside staring at the food being thrown away. She walked inside and ordered the most expensive steak the restaurant offered. She finished half but could not eat the rest. She began to cry. A waitress came over to remove the dishes. Yezierska grabbed the plate. Waiting until no one was looking, she took out her handkerchief, put the meat and potatoes in it, and covered it with a newspaper. At home, she fed the steak to Lily, an alley cat.

Samuel Goldwyn bought the rights to make the film and brought Yezierska out to Hollywood to work on it. But the determined Jewish writer from the Lower East Side could not conform to the Hollywood-style suggestions of the determined Jewish producer. She ultimately left Hollywood, though she continued to write, producing six books between 1920 and 1932. After that, living once again in poverty because she was unwilling to bend to Hollywood's rules, she was literarily silent for several decades until her memoir, *Red Ribbon on a White Horse*, was published in 1950.

Bread Givers was Anzia Yezierska's best novel. It is the story of a confrontation between Jewish tradition, as represented by the father in the Smolinsky family, and the driving urge for freedom represented by the protagonist, Sara. The book is unrelenting in portraying poverty and despair as well as the plight of a woman who needs an education and economic independence to survive emotionally.

JEWS WITHOUT MONEY (1930)

Irving Granich was born in 1893 and became a political radical. Desperate to escape his poverty, he attended a demonstration in Union Square in 1914. A police officer knocked him down, and the young man had a sudden realization: his poverty couldn't just be overcome by personal effort. The entire capitalistic system, he decided, was against the exploited workers. The workers' revolution was, for Granich, the messiah that had replaced religion.

Soon he began writing about the poverty he knew firsthand. He changed his name to Michael Gold during the Palmer Raids and began to work as an editor and writer for communist publications.

Jews Without Money was published just as the Great Depression hit. It therefore became one of the first novels to deal directly with a subject—poverty—then on every reader's mind. The book was an unflinching portrait of Jewish poverty on the Lower East Side and was filled with the death, crime, diseases, and prostitution that he had come to see as the outcome of capitalism. The book was a stirring call for workers to see their plight and rise against it.

CALL IT SLEEP (1934)

Henry Roth lived for only four years on the Lower East Side, but it became the setting for *Call It Sleep*, a novel that brought Jewish literature into the modern age. Influenced by the interior monologues in James Joyce's fiction, Roth tells the tale of the young boy David Schearl in the years before World War I. The boy is tormented by his chronically unemployed father, by anti-Semitic gangs, and by his own sexual desires. The book soon disappeared, and Roth went into a long period of literary isolation. Only near the end of his life did he publish more novels and reveal that part of his writer's block had come from the incestuous relations he had with his sister and a cousin.

OTHER NOVELS

There were many additional novels about immigrant life. Jerome Weidman's *I Can Get It for You Wholesale*, an extremely unflattering portrait of a Jewish scoundrel who rose from rags to riches in the garment industry, was published in 1937. Later the book was turned into a musical in which Barbra Streisand made her Broadway debut.

Sydney Taylor's *All-of-a-Kind Family* (1951) was the first major children's book about the Lower East Side. In the late 1970s and early 1980s, a succession of family sagas about the Lower East Side appeared, in the wake of the interest in finding one's roots and the success of *World of Our Fathers*. Those novels included Belva Plain's *Evergreen* (1978), Gloria Goldreich's *Leah's Journey* (1978), and Meredith Tax's *Rivington Street* (1982).

EARLY FILMS

The Lower East Side intrigued early filmmakers. Then it mostly disappeared in films for several decades before achieving a central place in the film *Hester Street*. The following were some of the most prominent early films set on the Lower East Side.

THE YIDDISHER BOY (1909)

This three-minute film was produced by Sigmund Lubin, the first American Jewish filmmaker. The film is about two boys, Moses and Ed, and how they help each other. It emphasizes the value of tradition and how kindness can overcome the harshness of immigrant life.

A CHILD OF THE GHETTO (1910)

The legendary and controversial filmmaker D. W. Griffith directed this fifteen-minute film. It centers on Ruth, a seamstress on Rivington Street, who is unfairly accused of stealing. She leaves the Lower East Side to hide in the country, where she falls in love with a farmer. Griffith prizes rural over urban values and is among the first to deal with interfaith relationships.

HUNGRY HEARTS (1922)

This is the full-length Samuel Goldwyn film based on Anzia Yezierska's collection of stories. The film doesn't capture the emotional power of the prose, but the relatively few authentic Lower East Side shots provide a dramatic record of the place.

HIS PEOPLE (1925)

This emotionally powerful film, directed by Edward Sloman, has some of the best photography of the Lower East Side in any film. It is the story of two Jewish immigrants' sons, one a lawyer and the other a boxer, and tells yet again of the struggle involved in leaving the values of the Old World behind while trying to adapt to those of the New.

THE RAG MAN (1925)

Little Jackie Coogan had become famous for his heart-wrenching scenes with Charlie Chaplin in *The Kid* (1921), but his work opposite Jewish silent film comedian Max Davidson in *The Rag Man* is just as moving. Coogan plays Tim Kelly, a Gentile boy at loose ends who meets the Lower East Side Jewish rag man Max Ginsberg. The two need each other desperately and develop a profound bond. As Coogan rides around the city, the camera follows and records some extraordinary images.

THE JAZZ SINGER (1927)

In 1922, while still an undergraduate at the University of Illinois, Samson Raphaelson wrote a story called "The Day of Atonement." In 1926, Raphaelson turned the story into a play starring the comedian George Jessel.

Warner Brothers bought the rights for $50,000 and hired Jessel for $30,000. Jessel either wanted more money or was tricked out of the part. Whatever happened, Jack Warner asked Eddie Cantor to play the part. Cantor, who was close friends with Jessel, refused. Warner then approached Al Jolson, who asked for $75,000 and got it, even though his acting talents were suspect.

The Jazz Singer is frequently referred to as the first talking picture. *Don Juan* (1926) had a musical score and sound effects, but *The Jazz Singer* was the first feature-length picture in which dialogue is spoken as part of the film. But its use of sound was not complete; only a quarter of the film is a "talkie." The first genuine all-talking film was *Lights of New York* in 1928. Also, Al Jolson was not even the first character to speak in *The Jazz Singer;* Bobby Gordon, who played the main character as a thirteen-year-old, speaks first. Jolson's famous words in the film were "Wait a minute, wait a minute. You ain't heard nothin' yet! Wait a minute, I tell ya! You ain't heard nothin'! You wanna hear 'Toot, Toot, Tootsie'? All right, hold on, hold on."

The story focuses on Jakie Rabinowitz, a cantor's son who leaves his family's tradition to become a star on Broadway. At the end of the film, Jakie, now Jack Robin, returns for a Yom Kippur service as his father is dying. The film depicts life on Hester and Orchard Streets primarily because Cantor Rabinowitz works at the Orchard Street Synagogue.

The film is widely interpreted as sympathetic to young Jakie, who only wants to succeed in America and would be held back if he pleased his Old World father. His rebellion was, on this understanding, a cry from the heart for personal freedom. But most of the entertainers who had lived the story saw the film as more painful.

THE ANIMATED LOWER EAST SIDE

In 1986, Steven Spielberg produced the animated movie *An American Tail*. The Jewish immigrant experience is retold through the eyes of a family of Russian Jewish mice as they flee pogroms and journey to America, only to work in a sweatshop, live in tenements, and bribe cats so they won't be eaten. The main character, Fievel Mousekewitz, has to search for the rest of his family after being separated from them on the voyage across the ocean. The movie eventually had a sequel about Fievel heading West, a television series, and two additional films.

The popular animated comedy *The Simpsons* also had an episode centered on the Lower East Side. First broadcast on October 24, 1991, the show's episode "Like Father, like Clown" was about the decadent but endearing Krusty the Clown—born Hershel Krustofsky. Krusty was depressed because his father, Rabbi Krustofsky, objected to his son's career choice. Lisa and Bart Simpson, learning a lot about traditional Jewish texts along the way, try to effect a reconciliation. The Orthodox rabbi, of course, lives on the Lower East Side. As in *The Jazz Singer* and so many novels, the Lower East Side serves not only as a practical locale but also as a perfect symbol of the Judaism from which Krusty has strayed.

George Burns said that he cried as he sat in the theater. The film made even the American successes aware of what they had abandoned.

THE MEANING OF THE LOWER EAST SIDE

There are conflicting trends in the Jewish American world today, including an energized Orthodox movement and increased ritual practices among some Conservative and Reform Jews, but overall assimilation has greatly increased, most prominently reflected in the intermarriage rate, especially among younger Jews.

If in the 1920s Jews were nostalgic for a time of community as they saw a rise in American anti-Semitism, and if in the 1970s Jews were buoyant and proud of their American heritage as best physically exemplified by the Lower East Side, and if at the beginning of the twenty-first century Jews were more confused, more uncertain about whether their children or grandchildren would even be Jewish, it is that very confusion that drives them to reconsider their story.

It is precisely at moments of greatest doubts that the story most needs to be told and most desperately needs to be heard. That is partly so because the journey the Jewish immigrants made was a heroic journey. They faced the perils of persecution and hunger and chose not to ignore them but to react by facing a different set of perils. They chose to flee their homes, endure an uncertain trip across an ocean, come to a new country where they didn't speak the language and had an uncertain economic future, and adapt to that new country. Theirs was the mythic adventure of ancient tales told about modern life. In that sense, the lessons they provide are not imprisoned by history but useful to all people at all times. But the lessons are especially valuable for American Jews.

The story of the Lower East Side is literally the story of the beginnings of many American Jews. But if it is the master story of the American Jewish past, its rich heritage, its vivid, outrageous, larger-than-life warm characters, and its inspiration also yield guidance for the American Jewish present and future.

Indeed, read correctly, the story of Jewish immigrants on the Lower East Side is the master story of hope for all people.

SOURCES

HERE ARE the sources not identified in the text. Full bibliographic information is provided in the References.

INTRODUCTION

Statistics on Jewish immigration: Samuel Joseph, *Jewish Immigration to the United States from 1881 to 1910*.

ONE: ESCAPING FROM THE OLD WORLD

Boxed Material

Proverbs and Curses: Lawrence J. Epstein.

Superstitions: Lawrence J. Epstein.

A Sister's Bravery: Lawrence J. Epstein, *A Treasury of Jewish Inspirational Stories*, pp. 196–199.

The Odessa Pogrom: Milton Meltzer, *The Jews in America*, pp. 115–116.

The Goldene Medina: Mary Antin, *From Plotzk to Boston*, p. 12.

Crossing the Border: Abraham Cahan, *The Education of Abraham Cahan*, p. 199.

Brody: Leo Shapall, "The Diary of Dr. George M. Price," p. 176.

A Stormy Crossing: Benjamin Gordon, *Between Two Worlds*, pp. 34–38.

Steerage: Morris Raphael Cohen, *A Dreamer's Journey*, p. 61.

First Glimpse of America: Anzia Yezierska, quoted in Meltzer, *Jews in America*, p. 62.

Quotations and Details

Mollie Hyman: Joel Kisseloff, *You Must Remember This*, p. 12.

"Streets paved with gold": quoted in Richard F. Shepard and Vicki Gold Levi, *Live and Be Well*, p. 70.

Jack Benny and Sophie Tucker: Lawrence J. Epstein, *The Haunted Smile*, pp. 3–4.

Robert Louis Stevenson: Wilton S. Tifft, *Ellis Island*, p. 23.

Soup: Stephen Fox, *Transatlantic*, p. 326.

Emma Beckerman: Emma Beckerman, *Not So Long Ago*, p. 9.

TWO: LANDING AT ELLIS ISLAND

Boxed Material

Castle Garden: Isidore Kopeloff, quoted in Milton Meltzer, *Taking Root*, p. 52.

Defending a Barrier to Immigrants: Henry Cabot Lodge, quoted in Tifft, *Ellis Island*, p. 58.

Ellis Island Chalk Marks: Lawrence J. Epstein.

The Angel of Ellis Island: *Heritage*, Fall 2005, pp. 4–5.

Famous Changed Names: Lawrence J. Epstein.

A Special Case: Philip Cowen, *Memories*, p. 148.

Quotations and Details

Ages of immigrants: Samuel Joseph, *Jewish Immigration*, pp. 127ff.

Odors: Ann Novotny, *Strangers at the Door*, p. 81.

THREE: LIFE IN THE TENEMENTS

Boxed Material

Ruth J. Abram: Lawrence J. Epstein and Ruth J. Abram.

The Levine Family Apartment: Lawrence J. Epstein and Lower East Side Tenement Museum.

Welcome to the Neighborhood: Samuel Chotzinoff, *A Lost Paradise*, p. 62.

Mama Feeds a Crowd: Lawrence J. Epstein, *A Treasury of Jewish Anecdotes*, p. 137.

Mother or Saint?: Zalmen Yoffeh, "The Passing of the East Side," *Menorah Journal*, December 1929, reprinted in Howe and Libo, *How We Lived*, p. 43.

Quotations and Details

Arnold Bennett: Meltzer, *Taking Root*, p. 75.

Martha Dolinko: Kisseloff, *You Must Remember This*, p. 28.

George Burns (privy): Herb Fagen, *George Burns: In His Own Words*, pp. 19–20.

Emma Beckerman: Beckerman, *Not So Long Ago*, p. 11.

Abraham Hyman: Kisseloff, *You Must Remember This*, p. 47.

Victrola: Stephen Birmingham, *The Rest of Us*, p. 48.

Blanche Lasky: Kisseloff, *You Must Remember This*, p. 41.

George Burns's father: George Burns, *Transcript*.

George Burns (washing): George Burns, *I Love Her, That's Why*, p. 12.

George Burns (gas lighting): Burns, *Transcript*.

FOUR: WORKING ON THE LOWER EAST SIDE

Boxed Material

A First Job: Louis Waldman, *Labor Lawyer*, pp. 22–23.

A Tenement Sweatshop: Jacob Riis, *How the Other Half Lives*, quoted in Meltzer, *Jews in America*, p. 79.

Quotations and Details

Marcus Ravage: Marcus Ravage, *An American in the Making*, p. 67.

Sam Levenson: Lawrence J. Epstein, *Haunted Smile*, p. 158.

William Fox: Epstein, *Anecdotes*, p. 77.

Rose Schneiderman: Shepard and Levi, *Live and Be Well*, p. 144.

FIVE: LIFE ON THESE MEAN STREETS

Boxed Material

Street Names: Lawrence J. Epstein.

The Ghetto Market, Hester Street: Milton Reigenstein, "Pictures of the Ghetto," *New York Times*, November 14, 1897, p. IWM3.

Immigrant Criminal Slang: Lawrence J. Epstein.

Quotations and Details

Michael Gold. *Jews Without Money*, quoted in *News from the Tenement Museum*, November 2005, p. 1.

George Burns (show business): Burns, *I Love Her, That's Why*, p. 12.

Harry Golden ("scalemen"): Harry Golden, *Only in America*, p. 90.

Tillie Taub and Rose Herz: Steve Koppman and Lion Koppman, *A Treasury of American Jewish Folklore*, pp. 163–167.

Jonah Goldstein: Jenna Weissman Joselit, "The Wonders of America: Pickpockets, Players, Prostitutes—Jews? *Jewish Daily Forward*, March 4, 2005, p. 16.

Harry Golden (prostitute): Harry Golden, *The Right Time*, p. 55.

SIX: ROMANCE IN THE NEW WORLD

Boxed Materials

Bad Business for Matchmakers: *New York Tribune*, September 30, 1900.

A Wedding on Ludlow Street: Irving Howe and Kenneth Libo, *World of Our Fathers*, p. 220.

Abandoned! Isaac Metzker, *A Bintel Brief*, pp. 83–84.

On Intermarriage: Metzker, *A Bintel Brief*, pp. 43–44.

Quotations and Details

Morton novel: quoted in Jenna Weissman Joselit, *The Wonders of America*, p. 43.

SEVEN: CHILDREN AND FAMILIES

Boxed Materials

A Father's Role: Harold Ribalow, *Autobiographies of American Jews*, p. 309.

Teachers: Chotzinoff, *Lost Paradise*, pp. 117–118.

School Discipline: Harry Roskolenko, *The Time That Was Then*, p. 27.

Ideals Learned from Books: Rose Schneiderman, *All for One* (1967), quoted in Howe and Libo, *How We Lived*, p. 132.

Quotations and Details

Jewish Daily Forward and Cantor on baseball: Howe and Libo, *World of Our Fathers*, p. 182.

Anzia Yezierska: quoted in Howe and Libo, *World of Our Fathers*, p. 269.

Morris Raphael Cohen: Morris Raphael Cohen, *A Dreamer's Journey*, pp. 82 ff.

Irving Berlin quotes: Lawrence J. Epstein.

George Burns (Peewee Quartet): Epstein, *Haunted Smile*, p. 18.

Ira Gershwin: Deena Rosenberg, *Fascinating Rhythm*, p. 5.

Robert Leslie: Kisseloff, *You Must Remember This*, p. 44.

George Burns ("hungry for food"): Burns, *Transcript*.

EIGHT: POLITICS AND STRIFE

Boxed Material

Votes for Sale: Abraham Cahan, quoted in Howe and Libo, *World of Our Fathers*, p. 218.

An Anarchist Speaks: Abraham Cahan, *Grandma Never Lived in America*, pp. 329–330.

Organizing a Union: Rose Schneiderman, quoted in Dorothy Hoobler and Thomas Hoobler, *The Jewish American Family Album*, pp. 63–64.

Busting a Strike: Howe and Libo, *World of Our Fathers*, pp. 299–300.

Quotations and Details

Statistics for 1911: Peggy Whitley, "American Cultural History: The Twentieth Century—1910–1919," http://kclibrary.nhmccd.edu/decade10.html.

Mel Lasky: Shepard and Levi, *Live and Be Well*, p. 43.

Clara Lemlich: Birmingham, *The Rest of Us*, pp. 71–72.

Tony Michels: correspondence with Lawrence J. Epstein.

NINE: THE OPPONENTS OF JEWISH IMMIGRATION

Boxed Materials

Turning Bias into Law: Lawrence J. Epstein.

Through a Bigot's Eyes: Hoobler and Hoobler, *Jewish American Family Album*, p. 73.

Anti-Semitism in Action: Lawrence J. Epstein.

Quotations and Details

Leo Frank: quoted in Hoobler and Hoobler, *Jewish American Family Album*, p. 72.

Scientific American: Meltzer, *Taking Root*, p. 159.

Julia Richman and Theodore Bingham: Ande Manners, *Poor Cousins*, pp. 211–215.

Jewish Daily Forward: Jenna Weissman Joselit, "Answer to Commissioner Bingham: New York Jews and Crime, 1907," *YIVO Annual of Jewish Social Science*, p. 124.

TEN: A HELPING HAND

Boxed Materials

Lillian Wald Case Notes: Courtesy of the New York Public Library.

Landsmanshaft Fundraising: Kisseloff, *You Must Remember This*, p. 52.

How Landsmanshaften Came to Be: Howe and Libo, *World of Our Fathers*, p. 184.

Quotations and Details

Rabbi Kaufmann Kohler: Meltzer, *Jews in America*, p. 101.

Rabbi Stephen Wise: Shepard and Levi, *Live and Be Well*, p. 170.

Henry Cohen: Epstein, *Jewish Anecdotes*, p. 51.

Lillian Wald: Lawrence J. Epstein.

Lincoln Steffens: Shepard and Levi, *Live and Be Well*, p. 159.

Jacob Riis: Shepard and Levi, *Live and Be Well*, p. 137.

ELEVEN: RELIGION AND ITS REBELS

Boxed Materials

One Family's Religion: Jacob Javits, *Javits*, pp. 7–8.

A Frustrated Rabbi: Howe and Libo, *How We Lived*, pp. 107–108.

Quotations and Details

Teachers: Roskolenko, *The Time That Was Then*, p. 165.

Wine: Kisseloff, *You Must Remember This*, p. 50.

TWELVE: REFUGE ON THE LOWER EAST SIDE

Boxed Materials

The Café: Roskolenko, *The Time That Was Then*, pp. 185–188.

Sach's Café Society: Meltzer, *Taking Root*, p. 199.

Quotations and Details

"We were 'Americanized'": Eugene Lyons, *Assignment in Utopia*, p. 4.

Library: *Evening Post*, October 3, 1903.

THIRTEEN: YIDDISH THEATER

Boxed Materials

Behind the Scenes: David Kessler, quoted in Howe and Libo, *How We Lived*, pp. 239–240.

Quotations and Details

Joseph Lateiner: Stefan Kanfer, "The Yiddish Theater's Triumph," *City Journal*, Spring 2004, http://www.city-journal.org/html/14_2_urbanities-the_yiddish.html.

Boris Thomashefsky: Howe and Libo, *World of Our Fathers*, p. 465.

Gordin and Adler: Howe and Libo, *World of Our Fathers*, p. 468.

FOURTEEN: YIDDISH JOURNALISM

Quotations and Details

Cahan on the Bintel Brief: Metzker, *A Bintel Brief*, p. 13.

Selections from the Bintel Brief: Metzker, *A Bintel Brief*, p. 53; Howe and Libo, *How We Lived*, p. 88.

FIFTEEN: YIDDISH LITERATURE

Quotations and Details

Morris Rosenfeld, "In the Shop": Howard Sachar, *A History of the Jews in America*, p. 380.

SIXTEEN: THE END OF AN ERA

Boxed Materials

Stepping into Show Business: Ann Banks, *First-Person America*, p. 208.

Burns and Allen Routines: Epstein, *Mixed Nuts*, pp. 9–11.

Quotations and Details

Sun and *Der Tag* quotes: Shepard and Levi, *Live and Be Well*, p. 18.

SEVENTEEN: THE LEGACY OF THE LOWER EAST SIDE

Boxed Materials

Lower East Side Memories: Courtesy of Hasia R. Diner.

Memoirs: Lawrence J. Epstein.

The Animated Lower East Side: Lawrence J. Epstein.

REFERENCES

><><

BOOKS AND ARTICLES

Adler, Jacob. *Jacob Adler: A Life on the Stage,* trans. and with commentary by Lulla Rosenfeld. New York: Applause, 2001.

"Aleichem Welcomed." *New York Times.* November 1, 1906, p. 9.

Antin, Mary. *The Promised Land.* Boston: Houghton Mifflin, 1912.

Antin, Mary. *From Plotzk to Boston.* Upper Saddle River, N.J.: Literature House, 1970.

Ausubel, Nathan, ed. *A Treasury of Jewish Folklore.* New York: Bantam, 1980.

Banks, Ann. *First-Person America.* New York: Knopf, 1980.

Baum, Charlotte, Paula Hyman, and Sonya Michel. *The Jewish Woman in America.* New York: Dial, 1976.

Beckerman, Emma. *Not So Long Ago: A Recollection.* New York: Bloch, 1980.

Bergreen, Laurence. *As Thousands Cheer: The Life of Irving Berlin.* New York: Viking, 1990.

Bial, Raymond. *Tenement: Immigrant Life on the Lower East Side.* Boston: Houghton Mifflin, 2002.

Birmingham, Stephen. *The Rest of Us: The Rise of America's Eastern European Jews.* Boston: Little Brown, 1984.

Borgenicht, Louis. *The Happiest Man: The Life of Louis Borgenicht as told to Harold Friedman*. New York: Putnam, 1942.

George Burns. *Transcript of an Interview with George Burns*. William E. Wiener Oral History Library. American Jewish Committee. Dorot Jewish Division. New York Public Library, 1977.

Burns, George, with David Fisher. *All My Best Friends*. New York: Putnam, 1989.

Burns, George, with Cynthia Hobart Lindsay. *I Love Her, That's Why: An Autobiography*. New York: Simon & Schuster, 1955.

Cahan, Abraham. *The Rise of David Levinsky*. New York: Harper, 1917.

Cahan, Abraham. *The Education of Abraham Cahan,* trans. Leon Stein, Abraham P. Conan, and Lynn Davison. Philadelphia: Jewish Publication Society, 1969.

Cahan, Abraham. *Grandma Never Lived in America: The New Journalism of Abraham Cahan,* ed. Moses Rischin. Bloomington: Indiana University Press, 1985.

Cantor, Eddie. *My Life Is in Your Hands*. New York: Harper, 1928.

Cantor, Eddie. *Take My Life*. New York: Doubleday, 1957.

Cantor, Eddie. *As I Remember Them*. New York: Duell, Sloan & Pierce, 1963.

Chotzinoff, Samuel. *A Lost Paradise*. New York: Knopf, 1955.

Coan, Peter Morton. *Ellis Island Interviews*. New York: Checkmark, 1997.

Cohen, Jocelyn, and Daniel Soyer, eds. and trans. *My Future Is in America: Autobiographies of Eastern European Jewish Immigrants*. New York: New York University Press, 2006.

Cohen, Morris Raphael. *A Dreamer's Journey*. Boston: Beacon Press, 1949.

Cohen, Rose. *Out of the Shadow: A Russian Jewish Girlhood on the Lower East Side*. Ithaca, N.Y.: Cornell University Press, 1995.

Cowen, Philip. *Memories of an American Jew*. New York: Arno Press, 1975.

Diner, Hasia R. *Lower East Side Memories*. Princeton, N.J.: Princeton University Press, 2000.

Diner, Hasia R., Jeffrey Shandler, and Beth S. Wenger, eds. *Remembering the Lower East Side: American Jewish Reflections*. Bloomington: Indiana University Press, 2000.

Dreher, Carl. *Sarnoff: An American Success*. New York: Quadrangle/New York Times Books, 1977.

Drinnon, Richard. *Rebel in Paradise: A Biography of Emma Goldman*. Chicago: University of Chicago Press, 1982.

"An East Side Artist Who Has Disappeared." *New York Times*. August 28, 1905, p. 12.

"East Side Mourns Jewish Mark Twain." *New York Times*. May 14, 1916, p. 9.

Epstein, Jacob. *Epstein: An Autobiography*. New York: Dutton, 1955.

Epstein, Lawrence J. *A Treasury of Jewish Anecdotes*. Northvale, N.J.: Aronson, 1989.

Epstein, Lawrence J. *A Treasury of Jewish Inspirational Stories*. Northvale, N.J.: Aronson, 1993.

Epstein, Lawrence J. *The Haunted Smile: The Story of Jewish Comedians in America*. New York: PublicAffairs, 2001.

Epstein, Lawrence J. *Mixed Nuts: America's Love Affair with Comedy Teams*. New York: PublicAffairs, 2004.

Ewen, Elizabeth. *Immigrant Women in the Land of Dollars: Life and Culture on the Lower East Side, 1890–1925*. New York: Monthly Review Press, 1985.

Fagen, Herb. *George Burns: In His Own Words*. New York: Carroll & Graf, 1996.

Feingold, Henry. *Zion in America*. New York: Twayne, 1974.

Feldberg, Michael. "The Angel of Ellis Island," *Heritage* (American Jewish Historical Society). Fall 2005, pp. 4–5.

Ford, Gertrude. *81 Sheriff Street*. New York: Fell, 1981.

Fox, Stephen. *Transatlantic*. New York: Perennial, 2003.

Friedman, Reena Sigman. "'Send Me My Husband Who Is in New York City': Husband Desertion in the American Jewish Immigrant Community, 1900–1926," *Jewish Social Studies*, 44, Winter 1982, pp. 1–18.

Gold, Michael. *Jews Without Money*. Garden City, N.Y.: Sundial Press, 1946.

Golden, Harry. *For 2 Cents Plain*. Cleveland: World, 1958.

Golden, Harry. *Only in America*. Cleveland: World, 1958.

Golden, Harry. *The Right Time*. New York: Putnam, 1969.

Golden, Harry. *The Greatest Jewish City in the World*. Garden City, N.Y.: Doubleday, 1972.

Goldman, Emma. *Living My Life*. New York: AMS Press, 1970.

Goldman, Herbert G. *Fanny Brice: The Original Funny Girl*. New York: Oxford University Press, 1992.

Gordon, Benjamin. *Between Two Worlds: The Memoirs of a Physician*. New York: Bookman Associates, 1952.

Goren, Arthur A. *New York Jews and the Quest for Community: The Kehillah Experiment, 1908–1922*. New York: Columbia University Press, 1970.

Graham, Stephen. *With Poor Immigrants in America*. New York: Macmillan, 1914.

Granfield, Linda. *97 Orchard Street, New York: Stories of Immigrant Life*. Plattsburgh, N.Y.: Tundra Books, 2001.

Grossman, Barbara Wallace. *Funny Woman: The Life and Times of Fanny Brice*. Bloomington: Indiana University Press, 1991.

Gurock, Jeffrey S., ed. *East European Jews in America, 1880–1920: Immigration and Adaptation*. New York: Routledge, 1998.

Handlin, Oscar. *The Uprooted* (2nd ed.). Boston: Little, Brown, 1990.

Hapgood, Hutchins. *The Spirit of the Ghetto: Studies of the Jewish Quarter of New York*. New York: Schocken, 1966.

Hasanovitz, Elizabeth. *One of Them: Chapters from a Passionate Autobiography*. Boston: Houghton Mifflin, 1918.

Heaps, Willard Allison. *The Story of Ellis Island*. New York: Seabury Press, 1967.

Heinze, Andrew. *Adapting to Abundance: Jewish Immigrants, Mass Consumption, and the Search for American Identity*. New York: Columbia University Press, 1990.

Higham, John. *Strangers in the Land: Patterns of American Nativism, 1860–1925*. New York: Atheneum, 1968.

Hillquit, Morris. *Loose Leaves from a Busy Life*. New York: Da Capo Press, 1971.

Hindus, Milton, ed. *The Jewish East Side, 1881–1924*. New Brunswick, N.J.: Transaction, 1996.

Hoobler, Dorothy, and Thomas Hoobler. *The Jewish American Family Album*. New York: Oxford University Press, 1995.

Horwich, Bernard. *My First Eighty Years*. Chicago: Argus Books, 1939.

Howe, Irving, and Kenneth Libo. *World of Our Fathers*. New York: Harcourt Brace, 1976.

Howe, Irving, and Kenneth Libo. *How We Lived*. New York: Marek, 1979.

Howells, William Dean. *Impressions and Experiences*. New York: Harper, 1896.

Hyman, Paula. "Gender and the Immigrant Jewish Experience in the United States." In Judith Baskin, ed., *Jewish Women in Historical Perspective*. Detroit: Wayne State University Press, 1991.

Jablonski, Edward. *The Gershwin Years: George and Ira*. New York: Da Capo Press, 1996.

Jablonski, Edward. *Irving Berlin: American Troubadour*. New York: Henry Holt, 1999.

Jacob, H. E. *The World of Emma Lazarus*. New York: Schocken, 1949.

Javits, Jacob J., with Rafael Steinberg. *Javits: The Autobiography of a Public Man*. Boston: Houghton Mifflin, 1981.

"Jewish Massacre Denounced." *New York Times.* April 28, 1903, p. 6.

Jewish Museum. *Lower East Side: Portal to American Life, 1870–1924.* New York: Jewish Museum, 1966.

Johnpoll, Bernard K. "Why They Left: Russian-Jewish Mass Migration and Repressive Laws, 1881–1917." *American Jewish Archives,* 67, Spring-Summer 1995, pp. 17–54.

Joselit, Jenna Weissman. "An Answer to Commissioner Bingham: A Case Study of New York Jews and Crime, 1907." *YIVO Annual of Jewish Social Science,* vol. 18 (New York: YIVO, 1983).

Joselit, Jenna Weissman. "Giving the Melting Pot Its First Stir." *Forward.* March 3, 2006, p. 17.

Joselit, Jenna Weissman. *Our Gang: Jewish Crime and the New York Jewish Community, 1900–1940.* Bloomington: Indiana University Press, 1983.

Joselit, Jenna Weissman. "Telling Tales: Or, How a Slum Became a Shrine." *Jewish Social Studies,* Winter 1996, 2(2).

Joselit, Jenna Weissman. *The Wonders of America: Reinventing Jewish Culture, 1880-1950.* New York: Owl Books, 2002.

Joseph, Samuel. *Jewish Immigration to the United States from 1881 to 1910.* New York: Arno Press, 1969.

Kacyzne, Alter. *Poyln: Jewish Life in the Old Country.* New York: Henry Holt, 1999.

Kanfer, Stefan. "The Yiddish Theater's Triumph." *City Journal,* Spring 2004 [http://www.city-journal.org/html/14_2_urbanities-the_yiddish.html].

Karp, Abraham, ed. *Golden Door to America. The Jewish Immigrant Experience.* New York: Viking, 1976.

Kasovich, Israel. *The Days of Our Years,* trans. Maximilian Hurwitz. New York: Jordan, 1929.

Kessner, Thomas. *The Golden Door: Italian and Jewish Immigrant Mobility in New York City, 1880–1915.* New York: Oxford University Press, 1977.

Kisseloff, Jeff. *You Must Remember This: An Oral History of Manhattan from the 1890s to World War II.* New York: Schocken, 1990.

Klein, Maury. "Life on the Lower East Side." *American History Illustrated,* November 1972.

Koppman, Steve, and Lion Koppman. *A Treasury of American Jewish Folklore.* Northvale, N.J.: Aronson, 1996.

Kramer, Sydelle, and Jenny Masur Kramer. *Jewish Grandmothers.* Boston: Beacon Press, 1977.

Lasky, Kathryn. *Dreams in the Golden Country*. New York: Scholastic, 1978.

Lederhendler, Eli M. "Jewish Immigration to America and Revisionist Historiography: A Decade of New Perspectives." *YIVO Annual of Jewish Social Science,* vol. 18 (New York: YIVO, 1983).

Lifson, David. *The Yiddish Theater in America*. New York: Yoseloff, 1965.

Limmer, Ruth. *Six Heritage Tours of the Lower East Side*. New York: New York University Press, 1997.

Lisitzky, Ephraim. *In the Grip of Cross Currents,* trans. Moshe Kohn and Jacob Sloan. New York: Bloch, 1959.

Lyons, Eugene. *Assignment in Utopia*. New York: Harcourt Brace, 1937.

Maffi, Mario. *Gateway to the Promised City: Ethnic Cultures in New York's Lower East Side*. New York: New York University Press, 1995.

Malkiel, Theresa S. *Diary of a Shirtwaist Striker*. Ithaca, N.Y.: ILR Press, 1990.

Malkin, Carole. *The Journeys of David Toback: As Retold by His Granddaughter*. New York: Schocken, 1981.

Manners, Ande. *Poor Cousins*. New York: Coward, McCann & Geoghegan, 1972.

Meltzer, Milton. *Taking Root: Jewish Immigrants in America*. New York: Dell, 1976.

Meltzer, Milton. *The Jews in America: A Picture Album*. Philadelphia: Jewish Publication Society, 1985.

Mendelsohn, Joyce. *The Lower East Side Remembered and Revisited. History and Guide to a Legendary New York Neighborhood*. New York: Lower East Side Press, 2001.

Metzker, Isaac, ed. *A Bintel Brief*. Garden City, N.Y.: Doubleday, 1971.

Meyerowitz, Rael. *Transferring to America: Jewish Interpretations of American Dreams*. Albany: State University of New York Press, 1995.

Michels, Tony. *A Fire in Their Hearts: Yiddish Socialists in New York*. Cambridge, Mass.: Harvard University Press, 2005.

Michels, Tony. Interview by Mort Mecklosky. WUSB. March 1, 2006.

Moscow, Henry. *The Street Book: An Encyclopedia of Manhattan's Street Names and Their Origins*. New York: Hagstrom, 1978.

Nadell, Pamela S. "The Journey to America by Steam: The Jews of Eastern Europe in Transition." *American Jewish History*. December 1981, pp. 269–284.

Novotny, Ann. *Strangers at the Door*. New York: Bantam, 1971.

Ornitz, Samuel. *Haunch, Paunch, and Jowl: An Anonymous Autobiography*. New York: Boni & Liveright, 1924.

Picon, Molly. *Molly: An Autobiography*. New York: Simon & Schuster, 1980.

Prell, Riv-Ellen. *Fighting to Become Americans: Jews, Gender, and the Anxiety of Assimilation.* Boston: Beacon Press, 1999.

Ravage, Marcus. *An American in the Making: The Life Story of an Immigrant.* New York: Harper, 1917.

Ribalow, Harold U. *Autobiographies of American Jews.* Philadelphia: Jewish Publication Society, 1965.

Rich, J. C. *The Jewish Daily Forward.* New York: Forward Association, 1967.

Riis, Jacob. *How the Other Half Lives.* New York: Garrett Press, 1970.

"A Riot on the East Side." *New York Times.* September 26, 1898, p. 7.

Rischin, Moses. *The Promised City: New York's Jews, 1870–1914.* Cambridge, Mass.: Harvard University Press, 1962.

Robinson, Edward G., with Leonard Spiegelgass. *All My Yesterdays: An Autobiography.* New York: Hawthorn Books, 1973.

Rockaway, Robert A. *Words of the Uprooted: Jewish Immigrants in Early Twentieth Century America.* Ithaca, N.Y.: Cornell University Press, 1998.

Rosenberg, Deena. *Fascinating Rhythm: The Collaboration of George and Ira Gershwin.* Ann Arbor: University of Michigan Press, 1997.

Rosenfeld, Lulla. *The Yiddish Theatre and Jacob P. Adler* (2nd rev. ed.). New York: Shapolsky, 1988.

Roskolenko, Harry. *The Time That Was Then: The Lower East Side, 1900–1914.* New York: Dial, 1971.

Rosten, Leo. *The Education of H*Y*M*A*N K*A*P*L*A*N*.* New York: Harcourt, Brace, 1965.

Ruskay, Sophie. *Horsecars and Cobblestones.* South Brunswick, N.J.: Barnes, 1973.

Sachar, Howard Morley. *A History of the Jews in America.* New York: Knopf, 1992.

Sanders, Ronald. *The Downtown Jews: Portraits of an Immigrant Generation.* New York: Harper, 1969. [Reprinted as *The Lower East Side Jews: An Immigrant Generation.* New York: Dover, 1999.]

Sanders, Ronald. *The Lower East Side: A Guide to Its Jewish Past in 99 New Photographs.* Photos by Edmund V. Gillon Jr. New York: Dover, 1979.

Sanders, Ronald. *Shores of Refuge: A Hundred Years of Jewish Emigration.* New York: Henry Holt, 1988.

Sandrow, Nahma. *Vagabond Stars: A World History of Yiddish Theater.* New York: Limelight, 1986.

Sarna, Jonathan. *American Judaism: A History.* New Haven, Conn.: Yale University Press, 2004.

Schoener, Allon, ed. *Portal to America: The Lower East Side, 1870–1915.* New York: Holt, Rinehart and Winston, 1967.

Shapall, Leo. "The Diary of Dr. George M. Price." *Publications of the American Jewish Historical Society,* December 1950.

Shapiro, Judah J. *The Friendly Society: A History of the Workmen's Circle.* New York: Schocken, 1977.

Shepard, Richard F., and Vicki Gold Levi. *Live and Be Well: A Celebration of Yiddish Culture in America from the First Immigrants to the Second World War.* New York: Ballantine Books, 1982.

Snyder, Robert. *Voice of the City: Vaudeville and Popular Culture in New York.* Chicago: Dee, 2000.

Sorin, Gerald. *A Time for Building: The Third Migration, 1880–1920.* Baltimore: Johns Hopkins University Press, 1992.

Soyer, Daniel. *Jewish Immigrant Associations and American Identity in New York, 1880–1939.* Cambridge, Mass.: Harvard University Press, 1997.

Spewack, Bella Cohen. *Streets: A Memoir of the Lower East Side.* New York: Feminist Press, 1995.

Stein, Leon. *The Triangle Fire.* Ithaca, N.Y.: Cornell University Press, 2001.

Sternlicht, Sanford V. *The Tenement Saga: The Lower East Side and Early Jewish American Writers.* Madison: University of Wisconsin Press, 2004.

Stolberg, Benjamin. *Tailor's Progress.* New York: Doubleday, 1944.

Tax, Meredith. *Rivington Street.* Urbana: University of Illinois Press, 2001.

Tifft, Wilton S. *Ellis Island.* Chicago: Contemporary Books, 1990.

Von Drehle, David. *Triangle: The Fire That Changed America.* New York: Atlantic Monthly Press, 2003.

Wald, Lillian D. Case notes on file at the New York Public Library.

Wald, Lillian D. *The House on Henry Street.* New York: Dover, 1971. (Originally published 1915)

Waldman, Louis. *Labor Lawyer.* New York: Dutton, 1944.

Weinberg, Sydney Stahl. *The World of Our Mothers: The Lives of Jewish Immigrant Women.* Chapel Hill: University of North Carolina Press, 1988.

Weinstein, Gregory. *The Ardent Eighties.* New York: International Press, 1929.

Wenger, Beth S. "Memory as Identity: The Invention of the Lower East Side." *American Jewish History,* 85. March 1997, pp. 3–27.

Wex, Michael. *Born to Kvetch: Yiddish Language and Culture in All Its Moods.* New York: St. Martin's Press, 2005.

Wirth, Louis. *The Ghetto*. Chicago: University of Chicago Press, 1962.

Wischnitzer, Mark. *To Dwell in Safety*. Philadelphia: Jewish Publication Society, 1948.

Wolfe, Gerard R. *The Synagogues of New York's Lower East Side*. New York: New York University Press, 1978.

Wolfman, Ira. *Jewish New York*. New York: Universe, 2003.

Yezierska, Anzia. *Bread Givers*. New York: Persea Books, 1975.

Yezierska, Anzia. *Red Ribbon on a White Horse* (rev. ed.). New York: Persea Books, 1987.

WEB SITES

Eldridge Street Synagogue: http://www.eldridgestreet.org

Ellis Island Immigration Museum: http://www.ellisisland.org

Hebrew Immigrant Aid Society:http://www.hias.org/Who_We_Are/120stories/120stories_complete.pdf

Henry Street Settlement: http://www.henrystreet.org

Jewish Women's Archive: http://www.jwa.org

Liberty State Park: http://www.libertystatepark.com/immigran.htm

Lower East Side Tenement Museum: http://www.tenement.org

Sigmund Breitbart: http://www.sandowmuseum.com/breitbart.html

Triangle Factory Fire:
http://www.ilr.cornell.edu/trianglefire/narrative1.html

FILMS AND VIDEOS

America. Episode 9, "The Huddled Masses." PBS. 1988

Ellis Island. A&E Home Video, 1997.

The Forward: From Immigrants to Americans. Direct Cinema. 1988.

A Laugh, a Tear, a Mitzvah. WLIW. 1997.

THE AUTHOR

✤

LAWRENCE J. EPSTEIN is a professor of English at Suffolk County Community College in Selden, New York. Formerly the chair of the college's Humanities Division, he has also taught courses in Jewish studies, the Holocaust, and journalism.

Dr. Epstein's books about Jewish life include *A Treasury of Jewish Anecdotes, A Treasury of Jewish Inspirational Stories,* and *The Haunted Smile: The Story of Jewish Comedians in America*. He has also written more than one hundred articles, stories, and reviews for various major Jewish periodicals. He frequently lectures on a wide range of Jewish subjects around the United States. Dr. Epstein also served as an adviser on the Middle East for two members of the United States Congress.

He and his wife, Sharon, live on Long Island. They have four children. All four of his grandparents and two of his great-grandparents were immigrants who lived on the Lower East Side.

INDEX

>✕<

A

Abandonment, of wives, 95–98

Abie's Irish Rose (Nichols), 101

Abram, R. J., 51

Abramowitz, S. J., 233–234

Actors, 210–215

Adenoid Riot, 114–115

Adler, J. P., 204, 211, 212, 215, 217

Adult learning, 133, 186–189

Aguilar Free Library Society, 195

Aid, for immigrants, 19–20, 31–32, 40–42, 156–168

Aleichem, S., 3, 136, 234, 235

Alexander II (tsar of Russia), 1–2, 8–9

All for One (Schneiderman), 139

All-of-a-Kind Family (Taylor), 265

Allen, G., 251–253

Amalgamated Clothing Workers of America, 141–142

American culture, dealing with, 104–105

American Jewish Committee (AJC), 156–157

American Protective Association, 146, 148

Anarchism, 130–133

Angel of Ellis Island, 38

Anglo-Jewish Association, 19

Anti-Semitism, 135, 142–150

Antin, M., 14, 137

Asch, M., 238

Asch, S., 237–238

Athletes, 247–248

Auster's, 193

B

Bagels, 54

Balfour Declaration of 1917, 256

Bargaining, 64

Baseball, 105–106, 248

Bathhouses, 190

Beckerman, E., 24, 50

Ben-Gurion, D., 134

Bennett, A., 45

Benny, J., 16, 253

Berkman, A., 131–133, 192

Berlin, I., 48, 108–109, 113, 249–250

Beth Israel, 164

Between Two Worlds (Gordon), 21

Bingham, T., 150–153

Bintel Brief, 227–229

Blanck, M., 137

Blaustein, D., 188

Boarders, in tenements, 56–57

Bolshevik Revolution, 133

Bookmakers, 193–194

Border crossings, dangers of, 17–18

Bovshover, J., 236

Boxing, 247–248

Brandeis, L., 141, 256

Bread Givers (Yezierska), 56, 106–107, 263–264

Breitbart, Z. (S.), 248

Brewster, M., 159

Brice, F., 58, 108

Bridges, 196

"A Brivele der Kale" (song), 154

Broder Zinger, 207

The Brothers Ashkenazi (Singer), 238

Buchalter, L., 85

Buchwald, A., 158

Bureau of Jewish Education, 163

Burns and Allen comedy team, 251–253

Burns, G.: dyslexia of, 113; and organ-grinders, 75; and poverty, 104; and start as entertainer, 109, 114, 250–253; and tenements, 47–48, 56, 57–58; as thief, 108

Buskers, 109

C

Cafés, 190–193

Cahan, A.: and baseball, 105; and border crossing, 17–18; burial of, 136; and dispute with Gordin, 214–215; and E. Goldman, 131; and elections, 125; and family separation, 96; and *Jewish Daily Forward*, 223–229; and L. Steffens, 167; as novelist, 238–239

Call It Sleep (Roth), 265

Camp Kinderland, 133

Candy stores, 193–194

Cantor, E.: bar mitzvah of, 180; and baseball, 105; biography of, 253–254; and Ellis Island, 43; and gangs, 82; photo of, 242; and tenements, 48, 58; as thief, 108

"Cantor's Carnegie Hall," 183

Castle Garden, 30–32

A Child of the Ghetto (film), 266

Chotzinoff, S., 53, 104, 111

Christmas, 105

Citizenship, learning of, 110–112

Civil War in America, effects of, 15

Clara de Hirsch Home for Girls, 156

Cleveland, G., 34, 148

Cloakmakers' Strike, 141

Cohen, J., 261

Cohen, M. R., 25, 114

Cohen, Rabbi H., 157

Coleman, M., 140

Communism, 133, 135, 230

Community centers, 162

Coogan, J., 267

Cowen, P., 41

Crime, 83–87, 150–153, 162–163, 193–194, 199

Curses, of Eastern European Jews, 5

D

Debs, E. V., 224

Democracy and Assimilation: The Blending of Immigrant Heritages in America (Drachsler), 98–99, 101

Der Tag (newspaper), 229, 231

Desertion, by husbands, 95–98

Di Yidishe Tsaytung (newspaper), 230

Di Yunge (group of poets), 236–237

Diner, H. R., 260

Divorce, 95–98

Dowry, and matchmakers, 92, 94

Dr. Brown's Cel-Ray tonic, 55

Drachsler, J., 98–99, 101

A Dreamer's Journey (Cohen), 25

Dreyfus Affair, 149

Drug use, 87

E

Eastman, M., 85, 86

Edelstadt, D., 230, 236

Eden Musée, 109

The Education of Abraham Cahan (Cahan), 125

The Education of David Levinsky (Cahan), 17–18

The Education of Hyman Kaplan (Rosten), 187

Educational Alliance, 188–189

Ellis Island, 34–43

Emigration, difficulties of, 15–20

English language acquisition, 113–114

Enlightenment (Haskalah), 233

Entertainers, Jewish, 108–109, 248–255. *See also individual entertainers*

Epstein, J., 167

Eugenics, 148

"Evil eye" (*ayin hara*), 4

Extortion, 85

F

Family, transformation of, 118–120

Fathers, as absent or weak, 106–108

Fein, B., 85–86

Fiddler on the Roof (musical), 234

Fields, L., 200

Films, 186, 266–268

A Fire in Their Hearts (Michels), 142

Fitzgerald, F. S., 85

Folksbiene Yiddish Theater, 218

Food, 24, 42, 54–56, 106, 173, 176

Ford, H., 152–153, 256

Fortune-tellers, 68–70

Fox, W., 65

Frank, L., 149

Freie Arbeiter Shtimme (newspaper), 230

Freiheit (newspaper), 230

From Plotzk to Boston (Antin), 14

Fur Workers Union, 141–142

G

Galitzianers, 3

Galveston Plan, 157

Gambling, 84, 85, 185, 193–194

Games, 82–83

Gangs, 82, 84

Garden Cafeteria, 197

Garment industry, 65, 124–130, 136–137, 225. *See also* Labor unions

German Jews, and attitudes toward Eastern European Jews, 155–156

Gershwin, G., 109, 254–255

Gershwin, I., 58, 109